DEFENDING
NOTTINGHAMSHIRE

T0323083

DEFENDING NOTTINGHAMSHIRE

The Military Landscape from Prehistory to the Present

MIKE OSBORNE

To David Sibley,
one of life's true gentlemen, who contributed
so much to recording the built environment.

First published 2014
Reprinted 2019

The History Press
97 St George's Place, Cheltenham,
Gloucestershire, GL50 3QB
www.thehistorypress.co.uk

British Library Cataloguing in Publication Data.
A catalogue record for this book is available from the British Library.

ISBN 978 0 7524 9955 0

Typesetting and origination by The History Press
Printed in Great Britain by TJ International Ltd, Padstow, Cornwall.

Contents

Acknowledgements

Thanks are due to the following:

Colin Alexander; Hilary and Richard Allton; Adrian Armishaw; Peter Allen and Alistair MacIntosh for information on *Margidunum* used by Margaret Sibley; Bassetlaw Museum; Steve Cox; David Flintham particularly for information on Hawton redoubt; Paul Francis; Bob Holland; Pauline Marples of Forest Town; Adrian Peters; Stewart Squires; Mike Suttill of the East Midlands RFCA; Judith Wright of the archive department at Boots; Margaret Sibley; Carol Wilkinson and Bowbridge Primary School; the staff at Burton Joyce, Newark and Nottingham libraries and at the archive collections of Nottinghamshire and the University of Nottingham; and, as ever, to my wife, Pam, for constant help and support, especially through the irrationalities of a digital world.

All illustrations are the author's unless otherwise credited.

Abbreviations

NB In several places, especially where RAF buildings are concerned, reference is often made to Drawing Numbers. These consist of a sequential number and a year: thus 343/43 refers to the Watch Office for All Commands, built to the 343rd design to come out of the Air Ministry drawing office in 1943. The term 'tb' refers to buildings with walls a single brick in width and officially known as 'temporary brick'.

AA	anti-aircraft
AAOR	Anti-aircraft Operations Room
ACF	Army Cadet Force
ADGB	Air Defence of Great Britain (1924 scheme)
AFS	Auxiliary Fire Service
ARP	Air Raid Precautions
ASP	Aircraft Servicing Platform
AT	anti-tank
ATC	Air Training Corps
ATS	Auxiliary Territorial Service (1938–49, then WRAC)
AVRE	Armoured Vehicle Royal Engineers
BEF	British Expeditionary Force
BHQ	Battle Headquarters
CBA	Council for British Archaeology
CD	Civil Defence
C-in-C	Commander in Chief
CO	Commanding Officer
CRO	Civilian Repair Organisation (aircraft repair workshops)
DFW3	Directorate of Fortifications & Works, Department 3
DL	Defended Locality
(E & R)(S)FTS	(Elementary & Reserve)(Service) Flying Training School
ELINT	electronic intelligence
GCI	Ground Control Interception (radar system Second World War+)
GDA	Gun Defended Area (AA)
GHQ	General Headquarters (GHQ Line, GHQ Reserve etc.)
GL	gun-laying (radar for AA artillery)
HAA	heavy anti-aircraft

ICBM	Inter-Continental Ballistic Missile (e.g. POLARIS)
IRBM	Intermediate-Range Ballistic Missile (e.g. THOR)
LAA	light anti-aircraft
LDV	Local Defence Volunteers, later Home Guard (HG)
MAP	Ministry of Aircraft Production
MOD	Ministry of Defence
MU	maintenance unit (RAF)
NCO	non-commissioned officer
NFF	National Filling Factory
OCTU	Officer Cadet Training Unit
OCU	Operational Conversion Unit
ORP	Operational Readiness Platform
OTC	Officer Training Corps
OTU	Operational Training Unit (usually RAF Bomber Command)
PAD	Passive Air Defence (ARP, decoys, shelters etc.)
PBX	Private Branch Exchange (telephones)
pdr	pounder (as in weight of projectile) 1 pound = 454 grams
POL	petrol, oil and lubricants
RAuxAF	Royal Auxiliary Air Force (until 1957)
RAC	Royal Armoured Corps
RAF	Royal Air Force (from 1 April 1918)
RAFVR	Royal Air Force Volunteer Reserve
RAMC	Royal Army Medical Corps
(R)AOC	(Royal from 1918) Army Ordnance Corps
(R)ASC	(Royal from 1918) Army Service Corps
RBL	Royal British Legion
REME	Royal Electrical and Mechanical Engineers (formed 1942)
RFC	Royal Flying Corps (up to 31 March 1918)
RFCA	Reserve Forces and Cadets' Association
RHQ	Regimental Headquarters
(R)OC	(Royal from 1941) Observer Corps
SAA	small arms ammunition
SAGW	surface-to-air guided weapons (e.g. Bloodhound)
SAM	surface-to-air missile (AA weapons)
SIGINT	signals intelligence
S/L	searchlight
SMLE	Short Magazine Lee Enfield (0.303in rifle)
TA	Territorial Army (from 1920–39 and 1947–present)
TAC	Territorial Army Centre (drill hall post-1947)
TAFA	Territorial & Auxiliary Forces Association
tb	temporary brick (single brick with buttresses in RAF buildings)
TDS	Training Depot Station
TF	Territorial Force (from 1908–18)

UKWMO	United Kingdom Warning & Monitoring Organisation
UP	unrotated projectile (as in Z battery, AA rockets)
USAAF	United States Army Air Force (Second World War)
USAF(E)	United States Air Force (Europe) (post-Second World War)
VAD	Voluntary Aid Detachment (First World War)
VP	vulnerable point
VTC	Volunteer Training Corps (First World War Home Guard)
WAAC	Women's Army Auxiliary Corps (1917–21)
WAAF	Women's Auxiliary Air Force (later WRAF)
WRAC	Women's Royal Army Corps (from 1949)
W(R)VS	Women's (Royal) Voluntary Service

Introduction

Nottinghamshire's position in the very heart of England has given it important strategic significance throughout two millennia. This is underlined by the number of roads, waterways, and later, railways criss-crossing the county – the Roman Fosse Way from Exeter to Lincoln via Newark; the Great North Road from London to Newcastle through Newark, Tuxford and East Retford; the River Trent and its associated canal network connecting Birmingham and the Black Country to the east coast; the central place of Nottingham as a nodal point on the routes connecting all the main cities of the Midlands; and two of the main north-south railway lines. An endless succession of armies has used the Great North Road: the Romans of Aulus Plautius, the Vikings of Ivar the Boneless, the Normans of William the Conqueror, the Lancastrians of Henry VI's queen, and the Jacobites of the Young Pretender. Strategic river crossings and road junctions have been guarded by Roman camps, Viking and Saxon burhs, medieval castles, Parliamentarian and Royalist forts, and the anti-invasion defences of the Second World War. The area has traditionally provided a rallying point for armies to be gathered, from Richard III's in 1485 to Kitchener's in 1914. Building on the experience of the great training camps of Clipstone and the Dukeries and the extensive munitions works of Chilwell and Nottingham, in the Second World War the county expanded such provision becoming home to a concentration of flying training centres, key components of the army's and the RAF's logistical support networks and further munitions plants.

Much of this military activity has left its mark on the landscape, some of it relatively untouched, and some adapted to meet the demands of change. Whilst the castles of Nottingham and Newark retained their defensive capabilities into the 1600s, Greasley Castle, licensed in 1340 had, by the end of the century, become a focus for industrial and agricultural activity. Built in 1792 and operational into the middle of the next century, by 1861, the cavalry barracks in Nottingham's Park was being used for public entertainments including a demonstration by Blondin, the famous tightrope walker. Mansfield's High Oakham House was built as a barracks in 1839, was a private residence from 1854, and was hosting evacuees from Sheffield in September 1939. Some monuments are of enormous national importance. Newark-on-Trent, as well as retaining its unspoilt medieval castle ruins, boasts the best single concentration of Civil War-period fortifications anywhere in Britain. Sadly, many undervalued monuments, particularly those on brown-field sites ripe for development, are fast disappearing. It can only be a matter of time before the watch office at Wigsley, for instance, recently denied statutory protection, disappears. Nevertheless, it is still possible to rediscover some which have been hidden. Any readers who might be lucky enough to uncover items of interest, are asked to observe three principles: to respect private property and privacy; to take appropriate care in potentially hazardous locations; and to report discoveries to local authority Historic Environment Officers or museum staff.

Nottinghamshire is a historical goldmine, often under-appreciated, and under-explored. This book is an attempt to shine some light on one particular aspect of this heritage.

Mike Osborne, 2014

one

Prehistoric, Roman and Saxon Nottinghamshire

Prehistoric fortifications in Nottinghamshire

Only scanty evidence survives of early settlement in the county. Bronze Age finds at Clifton may indicate a riverside settlement. A large number of oak stakes, spaced in the riverbed a yard apart, suggest that they may have served as piles to carry a platform structure, maybe for dwellings. Although weapons were also found, these may simply constitute evidence for a site where precious possessions were cast into the river as sacrificial offerings. Even flimsier evidence of a similar nature has been turned up in Attenborough and Holme Pierrepont where three dug-out canoes were found.

There are few signs pointing to Nottingham as a fortified site in the Iron Age, but some ditches, apparently dating from this period, may be interpreted as delineating enclosures. Much of the settlement in the Trent valley consisted of a quite dense concentration of discrete farmsteads, and whilst many of these were surrounded by banks and ditches, their main purpose would have been to keep domestic animals in, and wild ones out.

There are, though, a number of sites in Nottinghamshire which have previously been classed as Iron Age hill forts. Not only is there still confusion as to the purpose of these monuments generally: permanently inhabited settlements; refuges in times of danger; sites for social or ritual gatherings; or secure stores for stock or surpluses; but doubt has actually been cast on whether they deserve the classification at all. However, one factor common to all of them is the presence of defensive features. According to Mike Bishop's Archaeological Resource Assessment for an East Midlands Research Agenda in 2001, most of those sites designated as Iron Age hill forts may be neither Iron Age, nor hill forts. Nevertheless, there are a number of sites in Nottinghamshire which exhibit many of the characteristics of the class, usually taking the form of an enclosure with one or more banks, likely topped by wooden palisades, and fronted with one or more ditches. Such banks could be quite complex structures with timber or stone revetments, and earthen ramparts strengthened internally with stone, timber or clay. The palisade might be topped with a fighting-platform carried on a framework of timber poles, embedded in the bank, and there was the possibility for towers, at intervals along the ramparts, or spanning gateways. Ditches were deep, and often wet, set in marshy ground, or fed by a stream. Entrances could be quite complex structures, often set in re-entrants with banks overlapping to create killing-grounds in the dog-legged passageways between inner and outer gates.

Whilst some of the county's putative hill forts, such as Beacon Hill Camp at Gringley-on-the-Hill, for instance, are set in dominant positions in the landscape, there is none which can claim to be anything approaching the impregnable fortresses of the South Downs. Arnold's Cockpit Hill has double ditches, and Fox Wood at Woodborough, where the farmer, Grahame Watson, has reconstructed an Iron Age round-house, has two circuits of ramparts and ditches, but most, such as Scratta Wood at Shireoaks, Crow Wood, Styrrup, or Burton Lodge, all three of whose perimeter defences have been excavated, had only a single layer of defences. The camp at Combs Farm, Farnsfield, presents as a promontory fort, with its neck defended by a ditch. Probably the most impressive is Oxton, or Oldox (Old Works) Camp on Robin Hood Hill, a few miles west of Southwell. Covering 3 acres (1.2ha), it is univallate on the west but has triple banks and ditches on, what may have appeared as, the more vulnerable south-east. There were two entrances, on the north-west and the south-east, and a 20ft (6m) high barrow outside the camp. Although appearing from the north-western approach to be occupying a dominant position on the end of a steep-sided ridge, and enjoying panoramic views of the surrounding landscape, the camp actually lies in a dip, and can be overlooked from neighbouring high ground on three sides, seriously compromising its defensive value. Two further sites, that at Dorket Head near Arnold, and the apparent Roman fort found at Broxstowe in the 1930s have also generated discussion over their origins and status, possibly having earlier Iron Age histories followed by later Roman occupation.

1 Gringley-on-the-Hill, an Iron Age camp in a dominant position overlooking a wide swathe of countryside.

2 Oxton, Robin Hood Hill, an Iron Age camp occupying a prominent but vulnerable position.

Whatever the purpose or uses of these sites, they may be thought of as settlements which were built by people for whom some feeling of security mattered. The tribal area of the Corieltauvi took in Nottinghamshire and its neighbouring counties, but the major tribal centres were elsewhere: Leicester, Old Sleaford, Burrough Hill near Melton Mowbray, and Lincoln, and it would appear that there were no important tribal or clan strongholds within the county. It may be that the Romano-British settlement at Dunston's Clump, west of Retford, consisting of a series of rectilinear timber-framed buildings of the first and second centuries AD, surrounded by a substantial ditch, represented a continuation into a new era, of what had become the area's typical homestead.

Roman fortifications in Nottinghamshire

Shortly after the Romans' second excursion into Britain in AD 43, Aulus Plautius established a frontier, marked by the Fosse Way. This made use of the limestone escarpment and the rivers Avon, lower Severn and Trent, reputedly used as a prehistoric trackway known as the Jurassic Way. Once this line had become established, those tribes to its east were disarmed. The Fosse Way itself ran all the way from the Exe estuary in Devon, to Ilchester (Somerset) before heading in a north-easterly direction through Cirencester (Gloucestershire), Leicester, itself a possible Legionary fortress under Plautius, and on to Lincoln.

The Roman army constructed several types of fort to fulfil particular roles. Whilst their general shape and layout generally conformed to a uniform design, the size of each fort was dependent on the number of troops expected to be based in it. The most common shape for the majority of Roman forts was rectangular with rounded corners, resembling a playing card. An outer ditch was dug whose spoil formed an inner bank, surmounted by a timber palisade. Permanent forts could have quite sophisticated defences with earth or clay banks and timber, or even stone, walls with towers and gates. Timber towers would project internally within the rounded corners and, if the fort were sufficiently large, more towers would straddle the fighting platform along the tops of the walls. The forts were laid out on a grid pattern with roads connecting the four gates, centrally placed in each wall. In the centre was the house of the commandant with a strongroom. Barrack-huts, granary, stores, baths, stables and workshops occupied the blocks formed by the roadways. In large forts, a track, the *pomerium*, ran around the inside of the walls to permit the speedy reinforcement of threatened lengths of wall in the event of an attack. Often a civilian settlement, a *vicus* grew up outside the gates of a fort, providing goods and services for the troops, ranging from pottery and metalwork, to food, and rest and recreation.

Roman forts

Vexillation fortresses, covering an area of around 20-30 acres (8-12 has), were built to accommodate mixed forces of legionaries, cavalry and auxiliaries, numbering up to a couple of thousand men, tasked with the operation to disarm the tribes during the early stages of the Roman Conquest of Britain. Two such forts, possibly used as bases for elements of the Ninth Legion, are known in Nottinghamshire. Osmanthorpe is one, and the other is Broxstowe. This latter fort, now lying under housing, was excavated in the 1930s. It had been constructed between AD 50 and 60 as a base for expeditions to subdue the Brigantes of Cheshire and North Wales. Second and third phases lasted until AD 75. It is unusually shaped with a cut-off corner causing it to resemble a Welsh harp. A combination of this odd shape and some ambiguous finds have caused its origins to be questioned, and it may be a re-used site from pre-Roman times.

Forts were built along the Fosse Way for garrisons to secure the temporary frontier and the lines of communication, particularly river-crossings, and many of these were later to develop into civil settlements. A fort at Tillbridge Lane, Newton-on-Trent, on a cliff on the Lincolnshire side of the river, dates from the campaigns of the AD 40s and 50s, and guards the road linking Worksop and Lincoln as it crosses the Trent. A little to the north, on the west bank of the Trent, a fort at Littleborough (*Segelocum*), was built to house auxiliary troops. It was occupied during the first century AD, to guard a ford across the Trent on the Lincoln to Doncaster road, which branches off from Ermine Street just below Scampton. A corresponding earthwork has been reported on the eastern, Lincolnshire bank at Marton. A similar auxiliary fort, fulfilling the same role, once lay beside the River Don at Templeborough (Yorkshire), on the Roman road from Nottingham to Doncaster. Guarding the Fosse Way itself there were at least two early forts and a possible third one. At *Margidunum*, just to the north of Bingham, a fort may have been built by AD 50. Excavation has uncovered the stone foundations of the commandant's house, arranged around a courtyard with verandas and covered ways, and replacing an earlier timber version. There are indications that the fort had a large military supply base alongside, apparently evidenced by large quantities of slag associated with iron-working. However, it has been suggested that such a depot might not have been risked in, what was at that time, the front line, that a military presence existed only until the troops moved on sometime around AD 70, and that some of the industrial activity belonged to the later phase of the site. At Brough (*Crococolana*), a ditched enclosure to the north-east of Newark, the cheek-piece of a Roman cavalry helmet with a casting of Epona, the Celtic goddess of horses, has been found. Notwithstanding the isolated and circumstantial nature of this evidence, it could still point to an occupation by auxiliary cavalry. Thorpe (*Ad Pontem*), the likely site of a pontoon bridge across the Trent, lies south of Newark. Here it appears that a fort with a large annexe on its northern side was built around AD 50–75, the first in a sequence of four building phases. From a much later period, but still a time when it was imperative that important routes be safeguarded, comes a small rectangular, triple-ditched enclosure at Scaftforth, east of Bawtry Bridge by the River Idle. Finds point to this being from the late Roman period. Attempts are often made to infer from the Roman road layout and known forts the likely locations of further forts in the network. Postulated forts in the area here under consideration include one near Bardon (Leicestershire), a second near Bilsthorpe, and a third near Radcliffe on Trent. It has been suggested that there was a possible Roman bridge over the Trent at Cromwell.

The final category of Roman fort represented in the county is the marching camp, a temporary overnight stop rather than a permanent garrison, with the purpose of simply providing security against a surprise night attack. On the march, Roman legionaries each carried a sharpened stake which would be used to supplement the 6ft (1.8m) high bank and the 5ft (1.5m) deep ditch, carefully constructed at the end of the day's march. Five examples of these marching camps are known in Nottinghamshire: at Farnsfield, Gleadthorpe near Warsop, Holme north of Newark on the bank of the Trent, and two at Calverton, one within the other but on a slightly different alignment.

Roman defended settlements

Some of these early forts went on to be developed as civil settlements. It would appear that the military had moved on from *Margidunum* well before the end of the second century, and that industrial activity either continued from these earlier days, or started up subsequently. With the demise of the fort came a small, walled town of 5 acres (2 has) on a different alignment from the fort. By the fourth century it had become more of an official staging-post on the Fosse Way rather than a civil settlement, and by 500 it was deserted. The town straddled the road and was enclosed, towards the end of the second century, by a wide defensive ditch and, initially, an earthen bank, polygonal in shape consisting of six fairly straight stretches forming an irregular hexagon. A century later significant improvements were made to these defences when the earth bank was enlarged, and a

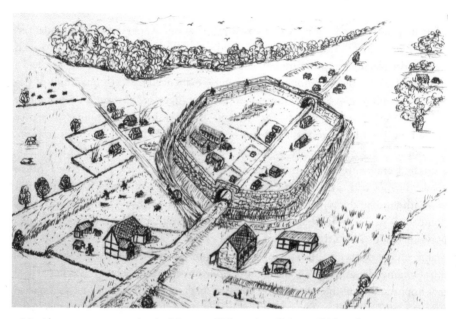

3 *Margidunum*, a reconstruction by Margaret Sibley, using all the available information; it shows the walled town straddling the Foss Way.

stone wall built into its forward face. In similar towns at this time this arrangement is known to have provided a stable fighting-platform, often of sufficient depth to carry defensive artillery such as heavy, bolt-firing crossbows and stone-throwing catapults. New outer ditches with an outer bank were also constructed and there were gates where the main road entered and exited the town in the north-east and south-west. Stone buildings stood both inside and outside the walled area. Like *Margidunum*, *Ad Pontem* was given its first defences as a non-military settlement towards the end of the second century. These consisted of a clay rampart with outer ditches on the lip of a terrace above the river, and a possible gateway may have provided access to the river-bank. Four circuits of widely spaced ditches suggest that the enclosed area was successively enlarged. Early in the third century a stone wall with a thickness of 8ft (2.4m), backed by a massive earthen rampart was built. These walls were pierced by a gateway, consisting of a timber-framed tower, and were continuously refurbished over the next two centuries. The settlement of Willoughby-on-the-Wolds (*Vernemetum*), on the other hand, remained an undefended roadside settlement, but continued in use into the Anglo-Saxon period.

Anglo-Saxon and Danish fortifications

There is evidence that a handful of Roman sites continued in occupation after the Romans had left around 410. The towns of *Margidunum*, *Vernemetum* and *Crococalana* have all yielded up Anglo-Saxon finds as has a villa site in Southwell. Whilst evidence of Saxon occupation at Newark-upon-Trent has led to speculation regarding the dating of the defensive bank and ditch surrounding the core of the medieval town, it is now known that these defences were raised shortly after 1066 along with the castle in its very earliest form. The Battle of Heathfield in 633 had seen King Edwin of Northumbria defeated and killed by the pagan king Penda of Mercia and when, in the 1950s, excavations beneath nearby Cuckney church, standing within the Norman castle earthworks, revealed up to 200 skeletons in mass-burial trenches, there was speculation that these might represent casualties from the battle.

Until around 865 the Danish raids on England had been hit-and-run attacks involving the gathering of loot and the destruction of property, after which the raiders would sail away to return another year. Sometimes Danish fleets over-wintered, drawing up their boats onto dry land alongside a suitable beaching-place, and surrounding their laager with a semi-circular enclosure defended by a bank and ditch. Such encampments were established at Repton (Derbyshire), and on the Lincolnshire bank of the Trent at Torksey. From this period onwards, however, the Danes showed every intention of colonising England. In 867 the Danish army had occupied York, where they defeated the Northumbrians attempting to dislodge them, and then moved south into Mercia, occupying Nottingham, where their ships could be protected. There is no real evidence of any significant earlier fortification, so a half-moon-shaped banked and ditched enclosure backing onto the Trent, and harbouring the Danish fleet, probably represented the first attempt to fortify this site. Its strategic significance lay in the strength of the high ground overlooking the Trent, and its status as the lowest point at which the river might easily be forded. Additionally, it commanded the Great North Road as well as the river. The Danish army, led by Ivar the Boneless and Halfdan Ragnarsson, was opposed by Burghred, King of Mercia, who, in 868, assembled a large army and invested the Danish fort. To maintain a full blockade, more troops were needed and so an approach was made to Wessex. Alfred and his brother Aethelred raised a large force of levies from Wessex and marched on Nottingham. However, the Danish defences were too strong and their warriors better armed and trained, and a truce was soon declared, after which the men of Wessex were grateful to head back home. It is possible that this early experience of having to compromise with a securely ensconced enemy determined Alfred in his future quest for victory on the open battlefield. Following a decade of often inconclusive warfare, Guthrum, the Danish leader, settled for peace and a share of the land, and the ensuing treaty partitioned England, setting up the Danelaw, to the north and east of a line drawn from Cheshire down to a point on the Thames, east of London.

Nottingham was soon established as an important Danish settlement beginning as an industrial centre with pottery kilns eventually producing a distinctive splashed ware, examples of which were found in a ditch filled in after 1066. However, the settlement was probably not fully fortified until around 900, possibly following the example of Alfred's Saxon burhs. Representing one of five separate jarldoms under the Kingdom of York, it became one of the Five Boroughs, along with Derby, Stamford, Lincoln and Leicester, and a centre of trade with Scandinavia and the Low Countries. Whereas Derby, Lincoln and Leicester had all previously been fortified by the Romans, there is only slight evidence that Stamford and Nottingham had been occupied to any great extent in the Middle Saxon period at all. At Nottingham the Danish strong-hold was surrounded by a bank and ditch, 19ft 6in (6m) wide, and 11ft (3.5m) deep with a U-shaped profile, later re-cut to become V-shaped. All this pre-dated the works of Edward the Elder. Traces of this early ditch were found near to Fletcher Gate (at SK574396), and bow-sided timber buildings, up to 100ft (35m) in length and usually described as halls, have been excavated near St Mary's church. These were similar to structures found in other Viking settlements in the east Midlands and were once wrongly thought to have derived from up-turned boats.

As part of his drive to reintegrate the Danelaw into a kingdom which comprised Wessex and Mercia, Edward the Elder captured Nottingham in 918, and organised a rebuilding of the town's defences, to be manned by both Mercian and Danish troops together. Two years later Edward returned and supervised the construction of a new burh, south of the river and linked to the existing one by a bridge, a very similar procedure to that he had carried out in Stamford. Nottingham's bridge, called the Hethbethebrigg in 920, would be rebuilt many times over the centuries, its final embodiment being demolished after 1871. A number of these 'double-boroughs' had been constructed on the Continent by Charles the Bald in the mid-ninth century, and there was an example at London, where Southwark represented a discrete burh on the south bank of the Thames. The establishment of these strongholds was part of a deliberate strategy by Edward, which involved the construction of some twenty-eight such fortresses, so sited as to deny the Danes the possibility of carrying out deep penetration raids into the heart of Mercia and Wessex, by blocking the river routes traditionally used by their longships.

There is no suggestion that Danish Nottingham represented a fully developed urban settlement but it did form the basis for a Saxon town after 920. Around St Mary's church, which may have been built as a Saxon minster, two of whose arches from the twelfth-century rebuild survive, there was a new Saxon enclosure. This was defended by a bank and ditch, and development on Barker Gate and Pilcher Gate exposed these Saxon defences in 1966. The area enclosed by Edward's defences is reckoned to have been 39 acres (15.5 has). The Wessex system of burhs was driven by an assess-ment of the land necessary to produce an adequate garrison for the local fortress. It has been suggested that Nottingham could draw manpower from around 1,300 hides which, applying the formula from Alfred's Burghal Hidage, would support a defended perimeter of about 1,500 yards, and the defences of what would become Nottingham's English Borough do indeed extend to a little under 2,000 yards, making these figures supportable. The town appears to have been dominant in the control of Edward's northern frontier, spreading its influence into Derbyshire. Throughout much of the tenth century, the mixed population of the Danelaw maintained a militia which effectively withstood attack from the north.

In 941 the Five Boroughs were taken back into the kingdom of York by King Olaf, and it is possible that a refurbishment of the earlier defences may date from then. In 1013 they submitted to Swein Forkbeard who was in the process of conquering England. By 1016, following the completion of the Danish conquest, Cnut created a new earldom.

4 Carlton-in-Lindrick, an eleventh-century Saxon church tower.

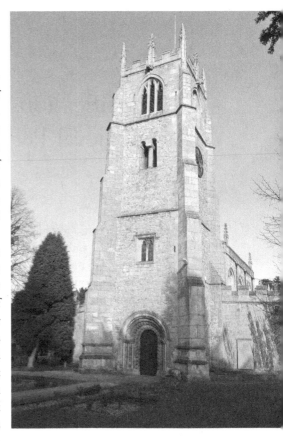

However, following unrest over newly introduced taxation under Earl Tosti of Northumbria and consequent representations to King Edward the Confessor, it was subsumed, after 1041, into the earldom of Mercia under Leofric. At the time of the Norman invasion, Nottingham was still confined to the eastern part with no evidence of any settlement on what would become the site chosen for new defences.

Anglo-Saxon church towers are thought to have played a part in secular as well as religious display, both as potentially defensive places of refuge, or as symbols of local authority where the local landowner might appear before his people, perhaps prior to dispensing justice. The word 'belfry' derives from words meaning height and strength. The west tower of St John the Evangelist at Carlton-in-Lindrick dates from the eleventh century and was added to an existing nave. It was originally of three stages with coupled bell-openings on two sides. The fourth storey was added after 1417. The ground floor of St Peter's, Clayworth, is also Saxon, and another, St Peter's, at Flawford, Ruddington, was demolished in 1773, but excavations have shown that a west tower had been added to the earlier church, in common with many other such towers, in later Saxon times.

Nottinghamshire exhibits a wide variety of features drawn from both Saxon and Danish cultures. There are Saxon place names such as Plumtree, Cuckney or Worksop, alongside Danish names which include Stragglethorpe, Welbeck and Kirkby. The moot known as the Thynghowe near Birklands, which was a place for applying the rules of the Danelaw, could not have been given a more Danish name, but it stands deep in Sherwood (Saxon: Shire Wood) Royal Forest. This may demonstrate how well-populated areas still absorbed incomers with their new customs and their new place names.

two

Fortifications in the Earlier Medieval Period 1066-1300

The campaigns which consolidated William I's conquest of England brought major changes to both the urban and the rural landscape. Although there had been examples of private fortifications in pre-Conquest times, the decades immediately following saw an explosion in castle-building with Nottingham as one of the earliest examples. As land was parcelled out to the new Norman nobility, castles were built as centres of these new estates and to epitomise the incoming regime. A century later, the Anarchy brought forth a further crop of castles, whilst general insecurity subsequently encouraged those with something to protect to build defensible residences.

Early Norman earth and timber castles

Very few castles share more than a superficial similarity. Although the received wisdom of the last 100 years stresses that the Normans built motte and bailey castles, the reality is much more complex. Although the castle, as a fortified private residence or a fortified centre of royal power was, indeed, a predominantly novel importation by the Normans, there were some existing precedents in England. A handful of castles had been built in the years preceding the Conquest by Normans resident in England under the patronage of Edward the Confessor. There were also some private fortified houses built by Saxon thegns, probably consisting of a timber hall and ancillary structures surrounded by a bank and ditch with a timber palisade and, perhaps, a gateway with a platform over it. This structure might be associated with an adjacent church with a stone tower. With the exception of a very small number, the Normans' early castles were built of earth and timber. In its simplest form, the castle consisted of a circular bank and ditch defended by a palisade, pierced by a defended gateway. Within this defended perimeter there might be a timber hall, stables, barns and workshops, and a chapel, space enough to accommodate the lordly family, the household servants, and half-a-dozen men who worked the land but, appropriately trained and equipped, could fight for their lord when called upon. This form of castle is known as a ring-work, which might have had an additional, outer enclosure, or bailey, differing little from the thegnly establishment it might have superseded, probably being only somewhat stronger. The motte was either a wholly artificial mound of earth, formed with the spoil from its deep surrounding ditch, or else a modification of an existing natural hillock or crag enhanced by scarping to make the sides steeper and more uniform, and isolated by the digging of a ditch. Either form could receive additional benefit from its natural surroundings – steep slopes or marshes for instance. It was sometimes necessary to strengthen the motte by layering it with timber, encasing it in clay, or terracing it and using stone revetments. Such techniques were most likely to be employed when the motte was intended to carry a heavy stone tower, but timber towers were often mounted on posts which were bedded on solid ground within the mound, and stone towers could be built on a foundation level or basement embedded in the mound itself. Much depended on the local geology and the nature of the soil. The motte-top might have a timber palisade with a fighting platform around the rim. If there was enough space, this shell-wall might have timber lean-to pentices built against it, forming a central courtyard, with or without a tower in its centre. Since mottes were less roomy than ring-works, they almost invariably had one or more baileys containing the structures which met the residential requirements of the household and garrison. Each bailey would be surrounded by bank, ditch and palisade, and have its own gateway. Often the inner bailey would be crescent-shaped, wrapping itself around the base of the motte, thereby maximising the defensive firepower of archers on the motte, whilst at the same time keeping attackers from approaching too closely to the base of the motte. Access to the motte would be by a flying bridge, by steps cut into the motte's side, or by continuing the bailey wall up the side of the motte to join the shell-wall, perhaps even with a tower at the junction. Some mottes had complex entry arrangements with gates and outer barbicans. Sometimes the choice of what type of castle to build was determined by the site, but other factors including purpose also came into play. The higher, more imposing, motte could be chosen as a means of overawing a subject population, for instance, in urban or rural setting. Choice could come down to local fashion or personal whim. Early attempts to quantify earthwork castle types in Nottinghamshire came up with a low ratio of ring-works to mottes, but more recent reinterpretations of sites and the application of improved criteria for the definition of castle-sites produce a figure closer to the national average.

Nottinghamshire's early Norman castles provide some good examples of many of the features described above. At Laxton a motte and bailey layout was adopted. The motte was large enough to have an imposing structure on top, providing a powerful message to the people of the forests whose administrative centre it soon became. The inner bailey was walled in stone and there has been speculation over the nature of the motte's crowning glory. In an article on computer games and virtual landscapes (Vista Centre in the Institute of Archaeology and Antiquity, University of Birmingham), Laxton was the recent subject of an investigation using cartographic, topographic and geophysical evidence, on the basis of which, hypothetical reconstructions were based. These are described as 'plausible' and reflect the arrangement of the earthworks and surviving fragments of masonry. A number of possible toppings for the motte were suggested, ranging from a shell keep à la Totnes (Devon), to a copy of St Leonard's Tower at West Malling (Kent) and to York's quatrefoil Cliffords Tower. Realistically the motte is unlikely to have supported the mass of masonry associated with towers, but a shell-keep is more feasible. The small mound which currently stands in the middle of Laxton's motte-top is thought to be a garden feature from several centuries later. The castle was ruinous by the late 1300s but a manor house occupied the inner bailey in Tudor times. The motte-top at Bothamsall has a sunken middle, quite large enough to hold a hall and detached kitchen. Prior to the Conquest it had been held by King Harold's brother Tostig, several of whose other estates acquired castles shortly after 1066. This begs the question as to whether these were developments of Tostig's own private fortified dwellings. If so, then Bothamsall may fall into this category, a hybrid motte/ring-work. The large motte at Egmanton appears to have a terrace to one side, and an appealing explanation for this is that it was a barbican, defending the entrance into the core defences on the motte-top. The connection between church and manor in Anglo-Saxon times has already been noted, and it would appear that this connection was to be continued under the Normans. Here at Egmanton the motte, with what appears to have been a wrap-around bailey, is built very close to the church. At Cuckney, whose motte is revetted in stone, the castle is likely to have been built around an existing church. At Southwell, the church itself became a castle for a short while. The proximity to the church at Shelford of a small, horseshoe-shaped earthwork may suggest a further example of this relationship of church to castle.

At Newark the stone castle of Alexander, Bishop of Lincoln was preceded by an earthwork castle soon after the Conquest. It is possible that this took the form of a motte and bailey, whose motte occupied the north-west angle between the present river-front and the approach to the bridge over the Trent. It would have been razed when the new gatehouse and angle tower were built in 1130. At Lowdham there are suggestions that the motte was crowned by a shell-wall, 4ft (1.3m) thick, inside which were buildings, connected by cobbled paths. Worksop Castle consists of a very large platform measuring 65 × 65 yards, with strong counter-scarp banks. This large

5 Egmanton motte showing the platform on the right which may indicate the presence of a barbican.

ring-work, possibly having a bailey to one side, would have accommodated significant ranges of buildings. At Aslockton there is a small motte with two baileys in line, but later garden landscaping may have altered these earthworks. Similar works at Haughton have rendered the large motte as a prospect mound with a spiral terrace, and obscured the arrangements of the bailey. Pancake Hill at East Bridgford is a small motte with a bailey. The earthworks at Annesley are too overgrown to interpret thoroughly but may be incomplete as they were abandoned soon after 1200 for the new hall. An example of the possible re-use of an earlier work is Beacon Hill, at Gringley-on-the-Hill, a prehistoric camp which may possibly have been brought back into use as a motte.

Nottingham and its castle after the Norman Conquest

Despite recent arguments regarding the rationale behind the siting of castles, listing a number of criteria ranging from schemes of national defence, the domination of established centres of population, and even random selection, it is likely that military and political, that is strategic, considerations underpinned the choice of Nottingham for one of William I's initial castle-sites. A castle at Nottingham could command the river-crossing and the major road north; it could dominate a resource-rich region; and it could provide a launch-pad for an offensive field army or a secure refuge for a force in retreat. At the same time it provided a dominant presence over a subject population; it housed a garrison which posed a permanent threat to those considering resistance to the new order; and it housed many of the legal, fiscal and administrative functions of local and national government. Nottingham lay on the most-used non-Roman road in the country, which would only lose this dense traffic when the Trent was bridged farther downstream at Newark in 1130. The royal castellan also had control of the castle at Tickhill on the road to York, and of those at Peveril and Bolsover in Derbyshire. Nottingham could therefore claim to be central to a strategy for controlling communications in the east Midlands. Additionally, in conjunction with castles at East Bridgford and Newark, the crossings of the Trent could be monitored.

Nottingham Castle occupies a strong position on a rocky crag above the River Leen, which may have been diverted to add a further layer of defence. It was established by William Peveril, on the king's orders, in 1068–69, in connection with William's campaign against a rebellion in northern England. The site is unusual in that, being removed from the earlier settlement, not only was it unnecessary to demolish houses to make way for the new fortress as was normal on urban castle-sites, but there was space for a number of enclosures and an adjacent park. The crag formed a natural D-shaped upper bailey, which was strengthened by the addition of a shell-wall, initially of timber, around its edge. A rock-cut ditch was crossed, on the northern side, by a fixed timber bridge, probably containing a drawbridge, leading to the middle bailey, 25ft (8m) lower and itself surrounded by a bank surmounted by a timber palisade and a ditch. The upper bailey, 50 yards across, would have contained timber lean-to buildings set against the shell-wall, possibly an imposing two- or three-storey tower with one or

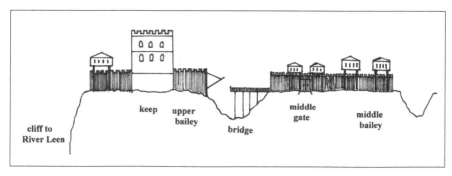

6 Nottingham Castle: conjectural cross-section of the earliest earth and timber defences raised in around 1068, seen from the east or town side.

two smaller ones astride the palisade and another over the gate-arch accessed by the bridge. Together, these defences provided ample protection against local unrest or even armed insurrection. The middle bailey contained most of the structures necessary to sustain the constable, his household and the garrison, installed to ensure that the populace of Nottingham obeyed the new king's injunctions.

Norman stone castles

The earth and timber defences of Nottingham Castle and the motte and bailey castle inferred from investigations at Newark lasted well into the next century. At Newark, Alexander, Bishop of Lincoln demolished the old castle, and commenced the construction of new works in the 1120s. This fortress consisted of a large rectangular bailey with angle towers, and a three-storey gatehouse in the middle of the northern curtain, noted as impressive in 1139. The core of the Norman south-west tower survives, and the line of the original ditch has been traced by excavation along three sides, the river marking the fourth. The curtain wall still adjoining the gatehouse was 40ft (12m) tall, and 6ft 6in (2m) thick and, as investigations have shown, was built at the same time, being tied together with transverse wooden beams, whose ghostly slots remain. Alexander's castle was built to the newly fashionable courtyard plan, with the hall, chambers and domestic offices ranged around the outer wall, some of them over vaulted under-crofts, and a cobbled yard in the middle. Whilst the gatehouse provided the strongest

7 Newark Castle, the gatehouse dating from the reconstruction of the castle, c.1130.

element of the castle, its layout gave rise to built-in vulnerabilities. Owing to its use as the bishop's private apartments and chapel, it was necessary to attach an external timber walkway in order to provide access to the en-suite chambers in the angle of the gatehouse and the north-east curtain at first-floor level. Along with a weakness in the drawbridge-raising arrangements, this would suggest that a further layer of defences, perhaps a small outer bailey or barbican, would have been desirable to the north of the gatehouse.

At Nottingham, it was probably Peveril's son who added the small, stone tower-keep by 1155, at the behest of Henry II. This keep, which projected into the upper bailey, and possibly replaced an earlier timber tower, was around 40ft (12m) square, and had three levels, one more than at Peveril's similar keep at Castleton (Derbyshire). The reign of Henry II saw a significant sum of money spent on the castle. After the keep, it is probable that the highest expenditure went on replacing the timber palisades with high, stone curtain walls, and the construction of a strong gatehouse for the middle bailey. The outer enclosure would have been left with only its original ditch and inner bank with timber palisade and gatehouse. Other improvements included a new Great Hall and chambers for the king and for his clerks, and a detached kitchen in stone. Money was also spent on a house for the king's falcons and for developing the park. 'Planking the tower', probably the medieval version of a loft-conversion, implies improvements to the keep's two main floors to make them more habitable. It may have been during John's seizure of the castle during Richard I's absence abroad that an outer barbican was erected. This was probably only of timber as it was captured by Richard who fired Henry II's outer gates prior to evicting his brother's garrison. Richard's and John's additions included stables, repairs to the castle's three chapels, and a further tower in the upper bailey, possibly at the junction of the shell-wall with that of the middle bailey.

Important royal castles were subject to a continuous process of development and modification. This ensured that defensive features were up-to-the-minute but, more importantly, that the castle was able effectively to fulfil its domestic, legal and administrative functions.

Under Henry III the wall of the outer bailey was rebuilt in stone and the twin-towered gatehouse which still stands was built. Five new towers, some of them open-backed and semi-circular, were built along the new walls of the outer bailey, including at the south-east and north-east angles. It must be remembered that the fortress still had to serve as a comfortable residence and so, in 1251, Henry III ordered the sheriff to have the queen's chamber, wardrobe and chapel whitewashed, and the king's great chamber wainscoted with vertical boards for painting. These improvements

8 Nottingham Castle: the outer gatehouse built by Henry III.

9 Nottingham Castle: Edward's Tower, one of those added to the masonry defences by Henry III.

were complemented by the rebuilding of the Great Hall in the middle bailey. Under Edward I, the substantial, three-storey cylindrical Black Tower was added to the curtain of the middle bailey's north-east angle, and the semi-circular east tower was built between it and the middle bailey gatehouse.

Many earth and timber castles were destined never to receive masonry defences, as only those important enough as military or administrative centres were consolidated in stone. Laxton's role as headquarters of the Keepers of Sherwood Forest ensured that its inner bailey was walled in stone, and that its motte was crowned with, most probably, a shell-wall, an arrangement possibly echoed at Lowdham.

The castle at war

We have to remind ourselves that, despite defensive features constituting the defining characteristics of the castle, war and violence could never be regarded as their default mode. At the twenty or so castles in Nottinghamshire, there were only nine occasions in the period from the Norman Conquest to the English Civil War, that any underwent

10 Nottingham Castle: the south-east tower, an angle tower of the outer bailey.

an attack. Two of those occasions fell in the early medieval period. The war between Henry I's nominated heir, the Empress Matilda, and her cousin Stephen lasted from 1135–54, and the fortunes of both parties waxed and waned, creating the state of anarchy which permitted lords, great and small, to terrorise their neighbourhoods. This was the time when many temporary castles were thrown up as bases from which robber bands might ride out to pillage and burn, with no effective central or regional authority to restrain them. Some lords, however, came to an accommodation, limiting the potential for destruction. The earls of Chester and Leicester, for instance, agreed the establishment of a demilitarized zone centred on Leicester with its northern boundary along the Castle Donington-Kinoulton-Belvoir line. Within this area no new castles could be raised and this may be one of the reasons for the scarcity of castles south of the Trent. Several Nottinghamshire castles did figure in the struggle. In 1140, Nottingham was attacked, apparently unexpectedly, by Duke Robert of Gloucester, Matilda's most powerful supporter, possibly out of a personal motive of revenge against the second William Peveril, Stephen's castellan. Fire destroyed much of the city and many citizens were carried off. The next year, Stephen and Peveril were captured by Matilda's forces at the Battle of Lincoln. Stephen handed over Nottingham Castle to Matilda who installed William Paynel as governor. This forced the evacuation of the royalist garrison which decamped to Southwell. Here, in the minster complex, they found a ready-made fortress. Begun in 1108, the church, with its two great west towers, was effectively complete by this time, and the addition of an outer circuit of banks and ditches would have made it well-nigh impregnable to anything but an army with a siege train. This was seen as a provocation by Paynel who left Nottingham in order to raise such a force to attack Southwell. This played right into Peveril's hands, providing the opportunity to retake Nottingham, and to reinstall its royalist garrison. Southwell was left in peace. The damage caused by these actions may have reached as far as Trent Bridge which was in need of repairs using timber from Bestwood around this time. Although too much has often been made of the notion of the adulterine or unlicensed castle, some of the less substantial earth and timber castles in the county may have originated from this time. There are strong local traditions that Thomas de Cuckney, a supporter of Stephen, threw up his fort around the pre-existing church at this time but there is no evidence to corroborate this.

The second occasion in which castles were called upon to earn their keep was during the disturbed reigns of Richard I and his brother John. On Richard's accession in 1189 he ensured that his brother John was well provided with lands which included the County of Nottinghamshire with the town but not the castle. Richard then went off on Crusade but was intercepted on his return through Europe and imprisoned, only being released in 1194 on payment of an enormous ransom. With Richard's return to England, those bishops and nobles upholding Richard's cause moved to besiege all those castles which John had ordered to be defended against Richard. These included Nottingham which John had seized using the excuse of acting as Richard's viceroy. The Earl of Huntingdon, brother of King David of Scotland, the Earl of Chester and the Earl Ferrers laid siege to Nottingham Castle, whose garrison appear to have been genuinely unaware of Richard's return. Concerned that such an important castle should be held against his forces, Richard rushed to Nottingham with an army to take personal charge of the attack. Fighting lasted for three days, during which time the timber outer gatehouse was stormed giving Richard possession of the outer bailey, and the timber barbican outside the gate to the middle bailey was burned. The outer bailey became the site for a gallows on which were hanged some captured sergeants (men-at-arms), and for a battery of siege engines. Richard's men attempted a frontal assault on the stone walls of the middle bailey, deploying shields or mantlets against the crossbow bolts fired at them at point-blank range. Eventually, word circulated in the castle that it actually was the real king himself attacking them and a delegation was sent out to confirm his identity. Capitulation soon followed, and the victorious Richard took his nobles off to Sherwood Forest for some hunting, vowing never again to allow such a dense concentration of lands around strategic centres like Nottingham to be held in potentially hostile hands.

When John succeeded his brother as king, he was faced with civil war, foreign invasion and power struggles with the Church. In 1206 he seized the Bishop of Lincoln's castle at Newark and installed a mercenary captain, Robert de Gaugy, as castellan. Only after John's death were steps taken to repossess the castle, and de Gaugy was ordered by Henry III, through his Regent William Marshall, to surrender the castle to the bishop. De Gaugy refused and the castle resisted both a bombardment by stone-throwing catapults and attempts by miners to weaken the walls. Finally, money talked, and de Gaugy surrendered for a payment of £100 in silver.

Whilst the actions described above involved many hundreds of soldiers, it was not the practice in peacetime to tie up large numbers of expensive troops in garrisons. When John seized Nottingham Castle, for instance, his men ejected just forty-one individuals, probably less than half of whom would have been full-time sergeants, probably under the command of a solitary knight. In 1267, the annual cost of keeping the garrison in Nottingham Castle came to £445 with the commander being paid nearly £100.

By the thirteenth century, Nottingham Castle was held to be one of the strongest royal castles in England, a fact underlined by its inclusion in the group of castles whose constables were reminded of the need for vigilance on the four occasions that royal warnings were broadcast (1223, 1258, 1260 and 1297). Despite these warnings, in 1264, during the Second Barons' War, the castle was occupied by Robert de Ferrers, Earl of Derby, a supporter of Simon de Montfort who was in rebellion against Henry III. It would appear that Ferrers was motivated less by a desire for constitutional reform than a hatred of Prince Edward (later Edward I) who held some Ferrers lands. Fortunately, unlike at some other Midland castles seized by Ferrers, here at Nottingham, the situation was retrieved peacefully.

Fortified manors

We have seen how the earth and timber castle at Annesley had been abandoned by around 1220, for the greater comfort of a more spacious manor house. The builder of this new house, brother of the Sheriff of Nottingham, was accused of upsetting the local power balance with his new fortified house, using ill-gotten gains made during the disturbances of 1216 at the end of John's reign, and this provides an example of how life was changing. Fewer outright fortresses were being built, but most manorial buildings were generally defensible. The most commonly built defensive feature was the moat, which would also serve a whole range of other purposes, including drainage and fishponds. Merely to build in stone invested a building with some protection against fire. At Stoke Bardolph, there was a stone hall with a possible two-storey addition of c.1200 at one end, perhaps a tower or a solar block, and traces of further foundations adjacent. Bestwood Lodge was a timber-framed hall with outbuildings and a stone tower of c.1200. It was surrounded by a fence, and had a deer-park, embanked by 1199. Clipstone was the site, from around 1180, of a royal hunting lodge. There was a timber chamber and a chapel, and both Henry III and Edward I later added further chambers, one in stone over an under-croft, stables for 200 horses and a timber hall. The whole complex was surrounded by a bank and ditch with a palisade, and a defended timber gatehouse. The ditch was 9ft (2.7m) deep and measured 14ft 6in (4.5m) across. The reconstruction drawing on site illustrates an extensive complex of stone and timber buildings with a stone gatehouse. A survey of the surrounding village appeared to have discovered the remains of such a gatehouse from the precinct walls, incorporated in a house. Another royal hunting lodge was Kingshaugh at Darlton, parts of whose masonry walls survive in a later house on the site. It was surrounded by extensive banks, ponds and ditches, and in 1193 was converted into a castle and held by adherents of John in rebellion against Richard I. John built a new house at considerable expense in 1210. Much has been written regarding the issue of licences to crenellate with regard to castles, defensible houses and monastic precincts. It would appear that, rather than a form of medieval planning permission without which building could not proceed, the licence was more a mark of royal approbation which the recipient could flaunt before his peers.

Many of the lesser nobility or yeomen made do with surrounding their property with a simple moat, and there are eighty-six moated sites in Nottinghamshire, of which, by 1978, a total of twenty-three had been scheduled as Ancient Monuments. The total includes three at Norwell, one of which supports a late medieval stone house. Another, at Sibthorpe, consists of an extensive complex which formerly surrounded a fortified manor. Within the moats are fishponds and a stone dovecote. A few of these moated sites have been excavated. One such, Epperstone, stands between Manor Hill Close and Nether Manor Close, at the bottom of the hill on which a later manor house was built. On excavation it was found to be quite empty, and sometimes gardens and orchards might be surrounded by a moat to prevent the theft of a valuable cash-crop. No medieval pottery was found in the 1950s excavation of Epperstone, so this may provide a plausible explanation. A moat at Bilborough was excavated prior to its disappearance under housing in the 1950s, and found to enclose a walled enclosure and other possibly substantial structures. Jordan's Castle at Wellow was long described as the county's only Norman ring-work but is assigned to the roll of thirteenth-century moated sites by Dr Sarah Speight. It is circular, about 30 yards in diameter and is linked to a licence to crenellate granted to Richard de Foliot in 1264 for Grimston, a village long ago deserted.

Town and village defences

Communities often deemed it advisable to provide themselves with some form of defensible barrier. Nottingham had been a Danish and an Anglo-Saxon burh. The original Saxon and Danish settlement on St Mary's Hill became known as the English Borough, soon to have added on its west side, the French Borough, both to be held by the king. Still further to the west, on what later became known as Standard Hill, around 500 yards from the English Borough, was one of the first of the Conqueror's new castles. This had prompted the establishment of the French Borough as both a source of provisions and as a magnet for attracting Norman settlers who would shift the balance in the town's demographic make-up, and finance the garrison of the castle. The Norman defences of the town extended from the northern outworks of the castle following the line of what are now Park Row and Parliament Street, before dropping down to join the original defences of the English Borough on its eastern side. The southern edge of the newly integrated town was marked by the cliff above the River Leen. This new circuit of defences increased the area enclosed four-fold from 30 acres (12 has) to nearer 125 acres (50 has). These earth and timber defences, possibly consisting of little more than a boundary ditch, lasted for two centuries. The town received its first murage grant in 1267 and a stone wall, pierced by gates, was constructed, using white sandstone which may have been excavated from below the castle. The construction appears to have been organised on a gang system which produced inconsistencies in the quality of different parts of the walls. Excavations at Park Row during the construction of Maid Marian Way uncovered significant

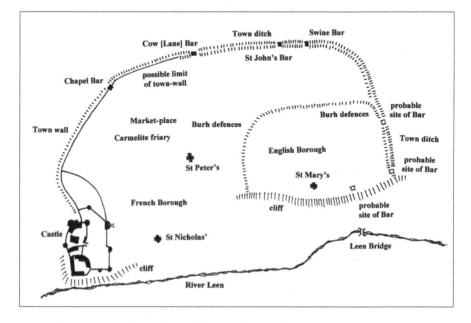

11 Sketch map to show the medieval defences of Nottingham.

lengths of wall, some of 7ft (2.1m) in thickness joined by a link wall to other lengths only 5ft (1.5m) thick. Various irregularities in the construction tend to point to the walls being built over a period of time, rather than in one concerted effort. Traces of interval towers have been found and there may have been up to seven fortified gateways, or bars. As in other towns with Danish origins, streets were known by the Norse *gata*, which was anglicised, for instance, as Pilcher Gate or Goose Gate, clouding the issue of the existence of actual town gates. It is possible that the eastern defences were only ever ditches, so their crossings may have been marked by little more than symbolic barriers.

Newark's medieval defended circuit formed a rectangle with the castle in the middle of the west side defined by the river. The first defences consisted of a bank and ditch which left the river near the Coffee Palace, the angle still visible though much rebuilt, running along Slaughter House Lane before turning south below St Mary's church along Appleton Gate and Carter Gate, thence to follow Lombard Street back to the river. These defences, probably still enclosing the core of the Saxon settlement, pre-dated the stone castle, so gates at Millgate, Bar Gate and Bridge Street were probably supplemented by one on the old Great North Road over the new bridge after 1130. A stone tower was excavated at Cuckstool Wharf, near the castle's south-west tower, and this may have been a watergate in the town wall. The existing circuit was walled in stone in the fourteenth century, and refurbished during the English Civil War.

As well as these town defences, some villages were also defended, and at least three retain some vestiges of these earthen banks and ditches. At Plumtree, a medieval bank and ditch stretches across the north-west edge of the village, and at Saxondale, a length of bank survives on the south side. Gorge Dyke, marks the extent of Wellow's village enclosure, and still consists of lengths of dry ditch running between the points SK671663-674662-671659.

Ecclesiastical fortifications

Falling into one other category of early medieval fortification, are those connected with the church whose temporal business could sometimes appear at odds with its spiritual mission. Lenton Priory, a Cluniac house built in the twelfth century, was accessed by a gatehouse which stood until the nineteenth century at the junction of Gregory and Abbey Streets, and on whose foundations the White Hart Hotel is said to be built. At Kinoulton there is a rectangular moat with traces of buildings on two sides, which is thought to have been a grange of either Launde (Leicestershire) or of Swineshead (Lincolnshire). The crusading order of Hospitallers or Knights of St John owned properties across England. They had granges in Nottinghamshire at Caunton (Dean Hall Farm), Ossington and Winkburn. Southwell was the site of an early palace of the Archbishops of York which had been rebuilt by the end of the fourteenth century, and then again by 1436.

three

The Later Medieval and Tudor Periods 1300-1600

This period is characterised by periods of anarchy and social change precipitated by fluctuations in the climate, by disease on an epidemic scale, by religious and dynastic upheaval, and by civil and foreign wars. England, though less affected than the lands of continental Europe by either full-fledged foreign invasion or mere casual raiding, was nevertheless an extremely dangerous place in the Middle Ages. It was all too tempting for nobility and gentry alike to resort to force to intimidate the peasantry or to resolve civil disputes over rights, ward-ships or property ownership, particularly when a pool of unemployed soldiery was generally available for hire, and human life was cheap. Unsurprisingly, those of sufficient wealth and standing often fortified their houses, not to the extent of being able to resist a determined assault or a siege, but enough to deter the casual band of predatory ne'er-do-wells. Meanwhile, the accent at royal and baronial castles alike was shifting further away from the military stronghold toward the administrative centre, or to a more domestic focus on comfort, or luxury. The dynastic struggle known since Victorian times as the Wars of the Roses involved attempts by each side to eradicate the opposition, and had little to do with gaining, or even retaining territory. So a succession of pitched battles, usually with particularly brutal and un-chivalric outcomes, rather than sieges of towns or castles, determined the fortunes of the protagonists.

Robin Hood and other outlaws

It has long been thought that Robin Hood was a composite character, made up of elements of a number of historical personages, living during the thirteenth century, and possibly around the reigns of Richard I and John. However, since the stories were not written down until at least 100 years later, it is not impossible that events and situations subsequent to those times were included. Although there are many ties to Yorkshire in all the legends, particularly those set down in the *Little Geste of Robyn Hode and his Meynie*, it is the Sheriff of *Nottingham*, not York, who is consistently the villain. It would appear that several of the same officers served as sheriff or Forest Justice in both counties at different times in the first quarter of the thirteenth century.

The *Geste*, written toward the end of the fourteenth century at a time of civil unrest, comprises five separate stories strung together to form a narrative. Nottingham itself figures prominently, with specific locations being named, and Sherwood Forest provides a plausible refuge for a gang of outlaws seeking a secure base.

Throughout the medieval period there were gangs operating in the forests, living off the land and committing opportunist crimes involving kidnap and ransom, highway robbery and extortion. Henry II offered rewards of 10d raised to 5s by John, for the apprehension and conviction of outlaws. Notorious gangs such as the Coterels and the Folvilles who operated in the east Midlands in the fourteenth century, often received help from influential landowners and even from those who were meant to uphold the law, and there is little to dissuade us from concluding that corruption was rife in these times. Simon Folville was actually Nottingham's MP in 1322. Just as Sir Richard at the Lee became Robin Hood's protector, then Sir Richard Foliot harboured Roger Godberd's following, and Sir William Aune of Gringley was one of those knights who sponsored the Coterel gang. Previous misdemeanours were no bar to royal patronage and the talents of both the leader of the Coterels and of Sir William Aune brought them employment under Edward III. Some of those actually implicated in the activities of criminal gangs held the offices of Mayor of Nottingham or Sheriff of Nottinghamshire. One sheriff was indicted for taking corn and livestock from villagers as well as extorting money, and taking bribes. Failing to appear at his trial, he was, himself, outlawed.

There may also be political dimensions to the stories. Some writers have sought to link the 'Disinherited', those who had fought on the wrong side at Evesham in 1265, with the outlaws in the forests, and they may not all have made it to the Isle of Ely. One such group was defeated by a force led by the deputy constable of Nottingham Castle, across the Leicestershire border in Charnwood Forest. Among them were a number of knights who had previously been members of the garrison of Nottingham Castle, but had been caught up in the subsequent free-for-all of royal and baronial alliances, generally characterised by the contested ownership of land. Those disputes between a king and factions supporting a rival claimant may have influenced the degree to which bands of outlaws were pursued or shielded. Members of the nobility and their followers fell in and out of favour, as their leaders' fortunes waxed and waned. Sir Roger Leyburn, for instance, was lord warden of the Cinque Ports under Henry III, reduced to the ranks by de Montfort, and then made constable of Nottingham Castle when Henry regained his dominance. Local knightly outlaws led a band in preying on, particularly, Church properties, and did not shrink from the odd murder if the situation demanded it. A skirmish with a force under Sir Roger Lestrange may have resulted in the capture and execution of one or more of them, but others, apprehended at Rufford Abbey, were treated leniently, possibly due to a friendship with the future Edward I. Another of them, Roger Godberd, finally came before the courts a mere twelve years later but, notwithstanding the capital crimes he was reckoned to have committed, it would appear that poaching deer at Bulwell and Bestwood was the most serious crime of which he stood accused, and even then he was acquitted for lack of evidence. Courts of the

Justices of the Forest were held in a number of places including Linby and Hucknall to hear all sorts of cases, but primarily those concerning poaching. Another group which contributed large groups of outlaws was the 'contrariants'. These had been the supporters of Thomas of Lancaster, whose rebellion had been crushed at the Battle of Boroughbridge in 1322, by Edward II, and who infested the forests of Yorkshire and Nottinghamshire.

There appear to be many parallels between the legends and documented history, but the one element missing is the charitable aspect, since the motive for robbery was invariably the enrichment of the perpetrator, an activity requiring no third-party beneficiaries. It may simply have been the fact that an outlaw leader was seen to be opposing the established order, exemplified by the popular canonisation of Simon de Montfort after the failure of his struggle against Henry III, that led to the invention of the legendary activity of robbing the rich to give to the poor.

Later medieval castles in Nottinghamshire

Nottingham was one of the few royal castles which continued to develop throughout the medieval period and Edward II carried out some improvements to the domestic facilities of the upper bailey. Sometime after Edward II's supposed death, the castle was the setting, it is said, for the young Prince Edward's bid for independent kingship in 1330, when he came up through the caves at dead of night to surprise his mother and her lover Mortimer. It was Edward III who embarked, in 1358, on the next major building programme under the supervision of the constable, Stephen Romylow. Along with a great deal of repairs arising from earlier neglect, Romylow's Tower in the middle bailey was built. This rectangular tower was flanked by new chambers, and a cross-wall was built linking it to the rebuilt middle gatehouse, creating, in the old moat, a courtyard with a range of service buildings to cater for the needs of the chambers on each side. Some of these may have housed important prisoners such as the King of Scotland who had been lodged there earlier in the century. Between this complex and the Great Hall, a new chapel was built.

From 1476, Edward IV began to build a sumptuous lodging attached to a new polygonal tower on the north-west angle of the middle bailey. Probably taking the Herberts' range at Cardiff Castle as the model, the three-storey, eight-bay block of apartments, with full-height semi-octagonal oriels to the front, curved around the inside of the curtain as far as the Black Tower. Behind them stood the semi-octagonal tower which, on its completion by Edward's brother Richard in 1483, bore his name. Richard's Tower rose up from the rock, topping the apartments by two storeys, had a turret and annexe to one side, and has been shown with machicolations, allying it to such contemporary donjons as built by the Herberts at Raglan (Gwent), and by Lord Hastings at Ashby-de-la-Zouch (Leicestershire). The castle was Richard III's main residence after his accession, and his principal military base from which he set out with his troops to his defeat and death at Bosworth (Leicestershire) in 1485.

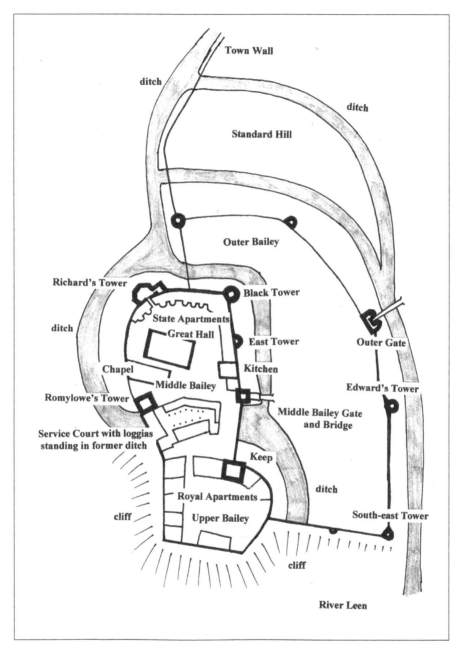

Town Wall

ditch

ditch

Standard Hill

Outer Bailey

Richard's Tower

Black Tower

ditch

State Apartments

Great Hall

East Tower

Outer Gate

Chapel

Kitchen

Middle Bailey

Romylowe's Tower

Edward's Tower

Middle Bailey Gate
and Bridge

Service Court with loggias
standing in former ditch

Keep

ditch

cliff

Royal Apartments

South-east Tower

Upper Bailey

cliff

River Leen

12 Sketch plan of Nottingham Castle in its most fully developed state in around 1490.

By the time that Smythson drew his plan in 1617, parts of the castle, including the Great Hall, had been demolished. Much, however, was to survive until after the Civil War, when it was slighted and replaced, from 1674, by the palace of the Cavendish Duke of Newcastle (under-Lyme).

Soon after 1300, the riverside wall of the castle at Newark was realigned in order to accommodate a range of new buildings to include two halls, one of them over an under-croft reached by a postern and passage from the riverside, two sets of chambers on two floors, and underground prisons. The south-west tower was strengthened by the addition of a plinth but the pentagonal north-west tower was completely new. It was four storeys high over a basement prison. A new central tower, projecting from the middle of the Great Hall was half-hexagonal in plan, and an oriel provided a window seat with a river view in the Bishop's Hall. All this work was carried out through to the end of the fifteenth century, by which time the defensive elements of the castle had been superseded by an emphasis on splendour and comfort.

Greasley Castle is a rectangular moated enclosure representing the main house built by Sir Nicholas de Cantilupe, third baron, who had fought for Edward III in Scotland and France. As a sign of royal approval he was granted a licence to crenellate in 1340.

The stone walling, the foundations of buildings, an arch reconstructed in outbuildings and part of the moat all survive. Sir Nicholas was also granted a licence to found the nearby Carthusian house of Beauvale Priory in 1343. Masonry still visible in the corner of a barn would suggest the remains of a circular angle tower, and analogous examples from the same period would point to a square plan with a tower at each corner and a gatehouse in the middle of one side. Quite elaborate architectural mouldings and tracery survive on site pointing to the level of craftsmanship on which the builder might draw. Wiverton Hall has a fifteenth-century gatehouse with narrow

13 Newark Castle: the riverside wall, of soon after 1300; in the centre may be seen the pentagonal north-west tower, with four storeys over a basement prison.

14 Newark Castle: the riverside wall with, on the right, the strengthened south-west tower on its plinth.

15 Greasley Castle showing traces of a circular corner tower.

cylindrical towers flanking a gate-arch with a groin-vaulted ceiling two storeys above, recorded by Smythson in 1615. The hall was probably built by Sir Thomas Chaworth sometime after 1440 and before 1460.

Fortified houses

Less ambitious than a courtyard castle like Greasley, were a series of stone tower-houses, appearing to date from the fourteenth or early fifteenth centuries, and quite unusual outside the marches of Wales or the Scottish borders. At Halloughton, a three-storey tower adjoins a timber-framed hall. The tower has an external entrance at ground-floor level and is connected to the hall only at first-floor level, with stairs then ascending to the second floor. The roof is gabled and appears not to have had a wall-walk. The tower measures 24ft (7.5m) by 17ft (5.2m) and retains some original features including an ogee-headed two-light window. Linby Hall now presents as a three-storey seventeenth-century house but encased within it at the south end is a 29ft (9m) square tower with walls 3–5ft (1–1.5m) thick. Again, some original features such as a chamfered doorway with its draw-bar hole survive. A third tower-house is hidden inside the corner nearest the church, of the late eighteenth-century Strelley Hall. The tower measures 23ft 9in (7.3m) by 22ft (6.8m) and lay inside a rock-cut ditch 22ft 9in (7m) across and 10ft (3m) deep, located by excavation in 2006. As at Greasley,

architectural details and pottery were recovered suggesting a date in the fourteenth century. A hall stood adjacent to the tower and a chapel was in use in 1356. The outbuildings alongside the road, rebuilt for the new house around 1790, incorporate medieval buttressed sandstone walls which would have been part of buildings belonging to the earlier tower. The original core of Clifton Hall was a late medieval tower-house. A seventeenth-century depiction of the hall includes a tall tower most likely to have been part of Smythson's remodelling but may be an extension of the earlier tower. Carr's complete rebuild of the hall in the eighteenth century would have seen the tower's demolition.

The royal hunting lodge complex at Clipstone was extensively repaired for Edward III in 1348, 1360 and 1367, but no

16 Halloughton Tower, a three-storey tower-house with only nods to defence.

substantial new buildings were added. In 1434, however, large sums of money were allocated, not only to repairs, but for the construction of new buildings including a tower, after which the palace was given to Henry VI's half-brothers. Thereafter little is heard until it is described in 1525 as decayed. Edward II had built another lodge nearby known as Clipstone Peel, now Beeston Lodge. This consisted of a timber chamber and a stone gatehouse which (allegedly) still stands in woodland. A number of other moated sites such as Gateford Hall on the outskirts of Worksop contained manor houses, in this particular case, incorporated into a later house. Sir Thomas Molyneux's moated mansion at Hawton occupied a strong position between the River Devon and the Middle Beck, and would be refortified in 1645 as part of the Parliamentarian siege-works around Newark.

17 Linby Hall: the later house conceals a three-storey fourteenth-century tower-house at one end.

An example of the need for a defensible home is the case of the Plumpton family, based in North Yorkshire but owning manors in Nottinghamshire including Kinoulton and Mansfield Woodhouse. Problems of inheritance, and debt, coupled with backing the wrong side at the Battle of Towton, brought them into conflict with powerful lawyers who enjoyed the favour of Crown and Church. In the unsettled times of the Wars of the Roses and the reign of the insecure Henry VII that followed, litigation led to armed conflict, skirmishes, land seizure, the persecution of the family's relations and tenants, and even a prolonged siege of the newly fortified Plumpton manor

18 Clipstone hunting lodge became an extensive and palatial centre for royal expeditions into the forest, but only fragments remain.

house itself, which had been stocked with weapons in anticipation. Dragging on for four generations, the affair reduced the family to penury, losing all its lands over the decades. Such evidence along with documents like the Paston Letters from Norfolk, underline the principle that, in the absence of strong government at either national or local level, might was right and possession nine-tenths of the law.

The earliest surviving element of Holme Pierrepont Hall is the entrance range, formerly the southern side of a late medieval courtyard house. In its centre is the brick gatehouse with three-storey gate-towers flanking an entrance archway with blank arches each side where pedestrian entrances might be expected. This may date from around 1510. This south range is made up of retainers' lodgings, self-contained rooms with fireplaces and garderobes, divided by stud partitions which rise up into the roof through the two storeys. In medieval houses, lords were advised to keep a central hall served by a single kitchen as it was more economical to feed the household communally. It was also one way of keeping an eye on things and of discouraging the formation of cliques. Members of the household were accommodated in private rooms on two floors, very similar to arrangements still existing at Oxbridge colleges, while the lordly family would inhabit a separate part of the establishment, easily isolated from the rest of the household, especially if retainers' loyalty was suspect. By the time of the paranoid Henry VII, great lords were being actively discouraged from housing armed retainers, with one or two going to the block for defying such injunctions. One notorious later example is supplied by Edward Stafford, Duke of Buckingham, whose stronghold at Thornbury (Gloucestershire) housed retainers in grand lodgings ranged around three courtyards. This perceived challenge to royal authority was sufficient to trigger Stafford's execution in 1521. No doubt the more lowly lords of houses such as Holme Pierrepont stayed well away from royal politics, but the insecurities brought about by lack of heirs to the throne and continuing religious uncertainties encouraged lords to walk the tightrope between personal security and attracting the wrong sort of royal recognition.

19 Holme Pierrepont Hall, built around three sides of a quadrangle, was entered by this imposing three-storey gatehouse.

Late medieval towns

Wealthy mercantile communities found it essential to safeguard themselves. The walls of Nottingham were maintained and improved throughout this period. The last surviving gate, Chapel Bar, its site now a traffic island in front of the Albert Hall and the Playhouse, was demolished in 1743. At Newark the earlier bank and ditch was replaced by stone town walls during the fourteenth century. Rich merchants were beginning to build stone houses, sometimes over vaulted cellars and exploiting the situation, peculiar to Nottingham, in which they could excavate cellars in the rock on which much of the town was built, creating caves. These subterranean strongrooms provided secure storage for stock, treasure or business records.

Ecclesiastical fortifications

At Beauvale Priory, a three-storey tower-house, possibly the prior's lodging, was included in the build of 1343. It stands at the west end of the church and has a ground-level door into the basement as well as a first-floor door accessed by external stairs. Like Halloughton it has a gabled roof and there is no evidence for a wall-walk. The blocked arches of the gatehouse range, with fascia walls to first-floor height, are incorporated in farm buildings and formerly used as a granary. The hunting lodge maintained by Lenton Priory at Aspley consisted of a timber-framed hall with an attached brick tower. This 22ft 9in (7m) square tower had walls a metre in thickness and a spiral stair in a projecting corner turret. It was destroyed in 1968. The Whitefriars or Carmelite house in Nottingham had been established on a site between St James's Lane and Moothall Gate by 1271. In the next century it expanded until, by 1495, the site had been enclosed by walls and gates and a prior's house had been added. The Archbishops of York had earlier built a palace at Southwell which was rebuilt around 1360 by Archbishop Thoresby, and then completed by Archbishop Kemp by 1436. The palace lies along the south side of the minster, and consists of four ranges of buildings around a rectangular courtyard. The west range has been successively restored and is in current use by the Bishop of Southwell. It contained the hall, entered through an external porch, a two-storey chamber block, a screens passage and service block with the usual buttery and pantry, and access to a now-vanished detached kitchen. The other three ranges, now ruined, contained two-storey lodgings, a chapel, and the archbishops' private apartments, and all retain original features such as chimneys and fireplaces. Projecting out at the south-east corner of the palace, well-away from the house, is the Garderobe Tower of around 1360. Up a flight of eight steps there is a chamber with a central pillar containing four apsidal closets with a circulatory passage and slit-windows in the outer wall, an unusual if not unique arrangement. The solid perimeter walls of the palace are raised on plinths, but there appears no evidence for a moat. Many members of the medieval episcopacy went out of their way to have chapels or residences either on islands or otherwise surrounded by water, observing a well-established

20 Beauvale Priory was defended by a gatehouse and this sturdy three-storey tower-house which probably constituted the prior's lodging.

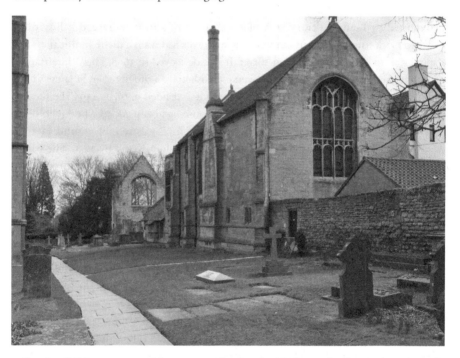

21 Southwell Palace was one of the many residences of archbishops of York; it presented mainly blank walls to the outside, here belonging to the North Chamber Block with the east end of the chapel visible beyond.

22 Southwell Palace: the east wall with the gable of a hall, and the projecting garderobe tower beyond.

23 Worksop Priory: the imposing fourteenth-century gatehouse.

tradition of Marian symbolism. The imposing gatehouse of the early fourteenth-century Augustinian house of Worksop Priory has a gate-hall with wings to each side. To one side is a chapel with a porch, and to the other, the guest-master's chamber and porter's room, with probable guest-chamber above. The gate-hall is divided halfway along by a cross-wall with coach and pedestrian arches. It is clearly intended to impress visitors, grand and humble alike, and to deter those threatening the monastic peace.

The Wars of the Roses

The River Trent was presented as the line below which the barbarous northern Lancastrians, bolstered by Scottish adventurers and French mercenaries, might pillage the civilised lands of the southern Yorkists, a belief given greater credence by the depredations of Queen Margaret's Lancastrian army on its southern progress in 1460. This would make the east Midlands a potential battleground. The northward advance of the Duke of York to meet the Lancastrian forces, for instance, involved a skirmish near Worksop, as York proceeded to his castle of Sandal prior to defeat and death at the Battle of Wakefield in December 1460. His son, by now Edward IV, used the facilities of Nottingham Castle to rest his army and to replenish their supplies on his way north to fight the Battle of Towton on Palm Sunday 1461, avenging the deaths of his father and brother. The final battles, Bosworth (1485) and Stoke Field (1487) moreover, were fought in Leicestershire and Nottinghamshire respectively.

The dynastic struggles between the houses of York and Lancaster threw up a number of power-brokers, whose forces often proved decisive in the pitched battles which punctuated the conflict. One such man was William Hastings, charged by the Yorkist king Edward IV with amassing an affinity in the Midlands, centred round the royal manors of Leicestershire and Nottinghamshire. In July 1469 Edward was in Nottingham when his cause suffered a setback. Opposition forces under Robin of Redesdale were advancing south from Yorkshire, whilst another hostile army under the Earl of Warwick was making its way northwards. Edward stayed in Nottingham awaiting reinforcements under the Earl of Pembroke. However, Pembroke became separated from his archers and was defeated at Edgecote in Oxfordshire. Edward was taken briefly but managed to get away and flee to Burgundy. By 1471 he was back in Yorkshire and, aided by Hastings, was assembling an army in the Midlands, which included 600 Nottingham men. He was also joined in Nottingham by Sir William Stanley, from a family whose colours were seldom nailed to any particular mast for very long. Edward's army advanced on Newark, where a force under Lord Oxford avoided contact, and then onwards to Barnet where the army of Henry VI was routed. As a reward for his vital contribution to the victory at Barnet, amongst other prestigious appointments, Hastings was made constable of Nottingham Castle. Magnates like Hastings naturally attracted some unsavoury characters, among them Grey of Codnor (Derbyshire) who was accused in 1471 of inciting a violent riot against the civic authorities of Nottingham. That same year, however, Grey was paid £100 by the Exchequer for bringing a strong and well-equipped force to Edward's army at Tewkesbury, fought a month after Barnet. Nottingham held a strategic importance during the conflict as a place from which threats from any quarter of the kingdom could be countered. Later on, this was the reason that Richard III spent so much time there, as it helped to calm his insecurity, and it was here that he received a Scottish embassy in 1484 in the castle's Great Hall and, a year later, assembled his army for the final battle at Bosworth. Hastings took the precaution of fortifying his own manors in Leicestershire, and managing his advancing family fortunes by judicious marriages. Ironically it was his enduring loyalty to Edward IV and his son the young Edward V that was his undoing.

Though a staunch ally in the Yorkist camp, Hastings could not be trusted to stand by while Richard III dethroned the rightful king, and so he was lured to the Tower, seized and summarily beheaded. Despite, or possibly because of, Nottingham's support for the Yorkist cause, the civic authorities were quick to find out the result of the Bosworth battle, and to declare their loyalty to the new regime, hosting a visit by Henry VII in 1486.

Even after his resounding victory at Bosworth, Henry VII was still far from being home and dry, and conspiracies, or the suggestion of conspiracies, were to cause him concern throughout his reign. In 1487, the Earl of Lincoln, nephew of Edward IV and Richard III, led an army raised in Ireland, supplemented by 2,000 German mercenaries under Martin Schwartz, provided by his aunt, Margaret of Burgundy, and containing die-hard Yorkists such as Sir Francis Lovell. His object was to attract support for a pretender, one Lambert Simnel, who, purporting to be Edward, Earl of Warwick, another Yorkist claimant who had disappeared into the Tower of London, had been crowned King Edward VI in Dublin. Lincoln's expedition failed to garner the anticipated support but nonetheless advanced southwards on London, skirmishing with Lord Scales's cavalry the length of Sherwood Forest and forcing Scales to retreat to Nottingham where Henry's troops were gathering. Lincoln's army crossed the Trent and the royal army advanced from Newark to intercept the rebels. Lincoln's 8,000-strong army was drawn up on high ground at East Stoke, between the Trent and the Fosse Way. Tactically, his only hope was to overwhelm Henry's main body with a sudden charge by his wild Kerns, lightly armed Irish tribesmen, but the better-equipped royal troops held their ground, and Lincoln, along with Schwartz, and many of their men were killed, few prisoners being taken or quarter given. Simnel was captured, and sent to work as a scullion in the royal kitchens. Lord Lovell fled the field, possibly heading for his mother's house at Stoke Bardolph, but was never seen again, perhaps having drowned attempting to cross the Trent. It is possible that he is buried in Gedling church. There were Lovells in Henry's army too. Thomas Lovell had joined Henry Tudor as a squire during his period of exile and, along with his brother Gregory, fought at Stoke where both were knighted. Sir Thomas was made constable of Nottingham Castle in 1489. He went on to hold high office as Speaker of the House of Commons and Chancellor of the Exchequer, and it was this national perspective which prompted him to break up the partisan allegiance to petty local lords which had plagued Nottingham throughout the troubles, and prompted Henry VII's laws against livery and maintenance.

Later medieval stone houses

Towards the end of the fifteenth century, manor houses grand and humble were gradually shedding serious pretensions to defensibility but often retained a symbolic nod to the past. At both Bleasby and Costock, stone hall-houses with two-storey cross-wings, one at Bleasby and two at Costock, were built in the early years of the sixteenth century. Even as late as c.1580, this style was used at The Gables, Little Carlton. At Hodsock, a house dating from c.1250, a three-storey brick gatehouse with polygonal turrets, reached by a

24 Hodsock Hall: the gatehouse provides a fine example of Tudor gentry continuing to use the vocabulary of the castle in their essentially peaceful country houses.

bridge across a moat, was built in the early 1500s. The turrets on the gatehouse carry blind machicolations to emphasize the quasi-defensive character of the building. Even into the early 1600s Smythson was building pseudo-medieval castles at The Lodge, later Worksop Manor, with tall slender towers on each side, and at Wollaton Park with its central keep and angle towers, possibly inspired by a book of French chateau plans. Wollaton was built for an extremely wealthy industrialist who may have wanted to remind people that he was cousin to the unfortunate Lady Jane Grey, with firm roots in the Quality.

Nottinghamshire under the Tudors

Both Henry VII and Henry VIII were well-received in Nottingham but were aware of dissenting voices, particularly at the time of the Reformation. This undermining of trust led to a neglect of Nottingham Castle, left without artillery or adequate garrison, and unprepared in 1536 to resist the unexpected advance from the north of armed rebels joining the Pilgrimage of Grace. This situation, fortunately, was rescued by the first Earl of Rutland who put the castle into a better state of defence and then equipped it as a base for later campaigns in Scotland. At Newark artillery batteries were thrown up around the town, a blockhouse was built at the Trent Bridge and a drawbridge inserted in Muskham Bridge.

A significant element of what Henry VIII perceived as the enemy within came from the monastic rump of the Church. Lenton Priory was seen as a hotbed of sedition and an example was made by the prosecution for treason in 1538 of the prior and eight of his community. Prior Heath and two brethren were executed. Following on from the earlier execution of two of the former Carthusian priors of Beauvale, the other religious houses in the county were dissolved relatively peacefully, with many of the former monks receiving pensions.

Resistance to threats from abroad

The reigns of Henry VIII and Elizabeth I were both overshadowed by the expectation of foreign invasion. Whilst inland counties were spared the particular anxieties which coastal communities permanently suffered, they were still required to furnish armed and trained men to the county militia. Records show that in 1530 quite considerable numbers were mustered from the various administrative districts of Nottinghamshire, still referred to by the ancient Saxon term of 'wapentakes'. Barssett Lawe provided 107 men equipped with 'harness', or armour, 270 archers, and 480 bill-men, or pike-men. Following a number of Acts of Parliament designed to promote military skills such as archery, to encourage the breeding of horses for cavalry use, and giving Lords Lieutenant powers to raise troops, the preparations for countering the Spanish Armada in 1588 included the raising of warning beacons, and assessments of the counties' militias. Inspections of forests, especially of royal enclaves such as those at Bestwood and Clipstone, were also carried out to assess the availability and quality of timber for the construction of warships. A network of warning beacons was re-established across the country to trigger the mobilisation of the militia. Locations of these beacons included obvious natural features such as Beacon Hill at Gringley-on-the-Hill, where the brazier would have stood on the top of the ancient earthwork and, where no such high spots existed, on church towers or other prominent structures. The over-riding principle was one of inter-visibility enabling the alarm to be relayed quickly across the country. The county's militia was assessed at a total of 1,800 men, of whom some 400 should already have received training, but at the time of muster it would appear that only 1,000 were available, but this did include the required element of trained men. These were all infantry as, unlike many other counties, no requirement for cavalry was recorded at this time. However, in a later abstract of the same year, the numbers

have been increased by 1,000 men overall, plus some specific additional categories: 100 pioneers; twenty 'launces' or armoured cavalry; sixty light horsemen for scouting and piquet duties; and twenty horses armed with 'petronelles'. Deriving from *poitrine*, the French for chest, this was a large pistol fired from the saddle and braced against the rider's breastplate, if he were lucky enough to wear one. From 1558, landowners worth more than £100 had been required to keep horses suitable for both light and heavy cavalry, items of armour including skulls (helmets), bills (pikes) and longbows with sheaves of arrows, for the training and equipping of the militia. Nottinghamshire's levies were to join with upwards of 110,000 militia-men from across the country, in proceeding to Tilbury on the Thames where they would be deployed to repel the expected Spanish amphibious invasion force.

25 Gringley-on-the-Hill was an obvious site for a beacon which would warn of invasion and summon the militia to arms.

four

Stuart and Hanoverian Nottinghamshire 1600–1815

Nottinghamshire in the Civil Wars

Both the opening and the closing acts of the First Civil War took place in Nottinghamshire. On 22 August 1642 Charles I raised his standard at Nottingham Castle, effectively declaring war on his own subjects. On 6 May 1646 Charles I, recognising that his field armies had been consistently defeated and that even his strongest garrison at Newark was on the point of capitulation, surrendered himself to the Scots army at Southwell. One of the acts which had precipitated the conflict in the first place had been the king's ill-considered attempt to enter the House of Commons in order to arrest five MPs whose views he was unable to tolerate. One of these five, charged with treason by Charles I but protected from arrest by the London mob and spirited away to safety, was Denzil Holles, MP for East Retford.

Newark-on-Trent, along with its satellite garrisons, had constituted the most enduring of Royalist strongholds throughout the war, undergoing three separate sieges: the first, more of a prolonged assault than a siege, lasting three days; the second, when the besiegers were forced to withdraw, lasting three weeks; and the final siege, resulting in the eventual fall of the town, lasting almost six months. Once again it was the strategic location that determined the town's importance. Guarding the lowest bridging point of the Trent and straddling both the Great North Road and the Fosse Way, Newark was a communications hub of the most vital importance to the Royalists. It was the link between the king's HQ at Oxford, and the mainly Royalist northern counties; it constituted a blocking point on the main route linking London and York; and it commanded the waterway connecting the west Midlands to the Humber. It was also well placed to disrupt communications between Parliamentarian bases in Derby, Leicester and Lincoln. There were more active roles for the fortress, when Charles Cavendish used it as a base for his cavalry sorties into Lincolnshire, and the Earl of Newcastle, William Cavendish, could always threaten an invasion of the eastern counties using Newark as a jumping-off point for his powerful army of the north. As well as being the best-known siege of the Civil War, Newark is blessed with the best-preserved remains of fortifications from the conflict. Nottingham, held by the supporters of Parliament, and only marginally less important strategically, was also subject to several assaults and sieges. Nottinghamshire was split between the two sides providing large numbers of troops and their leaders for both armies. The county, fortunately, figured only marginally in the Second Civil War.

The siege of Newark-on-Trent

Newark had always been an important stronghold and in 1642, when it declared for the king, it still retained its castle and town walls. The castle had been transformed into a comfortable country house, hosting royal visits by both James I and Charles I, but the timber-framed extensions of Lord Burghley could not detract from the solidity of its basic construction. The town's governor, Sir John Henderson, a professional soldier who had fought in the Thirty Years War, had governed the Imperial city of Ulm.

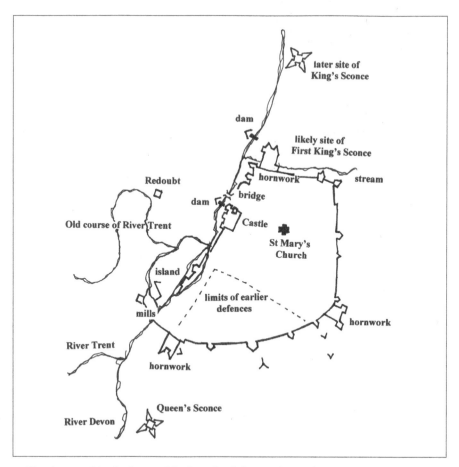

26 Sketch map of the final state of the Royalist defences of Newark-upon-Trent as they were in early 1645.

His first task at Newark was to bolster the existing fortifications with earthworks which might withstand the cannons of a besieging army. The by-then ruinous town walls were strengthened; the castle had a new ditch excavated on its northern side; new entrenchments to take in the suburbs of an expanding town were dug; barricades and outworks were added to the surviving town gates; and new earthworks secured the islands west of the castle. The 4–500 foot soldiers were commanded by Sir John Digby of Mansfield Woodhouse, High Sheriff of Nottinghamshire who had been with the king when his standard had been raised at Nottingham Castle. Digby had also raised an eighty-strong troop of horse. Outlying garrisons were established at Belvoir Castle (Leicestershire), Shelford House, Thurgarton Priory and Wiverton Hall.

The first threat to the town came in February 1643 when it was invested by a force of 6,000 Parliamentarian troops, drawn from the counties of the east Midlands, under Major-General Ballard. Although the numbers of defenders had increased since the start of hostilities, they were still outnumbered three to one. Had his officers been able to persuade him to press his attack, then the war could have taken a different course, for despite being out-thought and out-fought by the defenders, Ballard's troops had poured eighty shot into the town, and reached within pistol-shot of the inner defences. One more push might have done it. Unaccountably, Ballard declined to make that final effort, and withdrew his force. He was later accused of being in league with the burghers of Newark, was relieved of his command and allowed to go abroad where he died in Rouen in 1645. Newark's defenders had survived their first test and it would be another year before a further serious challenge was mounted. One lesson they had learned was that houses encroaching on the inner defences provided cover for attacking troops, so Henderson had those outside the North Gate demolished. In May 1643 the influence of Newark on the enemy's strategy was clearly shown. Forces from Lincoln, Leicester and Derby under Cromwell and Grey met at Nottingham with the intention of marching north to meet up with Fairfax and then to support him against the superior forces of the Earl of Newcastle. However, the threat of a concerted attack on Lincolnshire by the combined Royalist forces in Newark and Gainsborough presented a severe restraint to this plan. Cromwell was forced to abandon his plans either to reinforce Fairfax in Yorkshire, or to intercept the queen's munitions convoys from Newark to Oxford.

The Parliamentarians' next expedition against Newark was to end in disaster for them. The veteran, Sir John Meldrum, and Lord Willoughby, with an army of 7,000 men, and thirteen guns including a 32-pounder called 'Sweet Lips', moved on Newark in the spring of 1644. Sir Richard Byron of Strelley had been campaigning around the country as a cavalry leader when by January 1644 he was made governor of Newark. He continued the improvements to the defences begun under Henderson, pushing the defence line out to Millgate, particularly important to the defenders, dependent on the mills for both flour and black-powder. Meldrum's force began well by storming Muskham Bridge and constructing a bridge of boats across the river to maintain communications and deploy troops where they were needed more easily. An attempt by Colonel Gervase Lucas from Belvoir to relieve the town was also repulsed. The town was now completely blockaded but relief in the form of an army led by Prince Rupert was on the way, and Meldrum's repeated attempts to thwart its progress failed. It would appear that some complacency had crept into the Parliamentarian leadership and Meldrum's army was routed on Beacon Hill, the dominant feature east of the town, on 21 March. All the ammunition, the artillery which included two mortars and the famed 'Sweet Lips', and 3,000 muskets were lost to the victorious Royalists. Meldrum's men were lucky to be allowed to march away unhindered and with their dignity intact.

Throughout the rest of 1644, the Newark garrison was involved in providing troops for the field armies, and in both large- and small-scale raiding operations, some causing problems for the Parliamentarians, others, like an attempted relief of Crowland (Lincolnshire) ending in defeat. In December, all the local Parliamentarian cavalry gathered at Mansfield to march on Newark, storming Thurgarton on the way, and proceeding to Southwell. It was joined there by three regiments from Yorkshire, but they were surprised by a Royalist force from Newark, and lost a considerable number of men captured. Byron was replaced as governor in the autumn by a protégé of Prince Rupert's called Willys. The spring of 1645 saw a cordon drawn around the town but Royalist manoeuvres managed to disperse it although a new Parliamentarian garrison at Grantham remained in place. It was amongst mutual recriminations involving Rupert and the king that Willys was dismissed as governor and replaced by Lord John Bellasyse. A major strengthening of the town's defences was now put in train, expanding the defensive perimeter with stronger walls and bastions, constructing hornworks at the gates, building a redoubt on the island, and deploying the artillery, including the captured 'Sweet Lips', at strategic points. The most significant of the new works were two large, square, bastioned artillery forts, one at each end of the town. At the south-west end was the Queen's Sconce, whilst the King's Sconce guarded the approaches from the north.

27 The Queen's Sconce, raised in early 1645 to guard the southern approaches to the town and the confluence of the rivers Devon and Trent; the four corner bastions mounted cannon intended to keep the Parliamentarian batteries away from the inner defences of the fortress.

The ditches were cleared out anew, and dozens of camouflaged pits dug in front of them, with sharpened upward-pointing stakes in the bottom. The moated Norwell Manor became a new northern outpost. The town was now very much better-fortified under Bellasyse than under any of its three previous governors.

This upgrading of the defences was not before time, for at the end of November 1645, Colonel-General Poyntz and Colonel Rossiter, having completely cut off the outlying Royalist garrison in Belvoir Castle, had moved their troops nearer to Newark.

Poyntz approached from the south-west, captured the village of Farndon, and then took Hawton which he fortified. His redoubt, occupying a medieval moated site protected by the River Devon on two sides and a diverted beck on a third, was surrounded by a ditch now 20ft (6m) wide and 3ft deep, and measured 175 yards across. Importantly, it mounted artillery within range of the Queen's Sconce. The tower of Hawton church, traditionally Henry VII's viewpoint for the Battle of Stoke, would have provided an opportunity to observe the fall of shot. Meanwhile the Scots army under the Earl of Leven had arrived to seal the northern approaches. In January 1646 Belvoir surrendered and Parliamentarian troops from Cambridgeshire arrived to complete the encirclement. In all, the besiegers numbered around 16,000, and the besieged, about 2,000. However, the Parliamentarians were spread thinly along a perimeter of over

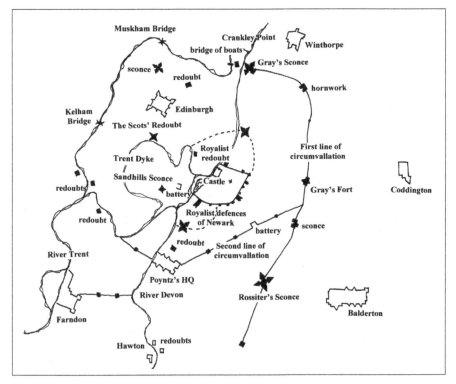

28 Sketch map of the Parliamentarian siege-works which surrounded Newark-upon-Trent; these are shown in their final state in early 1645, and include village defences, lines of circumvallation, redoubts and batteries.

10 miles (16km) so that they were heavily outnumbered at any particular spot, whenever the Royalists sent out a raiding force. In this way, Royalist raids were usually successful and managed to maintain a high level of morale. The besiegers' answer was to resort to classic siege-craft, constructing concentric lines of circumvallation around the whole town. These lines consisted of continuous banks and ditches linking armed camps, redoubts, batteries and places d'armes – areas in which assault parties might congregate under cover. They also provided covered ways for throwing saps or trenches towards the town's fortifications so that batteries might be advanced to positions where effective fire could be brought to bear. Bridges of boats were set up at Crankley Point, and a small boat mounting two guns was sailed up the Trent to within 800 yards of the town. Winthorpe, Coddington, Balderton and Farndon, marking the outer line of circumvallation, were surrounded by entrenchments with bastions and flankers. On the Island, the land between the two branches of the Trent, the Scots built a large square camp called 'Edinburgh', with arrow-head bastions at each corner, and fleches in the middle of each side. All this construction was more-or-less complete by the end of March. By this time, the town was in dire straits. Plague had broken out and over the next few weeks the besiegers were inching closer to the town – within musket range in many places. Lacking an effective artillery train which might render the defences untenable, the besiegers were forced to reduce the defenders by attrition, and then prepare to storm the defences in a concerted assault. This would have been an extremely risky enterprise, as the defenders would expect no quarter so would fight to the death, probably exploding their munitions in order to take as many of the enemy with them as possible. Both sides were now overtaken by events as the king turned himself in at Southwell on 5 May 1646 and gave the order to surrender Newark. On 8 May, the garrison marched out with full honours.

Nottingham in the Civil War

Although the Earl of Rutland had sought to strengthen the castle as a secure military base in the late 1530s, the castle had slipped back into decay and neglect through the reign of Elizabeth, and his successor-earls from Belvoir (Leicestershire) stripped out building materials from 1622, ensuring that by the start of the Civil War, it was ruinous. Nottingham's town walls had also been steadily disappearing because of the town's outward expansion, and the walls had been robbed for building stone. In 1625 citizens were prosecuted for such demolitions, but this was too late, as little by now remained except the odd gate. Along the northern circuit, for instance, the walls had completely disappeared under what became Upper and Lower Parliament Streets. By 1640, only Chapel Bar, still joined to the wall running along Park Row, and the completely isolated Cow Lane Bar, remained. Under intermittent threat from the Earl of Newcastle's army, Nottingham was extremely vulnerable. In June 1643, on the recommendation of Sir John Meldrum, Colonel John Hutchinson was appointed as commander of Nottingham's garrison. Determined to deny the Royalists an easy conquest, he set out to improve the town's defences but was hampered by a shortage of manpower. Nevertheless, he proceeded with his plans and had a drawbridge inserted into the bridge over the River Leen and surrounded the town with earthworks, with a rota drawn up for the townsfolk to man both them, and the re-fortified remaining gates. However, prior to the first Royalist attack on the town, these plans fell apart as Hutchinson realised that there was insufficient manpower adequately to man the defences. He therefore took his 400 troops and fourteen cannon into the castle, to the dismay of the townsfolk, several of whom were arrested and despatched as subversives to Derby. In September 1643 Newcastle's Royalists were poised to attack Nottingham and a summons to surrender was delivered. At the last moment this force was diverted to Hull, but Hutchinson was well aware that his small force was vulnerable to an enemy, not only superior in numbers but also able to count on a fifth column inside Nottingham itself. Indeed, in September 600 Royalists from Newark were covertly let into the city by Alderman Toplady, and surprised the tiny garrison holding the castle. Hutchinson and his men barred the gates and brought fire to bear on his attackers, managing to hold out for five days, long enough for relief in the form of a cavalry column from Leicester and Derby to arrive. The Royalists had come unprepared for a siege but did build a small bastioned sconce at Trent Bridge, with the intention of keeping control of the crossing. They also enlisted the help of the many disaffected townspeople in throwing down the town's earthwork defences.

The Royalists returned to Newark, leaving a small garrison in the Trent Bridge fort under Captain Rowland Hacker, and Hutchinson was able to rebuild his defences. The tower of St Nicholas's church, from which Royalist musketeers had been able to command the castle's outer courtyard, was torn down, as was Leen Bridge. Given that the castle provided the only tenable position, it was important that its approaches were barricaded to prevent infiltrators getting too close. To ensure that the northern part of the outer bailey was protected, two great ditches were dug on what would become the General Hospital site. The inner one measured 50ft (15m) wide by 20ft (6m) deep, whilst the outer one was 16ft (5m) wide and 8ft (2.5m) deep. Both probably also had ramparts. A fresh attempt was made to surround the town with an enlarged circuit of earthworks, on a new line running north from Chapel Bar and then due east past where the Guildhall and Trinity church would stand, as far as The Bek which ran down to the Leen. Where roads entered the town, barricades which could be closed against an attack were set up. By October, Hutchinson was in a position to clear Hacker and his eighty men out of the Trent Bridge fort. After a bombardment, musketeers pushed forward protected by moveable breastworks but before the final assault could be launched the Royalists slipped away, demolishing two spans of the bridge behind them. Hutchinson promptly garrisoned the fort and felt much safer for having the Trent crossing under his control once more, and built up the town's arsenal, casting mortars, and stockpiling arms in the old Gild Hall armoury on High Pavement.

By December, Newcastle was at Welbeck Abbey having occupied the whole county. Hutchinson prepared for a siege, aware that his new defences were still incomplete. Inexplicably, instead of attacking the town, Newcastle tried to bribe Hutchinson and his officers to give it up. The governor was offered £10,000, a title and the hereditary

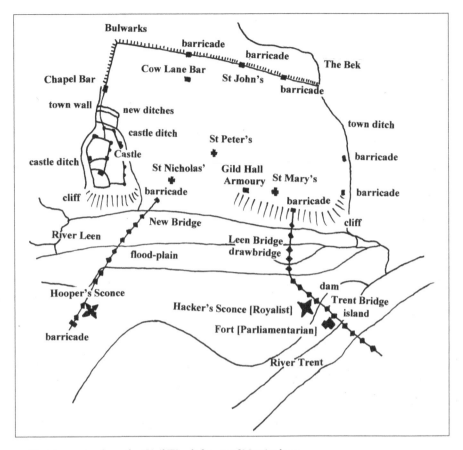

29 Sketch map to show the Civil War defences of Nottingham.

governorship of the castle; his brother George Hutchinson was offered £3,000, and Captain Poulton was offered £2,000 as go-between, all to be effected on the surrender of Nottingham to Colonel Dacre whose regiment was bivouacked at Watnall. The offers were declined and Newcastle's continued inactivity provided further opportunities for reinforcing the garrison, raiding with the cavalry, and strengthening the town defences. Although there was no hammer-blow, there were plenty of pinpricks. First, a convoy of booty from Newstead Abbey was attacked at Bestwood Park by a force from Wingfield under Colonel Frescheville. Next, a night-attack in the January snows saw a Royalist force enter through the unfinished earthworks and occupy the town before they were chased out by the castle garrison and Thornhaugh's cavalry fighting on foot. Next, an attempt was made by subterfuge to retake the Trent Bridge fort. Hacker's men approached the fort disguised as country-folk coming to market with arms hidden in carts and under women's shawls, but they had been betrayed and the Parliamentarian guards were expecting them. Most were captured but a few were drowned trying to escape by jumping into the Trent. In February 1644 Newcastle moved his forces away north to meet the threat posed by a Scottish army.

In March 1644, Hutchinson built a small fort, known as Hooper's Sconce, to guard the dams which could be opened to flood the meadows near the Leen Bridge, a measure which would shield the southern approaches from attack. The next month another raid from Newark seized the Trent Bridge fort from a garrison depleted through idleness and apathy. In order to retake it a further fort was built by Hutchinson's men, possibly between the two channels of the Trent, designed to cut off the enemy. Under cover of an attack on this new work the Newarkers withdrew and the town suffered no further attacks as the tide, at least in Nottinghamshire, began to turn in the Parliamentarians' favour. Towards the end of the war a million bricks from the local clay pits were donated by the second Earl of Clare to repair the castle defences.

Outposts and garrisons

Unlike previous wars in Britain, the Civil War involved sieges and the widespread use of interdependent strongholds to retain territory as well as the well-remembered set-piece battles. The importance of Newark to the Royalists was underlined by the outer ring of garrisons which defended the approaches, and the corresponding ones of the Parliamentarians which sought to maintain a blockade. These outposts can be put into three categories: those which served as Royalist garrisons for the protection of Newark throughout the struggle: Shelford House, Wiverton Hall, Thurgarton Priory and Belvoir Castle (Leicestershire); those which served as garrisons for shorter periods of time: Felley Priory and Newstead Abbey in 1643, and Norwell Manor and Staunton Hall during 1645; and those which changed hands several times during the war such as Welbeck Abbey and South Wingfield House (Derbyshire). The corresponding Parliamentarian garrisons lay mainly to the south and east, on the borders of their Eastern Association heartlands, but they too had outliers such as Castle Hill Camp at East Retford, a prehistoric earthwork, with ditches deepened and banks heightened.

Many of the Royalist garrisons fell during the Parliamentarian campaigns which followed their victories at Marston Moor in July 1644, and Naseby in the following June. The church and stables of the medieval Thurgarton Priory, later converted into a house demolished c.1900, were garrisoned by Sir Roger Cooper, with forty men. In December 1644, the garrison foolishly fired on a passing force of Parliamentarians from Nottingham, killing a Captain Heywood. The place was stormed and then fired by troops under Colonel Thornhaugh. Welbeck Abbey had been fortified by order of the Earl of Newcastle in 1642. Only a small part of the extensive courtyard house, planned by Smythson, had been built by then, but wet moats crossed by drawbridges made it a difficult place to attack without heavy guns. In 1642 Welbeck was the first stop for the convoy of munitions being taken by Queen Henrietta Maria from the port of Bridlington (Yorkshire) via Newark to her husband's headquarters at Oxford. At Welbeck she was supplied with an escort of 1,500 men. It remained in Royalist hands until taken in August 1644 and garrisoned by 200 Parliamentarian troops who

30 Shelford
House, successor
to that destroyed
in the Civil War.

were constantly being raided by Newark-based cavalry. Finally, in July 1645, it was
taken in a daring raid by 250 horsemen, whose advance-guard contrived to grab hold
of the drawbridge as it was being raised. These men, under Major Jarnot, were from the
regiment of Sir John Frescheville, previously in charge at Staveley and Wingfield, both
of which had fallen to Parliamentarian forces. As Welbeck's governor, in October 1645
he hosted a visit by Charles I who had an angry confrontation with his nephew
Rupert who was in disgrace for surrendering Bristol. The next month Frescheville
entered into negotiations with Poyntz aimed at disarming some of the local garrisons.
Poyntz must have wanted to reduce the screen around Newark as what was to become
the final siege was about to commence, and Frescheville must have been under orders
to reinforce the Newark garrison but to try to gain a bonus by denying the enemy
dangerous footholds. Poyntz needed to retain the fortified manor of South Wingfield
(Derbyshire) as an essential link in the northern blockade of Newark. It had changed
hands several times before finally, in August 1644, falling to Parliament. In return for
the surrender of Welbeck, he settled for giving up Tickhill (Yorkshire) and Bolsover
(Derbyshire), both taken by Parliament in July and August 1644. An agreement was
reached and all three strongholds were then evacuated and slighted in November 1645.
A late addition to Newark's outposts from February 1645 had been Norwell Manor,
located to the north-west. The moated house with its garrison of sixty musketeers,
under Lieutenant-Colonel Kirby, withstood one attack mounted by Parliamentarian
troops from Retford, but later fell to the Scots army besieging Newark. Staunton Hall
was a semi-fortified house of 1554. In 1645, its owner, William Staunton, was away
commanding first a troop of horse he had raised locally, and then a new regiment of
1,200 foot, as part of the Newark garrison, leaving his wife and their household of
twenty servants to hold the fort. Although the alarm was given when approaching
Parliamentarian troops were spotted by a lookout in the next-door church tower,
resistance was brave but futile. The attackers set fires to smoke out the defenders, badly
damaging the house which they then looted. The present house is a much later rebuild.

Two of the original Newark outposts were the last to fall. Shelford House, built by the Stanhope family on the remains of an Augustinian priory in 1537, was garrisoned by the Earl of Chesterfield as an outpost of Newark. In 1645 it was held by his son, Colonel Philip Stanhope, with around 200 men. The house, which already had a wet moat, had been further fortified by being surrounded by a palisaded rampart, partly raised on the ruins of the priory buildings, these outer works being commanded from the windows of the house. Despite disregarded orders to evacuate the house back in August, and the offer of favourable terms of surrender from Hutchinson, Stanhope chose to stand fast, even when offered terms again by Poyntz late in October. A superior Parliamentarian force under Poyntz and Hutchinson was initially harassed by a party of Stanhope's musketeers ensconced in the church tower. These eventually having been smoked out, the hall was then invested. Storming parties filled up the ditches with faggots, or fascines, and then attempted to scale the walls using ladders which the defenders dislodged by knocking them away with beams. Finally, as the defenders were whittled away and Colonel Stanhope was mortally wounded whilst attempting to shore up the defences under fire, the house was stormed. The last fierce resistance was overcome with losses on both sides, and Stanhope's stubborn determination to resist to the end must have contributed to the denial of quarter. In some accounts only forty of the garrison were left alive when the Parliamentarian troops were finally restrained; in others, around 140 were taken prisoner. The house was burned to the ground, possibly, as Lucy Hutchinson somewhat disingenuously suggests, by the locals who had been forced to feed the garrison those long years, but more likely by the negligence, rather than the malice, of the victors. Contemporary accounts refer to cavaliers, raised batteries within the defences, and half-moon batteries astride the rampart, but few traces remain. Some ditches are thought to be for the drainage of the priory grounds, but one length of bank may be the remains of a defensive rampart from the time of the siege. Excavations by Tony Pollard and Neil Oliver for the first series of BBC TV's *Two Men in a Trench* uncovered musket balls and other artefacts from the action. After the successful reduction of Shelford Manor, Poyntz and Hutchinson led their troops, some 2,000 of them, off to nearby Wiverton Hall. The hall under John, Lord Chaworth had previously been threatened by Parliamentarian troops but although they had dislodged the defenders from some outworks, rumours of a relieving force being on their way from Newark prompted disengagement. This time the garrison was unprepared to resist the force Poyntz brought with him. Sir Robert Thervill, apparently swayed by his wife's entreaties, and influenced by the fate of Shelford just a week previously, surrendered without a fight. The house had been strongly fortified with two half-moon batteries to the south, one of which can still be seen on the lawn in front of the Gothicised medieval gatehouse.

Two further footnotes are worth recording. First, one other casualty of the war was the archbishops' palace at Southwell which was slighted; and second, Colonel Hacker of East Bridgford was given the task of managing the king's execution in 1649 and he, himself, as a regicide, was hunted down and executed at Tyburn in 1660. His two brothers had fought for the king, one of them being killed in a skirmish at Colston Bassett.

31 Wiverton Hall: the fifteenth-century gatehouse which survived the siege of 1645 may be seen in the present Gothic building; the Hall housed the HQ of a searchlight battery during the Second World War.

Royalist revivals

In 1648 the Second Civil War broke out and a Royalist army marched south into Nottinghamshire under Sir Philip Monckton, all the while shadowed by a Parliamentarian force under Colonel Rossiter, an experienced leader of the New Model Army. At Willoughby-on-the-Wolds the two forces clashed and Rossiter's battle-hardened troops prevailed. Seven years later the local organisers of a projected Royalist uprising chose Rufford Abbey as the meeting-place for their Nottinghamshire contingent. An estimated 3,000 men gathered there on 8 March 1655, but dispersed without taking any other action. The next year Sir Richard Byron of Newstead, once governor of Newark, was chosen to lead the county's Royalists in the event of a rising but when the time came in 1659 he raised 100 horse but they quickly dispersed. Only a year later, Charles II had been restored to the throne.

The Glorious Revolution of 1688

Nottingham first became a focus of attention when a Scottish regiment, posted south to aid the beleaguered James II, mutinied while passing through the town. A number of those conspiring to replace James, including the Earl of Devonshire, occupied the town, and it was here that Princess Anne, James's second daughter and later Queen Anne, was brought covertly. Responding to what turned out to be a false alarm, many citizens armed themselves against a royal force thought to be closing in on Nottingham. Not everyone was pleased by the accession of William and Mary, and recriminations and factionalism continued for some years after.

The eighteenth century

In 1745 the country was threatened on two fronts. Fear of an invasion by the French, Britain's opponents in the War of Austrian Succession (1740–48), prompted efforts, even in inland towns, to round-up deserters from the navy. At the same time a Jacobite army under Charles Stuart, Bonnie Prince Charlie or the Young Pretender, invaded England and was making rapid southward progress. Nottingham was identified by the government as the centre of resistance in the Midlands should the Highlanders get that far south. A number of convoys of troops and artillery passed through the town on their way north to join General Wade, dropping off quantities of arms and munitions to be stockpiled in Nottingham Castle for distribution to volunteer forces. A Defence Association to recruit local volunteers was funded by subscriptions of over £2,000, and administered by Newcastle, the Lord Lieutenant, but only 140 volunteers were forthcoming and little seems to have happened. However, Evelyn Pierrepont, from 1726 the second Duke of Kingston (-upon-Hull), raised and financed his own regiment of light dragoons. This was an innovative unit, based on the various hussar formations to be seen in European armies. It served with Cumberland's army in the north-west until the Jacobites veered eastwards toward Leek and Derby, the furthest south that they finally penetrated. During the Jacobite retreat, they were part of the army which tracked them back to Scotland, skirmishing all the way. At the final battle at Culloden Moor, Kingston's men attacked the Highlanders' left flank as it collided with the troops in the centre. Lacking the discipline of regulars, Kingston's troopers were guilty of cutting down fleeing civilians including women and children. On their disbandment, Cumberland nevertheless recruited all but a handful into a new regiment which would ultimately become the 15th Hussars. Despite any previous military training or experience, Kingston went on to become a full general, and was appointed Lord Lieutenant of Nottinghamshire in 1763.

In common with other areas of the country, in 1757 anti-militia riots broke out in Mansfield, with call-up papers being publicly burned. A further attempt to re-establish the militia was made in 1759 but the natural local leaders preferred to pay a fine rather than take up their commissions. In 1775, a meeting of deputy lieutenants from the Midland counties at the Swan Hotel in Mansfield finally raised a Nottinghamshire Regiment of Militia. The next year, a grand ball was held in Nottingham Castle by the officers of the regiment.

Thoughts of security, if only at a fantasy level, clearly exercised the minds of the aristocracy. At Newstead Abbey, the fifth Lord Byron, a former officer in the Royal Navy, built a castellated fort by the lake and another with an accompanying gun-emplacement on the hill above, called Folly Castle. He later, in the 1770s, rebuilt the stables as a toy fort, and maintained a 20-gun boat on the lake.

The Napoleonic Wars

It was fear of the French revolutionary virus spreading to Britain which initially prompted the government to garrison industrial towns, and the bourgeoisie to organise units of armed volunteers. In 1792, on a site along the west side of The Park and leased for sixty years, Nottingham Cavalry Barracks was built. The rectangular site consisted of apartments for officers, stabling for three troops of cavalry with the troopers' quarters above, hay-barn, granary, canteen, hospital, infirmary stables, magazine, harness-rooms and forge, all in a yard surrounded by a stout brick wall.

Earth removed for the construction of the barracks was used to fill in the castle fishponds, creating Fish Pond Gardens by 1794. The barracks received additions in 1797–99, increasing its capacity to a full regiment. The townsfolk felt some relief that, with the construction of these permanent barracks, they would be spared having soldiers billeted on them.

On 10 June 1794 a meeting was called at Mansfield's Moot Hall to raise a troop of yeomanry cavalry, collecting subscriptions of £8,000, sufficient funding for four troops of sixty men to be known as the Sherwood Rangers. The new regiment was presented

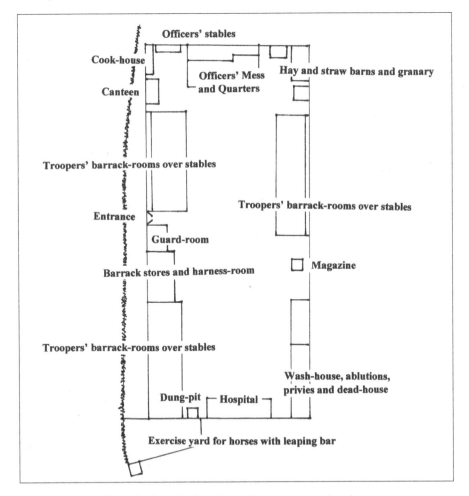

32 Nottingham Park cavalry barracks. A conjectural reconstruction based on contemporary plans and surviving elements of other similar establishments at Christchurch, Windsor, Exeter and Dorchester.

with royal colours in front of the Exchange Hall in Nottingham, the troop raised in Nottingham being led by Colonel Ichabod Wright of Mapperley Park. Four years later 'a respectable volunteer corps' of infantry was raised, and a yeomanry riding school was built next to the outer gateway of the castle. In 1803 the militia were employed on garrison duties in Ireland in order to release regular troops for active service.

Civil disorder

Following a poor harvest in the previous year, food prices rose and by August 1800, there were riots and attacks on mills and granaries, fighting in the Meadows and an attack on a trooper of the Holme Pierrepont Yeomanry as he guarded a grain shipment. Other troopers were stoned by angry crowds, and troops were sent from Northampton in September to restore order. Further riots at Christmas brought troops from Birmingham, and this situation was repeated throughout the winter and spring of 1811–12, and then into the autumn of 1812. Nottingham had established a tradition of elections being accompanied by violence. In 1747, for instance, troops had opened fire, killing a male bystander, and the town had experienced continuous unrest, with radicals only giving way to self-proclaimed patriots on the declaration of war in 1793. Both sides were reported to be under arms and drilling and rioting again broke out, with patriotic fervour quickly changing to opposition to the war as the deepening recession hit the textile workers. The short-lived Peace of Amiens of 1802 was followed by the recruitment of 750 men forming two battalions of an armed volunteer force with an armoury in the Exchange Building of 1725, standing in the Market Square. Muskets were issued to volunteer units from, amongst other places, Strelley, Beeston and Wollaton. The fear of invasion, only calmed after Nelson's victory at Trafalgar in 1805, brought out most able-bodied males either to be trained in the use of arms or to be sworn in as special constables, but most volunteers had drifted away by 1809.

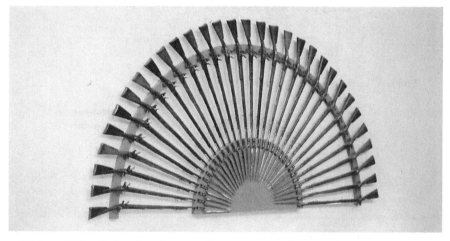

33 Wollaton Hall: a display of muskets issued in 1803 to the Volunteers of Beeston, Strelley and Woolaton (*sic*) and now in the house's armoury.

five

Nottinghamshire in the Victorian Period 1815-1914

After the end of the Napoleonic Wars there came a long period of social unrest caused by depressed living conditions, unemployment and frustrated attempts by the populace to expand their political involvement. Periods of domestic instability were succeeded later in the century by threats of foreign invasion, with both these factors provoking a military response.

Continuing civil unrest

The threat of rebellion, amongst working people, in the years after 1815, was to trigger a strong military reaction from the ruling classes. Nottingham's town clerk, fearing revolution, lobbied unsuccessfully for an increase in the town's garrison of one cavalry regiment. In 1817 an out-of-work stockinger named Jeremiah Brandreth of Sutton-in-Ashfield had previously been suspected of Luddite activities in 1811. Egged on by a government *agent provocateur* who told him he would be part of a co-ordinated national rising, Brandreth gathered fifty, or in one account, 300 rebellious, but poorly armed, men at Wingfield Park and marched them toward Eastwood en route for Nottingham where a further 100 or so had gathered on the Forest to await their arrival. They were quickly rounded up by regular troopers of the 15th Light Dragoons at Hill Top and brought before the magistrates. Of the eighty-odd apprehended and indicted, Brandreth and two others were sentenced to be hanged, drawn and quartered, a sentence commuted to beheading by a magnanimous Prince Regent. Fourteen others were transported, and the rest were released. As Brandreth's severed head was held aloft and the watching crowd failed to show its approbation, cavalry standing nearby made every appearance of preparing to charge, an early Peterloo only narrowly being avoided. Incidents such as rick-burning and the destruction of machinery, Brandreth's rebellion, and the activities of the Chartists, all contributed to the resurrection of the yeomanry cavalry.

In 1826 the Sherwood Rangers was reorganised from troops of yeomanry from Newark, Clumber and Mansfield and, two years later, the South Nottinghamshire Hussars from troops raised at Holme Pierrepont, Watnall, Nottingham, Bingham and Wollaton. In the 1830s the east Midland counties had more troops of yeomanry than the rest of the country, Derbyshire, Leicestershire and Nottinghamshire fielding a total of twenty troops against none at all in the industrial areas of Durham or Lancashire for instance. This air of unrest even had an effect on domestic architecture. In 1823, Lord Middleton, fearing a popular uprising, rebuilt the boundary wall at Wollaton House, incorporating Beeston and Lenton Lodges in a decorative sixteenth-century style with castellated towers and machicolations, but also exhibiting thick walls and an absence of ground-floor windows, demonstrating a serious intent to defend the house from the mob. A few years later, such precautions were vindicated.

In October 1831, Parliament was debating the Reform Bill, and when word reached Nottingham that the Duke of Newcastle, described at the time as the most hated man in England, had voted against it, Nottingham Castle was set ablaze and destroyed by a rioting mob. Newcastle retreated to Clumber Park which he proceeded to put into a state of defence. He is reported to have gathered together a force of 400 men, which included a troop of seventy yeomanry cavalrymen armed, not only with muskets and sabres, but also with three 3-pounders, and fourteen little ship's guns, presumably from the 40-ton, one-third-scale frigate *Lincoln* which had been launched onto the lake in 1814. Other landowners also took steps to protect themselves from the fury of the mob.

From the end of the Napoleonic Wars, Nottingham's Park Cavalry Barracks had housed a regiment of cavalry as a permanent garrison, primarily to counter political

34 Lenton Lodge, along with Beeston Lodge, one of two built in 1823 by Lord Middleton to restrict access to his Wollaton Hall estate at a time of civil unrest; note the size and scarcity of windows in the lower storey.

unrest, regularly rotating units. In 1820, for instance, a detachment of ninety troopers of the 9th Lancers returned to London after their stint of duty, travelling up the Trent and then entering the canal system via the Loughborough Navigation. The 1840s saw fresh outbreaks of violence associated with the Chartists, peaking with 'The Battle of Mapperley Hills' in August 1842, when the cavalry were once again called out to disperse what had begun as a peaceful gathering but had escalated into wholesale arrests and confrontation with the authorities. Six years later, up to 5,000 Chartists gathered on the Forest to celebrate the presentation of a petition to the government in London. The authorities, fearing a repetition of earlier disturbances, brought out the Irish Dragoon Guards from the Park Barracks along with four troops of yeomanry at Trent Bridge, Gamston, Wollaton and Gedling, with 1,500 specials also mobilised for duty. Fortunately the event passed without trouble. Elections continued to provoke fights and riots, and the mayor was forced to send for troops from Sheffield in 1865 when campaigners from Mansfield and elsewhere were attacked as they arrived by rail for a rally. As late as 1885 there were occasions on which it was necessary for the Riot Act to be read, followed by police baton charges. All this turbulence gave Nottingham the reputation of being a riotous and disorderly place, by some commentators attributed to radical politics and class struggle, but by others, as just the local way of conducting political activities.

The army in the Victorian period

The nineteenth century saw enormous structural changes in the army. As well as efforts to alter the way in which its officers were recruited, trained and promoted, there were also attempts to rehabilitate the common soldier in the eyes of the public. After the Napoleonic Wars soldiers were generally seen as the dregs of society, led by titled buffoons who had neither interest nor competence in soldiering and showed minimal commitment to the welfare of their men. These concerns came to a head with the reporting of the Crimean War in the 1850s, highlighting the complete lack of any organisation in the feeding, clothing or medical treatment of the soldiers fighting in the extremes of the Sevastopol climate.

The regular army

The regional affiliations attributed to the infantry units of the British Army at this time held little significance. Thus the 45th Foot was only notionally connected to Nottinghamshire and the 95th to Derbyshire. Made necessary by the scarcity of barrack accommodation, one of the most unpopular habits of the army was the billeting of troops in private houses or, in some respects worse still, in public houses. A further problem was that regiments could be posted abroad for periods of up to ten years, completely severing any links they might have had with any community. The solution lay in a programme of localisation, which tied regiments to specific localities.

This was expected to foster local pride, to aid continuity in recruitment, and to provide each regiment with a permanent home-base. In 1881, the 45th and 95th Foot were amalgamated as the Sherwood Foresters (Derbyshire Regiment) with their regimental depot, built in 1877, established at Normanton Barracks, Sinfin Lane in Derby. Most regiments had two regular battalions, which alternated carrying out a tour of overseas duty, and staying at home in the regimental depot to train new recruits. Only in 1903 was 'Nottinghamshire' included in the regimental title when the Sherwood Foresters became the Nottingham and Derby Regiment.

The militia

Having fallen into abeyance after 1815, the militia was revitalised with its county regiments being ranked in order of precedence at a conference convened by George IV in 1833. The 59th Nottingham or Royal Sherwood Foresters Regiment of Militia was based in Newark-upon-Trent. The 62nd Derby Regiment of Militia was joined in 1855 by a second regiment known as the Chatsworth Rifles. After 1881, these were renumbered as the 3rd and 5th Battalions of the new Sherwood Foresters, with the Nottingham Militia constituting its 4th Battalion. In 1891 the two Derbyshire Militia battalions amalgamated as the 3rd Battalion. The Nottingham Regiment volunteered for foreign service during the Crimean War, thus releasing garrison troops from such places as Gibraltar, Malta and Corfu, for active service. Again in 1900 a contingent of thirty-two officers and over 650 men volunteered to go to fight the Boers in South Africa, and suffered significant casualties which included their CO, three other officers and over forty NCOs and other ranks.

The yeomanry cavalry

In many parts of the country, the yeomanry corps raised during the French Wars would lie dormant for several generations, but in several Midlands counties, yeomanry regiments were consolidated in the 1820s. The Sherwood Rangers had stayed in continuous service from its foundation in 1794, and the South Nottinghamshire Hussars were re-formed in 1828, partly as a response to civil disorder. The officers were drawn from the gentry with the majority of the troopers coming from amongst their tenantry, mainly farmers with a few useful artisans such as saddlers and cartwrights. The Hussars numbered the owners of Flintham Hall, Chilwell Hall, Nuttall Temple, Bestwood Hall and Rufford Park amongst their officers, whilst the Rangers' officers included the proprietor of Kelham Hall, and Major the Earl of Lincoln. Many of these officers had served in fashionable regiments such as the Life Guards, the 12th, 16th and 17th Lancers and the Rifle Brigade. The Hussars' adjutant alone boasted '27 years' (full-pay) service' with dragoon and hussar regiments. Together, they fielded a complement of around forty-five officers and 700 troopers. Both regiments were recorded as turning out in aid of the civil power in 1831, the year of the Reform Bill riots, again in 1839 and then in 1848, the year of European revolution. The Hussars were based in Nottingham and the Rangers in East Retford. Although the terms of their existence precluded wholesale overseas postings for the yeomanry regiments, there was nothing to prevent the formation of volunteer companies from within their establishment. The Rangers and the Hussars respectively raised the 10th and 12th Companies in the 3rd Battalion of the Imperial Yeomanry for service in the South African wars. At Welbeck Abbey, the 5th Duke of Portland had built the second largest riding school in Europe, measuring 385ft (120m) by 112ft (35m), by 52ft (16m) high, with cast-iron columns, and an iron and glass vaulted roof. It may possibly have been made available to the Sherwood Rangers and/or the South Notts Hussars for equitation exercises or mounted drill.

The Rifle Volunteers

By the end of the 1850s there were many in the growing industrial cities who resented the claims of the yeomanry cavalry to be the guarantors of the nation's security. Despite their superior social standing in rural communities, it was their perceived reactionary leanings and their apparent mission to maintain the status quo which meant that their dominance could not remain unchallenged. Urban professionals and artisans alike also wanted to do their bit for the country. After the fiasco of the Crimean War and the challenge to imperial power in India, there was also a perception that Britain was somewhat lagging behind in the development of military skills, particularly some as basic as marksmanship. In the end, it was the threat of an invasion by Napoleon III which precipitated the establishment of a National Rifle Association, and this naturally led to a movement promoting a corps of volunteers to be trained in the military sciences. With the support of the Duke of Newcastle, Lord Lieutenant of Nottinghamshire, who convened a meeting of magistrates and deputy lieutenants at County Hall, a number of initiatives were advanced. An Angel Row bookseller named Simpkins enlisted the services of Jonathan (Jonty) White, a former sergeant-major in the 2nd Queen's Royals, as a drill instructor for himself and five friends. Their numbers rapidly increased and the mayor requested that Captain Simpkins form a corps which, by August 1859, had grown to over 400 men. By October 1859 there were five such corps in Nottingham, quickly coalescing into the Robin Hood Rifle Volunteer Corps. White, later a major, became the unit's adjutant, with his eleven-year-old son as a bugler. Drills were held in the Castle Yard, at the Park Barracks, Trent Bridge Cricket Ground and at the police station, with a firing-range at Mapperley Plain. On 24 May 1860, the Robin Hoods, 500-strong, celebrated the queen's birthday by performing all their set-piece manoeuvres in front of a crowd of at least 20,000 spectators in the Park. Along with a *feu de joie*, the display ended with a headlong charge towards the crowd and, the order to halt being inaudible in all the shouting and cheering, a dangerous situation was only narrowly avoided. The next month, on 23 June, the battalion was present at the first royal review of rifle volunteers in London's Hyde Park and two years later they attended a further review held at Warwick Racecourse. By 1866 the Robin Hoods were parading as a complete battalion with a band and a company of pioneers. In contrast to the gentlemen who officered the yeomanry many of the officers of the Robin Hoods were tradesmen. They included Thomas Starey, a coach-builder, William Lambert, a lace dresser and Abraham Pyatt, a timber merchant, who each later went on to hold such public offices as Mayor of Nottingham and JP. Captain Anthony Mundella, one of the original six and a partner in a hosiery company, would become MP for Sheffield and Minister of Education. Joseph Wright, a lace dresser from Sneinton, served in the Robin Hoods from its inception, in every rank from private to lieutenant colonel, commanding the 2nd Battalion on its formation in 1900. The CO from 1861–75 was Lieutenant-Colonel Charles Ichabod Wright of Stapleford Hall whose father had raised the Nottingham troop of yeomanry in 1798. He was succeeded by Colonel Sir Charles Seely who made his estate at Sherwood Lodge available for the Robin Hoods' annual camps in 1886, 1887 and 1890. Other venues for camps included Wainfleet with its firing-range and Skegness with its eagerly anticipated donkey derby.

Alongside the Robin Hoods, similar corps were being recruited across the county. A total of seven corps had been formed by July 1860 in most of the county's major centres of population including East Retford (2nd Corps), Mansfield (4th Corps) and Worksop (7th Corps). These seven corps formed the 1st Administrative Battalion in 1861, with HQ initially at Newark (home of the 3rd Corps) and from 1865 at East Retford.

Unsurprisingly, shooting was regarded as the primary activity of the Rifle Volunteers, but the provision of suitable ranges could be problematic. One solution was to insert a Morris Tube into the barrel of the rifle which allowed smaller-bore ammunition to be fired on a shorter indoor range with marksmanship skills being only minimally compromised, but there was really no substitute for shooting outdoors in all weathers on a range of over 400 yards. The Old Coppice range at Mapperley was acquired in 1860, and a lodge bearing the Robin Hoods' motto over its porch was built, along with a brick fort and a firing platform. The range started out at 200 yards and was steadily extended to reach 1,000 yards, but unfortunately at the cost of endangering the workers on the neighbouring farms. This forced a serious look at safety measures entailing a retreat to 200 yards, with shooting only taking place after 5.30 p.m. Further incidents with stray bullets brought about permanent closure in 1890 and, until new facilities could be organised, outdoor shooting only took place at the annual camps such as Grimsby and Wainfleet where ranges were available, or on borrowed ranges at Retford, with a 300-yard range, or Newark. Nevertheless, the Robin Hoods' teams continued to perform outstandingly at the national shooting competitions held initially at Wimbledon and then at Bisley (Surrey). In 1895 a new range on the banks of the Trent was started, with firing platforms and shelters at 200, 500, 600 and 800 yards. The range lodge, currently (2013) undergoing a refurbishment as a family home, contained living quarters for the sergeant instructor, an officers' room, an upstairs committee room which doubled as a mess on firing-days, and an armoury/ammunition store. The range was officially opened by Field Marshall Viscount Wolseley, C-in-C of the British Army, in November 1895 when over 500 men paraded and a Maxim Gun was demonstrated. Other Nottinghamshire corps made their own arrangements, with

35 Trent rifle range lodge was built for the sergeant instructor of the Robin Hood Rifles, and to provide administrative and social facilities on shooting days; the brick single-storey structure was the armoury and magazine.

30-yard ranges at Collingham, Epperstone, in use from at least 1887, Burton Joyce from 1907, and Southwell for instance. At Kimberley there was an indoor range at the Brewery; used by the Rifle Club and the Volunteers, most likely with overlapping membership and interests.

Like the militia and yeomanry, a number of Rifle Volunteers elected to go to South Africa in 1899. Although some 200 men from the four local battalions volunteered, just thirty from each were selected to make up a composite company. Although many troops serving in the Boer Wars found themselves on lines-of-communications and garrison duties, it would appear that the men of Nottingham were exposed to more active operations, coming under fire many times and marching long distances as part of the field army under Lord Roberts.

36 The distinctive magazine of Upton rifle range, Southwell.

The Territorial Force (TF)

The Volunteer Movement had begun life in 1859 as a popular initiative, a response to a perceived external threat, and had been accepted by the military establishment only with extreme reluctance. Few beyond the Prince Consort had attempted to define its purpose, and little was ever done towards its integration into the nation's defences. From time to time this purpose was raised and in 1874 it was a Nottinghamshire officer, Lieutenant-Colonel Eyre of the 1st Nottinghamshire Administrative Battalion, who, as part of his argument in favour of conscription, resurrected the idea of the Volunteer Force being constituted as entirely independent of the Regular Army. However, no action was taken to implement this or any other idea until the Boer War had alerted the government to the danger that successive and simultaneous overseas deployments of the regular army would leave the home country unprotected and vulnerable to attack from any one of a number of menacing neighbours. It was therefore decided that an official, complementary Home Army would be set up, to be called the Territorial Force. From 1908, this would consist of fourteen, regionally based, self-contained divisions containing infantry, artillery, engineers, service corps and medics, into which existing volunteer units could transfer piecemeal. The Nottinghamshire units were all part of the North Midland Division (TF) whose HQ was at Lichfield. One of the division's three infantry brigades was made up of the four volunteer battalions of the Sherwood Foresters, and there was a section of an RE Divisional Signals Company based in the county. Alongside the infantry division was the Notts and Derby Mounted Brigade comprising the South Nottinghamshire Hussars, the Sherwood Rangers and the Derbyshire Yeomanry, supported by the Nottinghamshire RHA and supply and medical units. All these units were administered by the Nottinghamshire TF Association with offices in Clinton Terrace opposite the Derby Road drill hall.

Also affiliated to the TF, and generally established by 1910, were cadet units. A senior OTC contingent was raised at Nottingham University with junior ones at the High School and at Worksop College. The High School's contingent had formed in 1900 as one of only fifty such school-based units. Within a year there were over 100 cadets, with shooting on the Trent Range and, by 1906, attendance at annual camps. In that year the school got its own range, opened by the Duke of Portland, with Lord Baden-Powell in attendance. Both the Boys' Brigade, introduced into Nottingham in 1888, and the Church Lads' Brigade had paramilitary identities and a photograph of c.1910 exists showing members of the Boys' Brigade in Retford parading with rifles. Mansfield already had a Boys' Brigade company and the drill hall at Forest Town was built in 1908, by the Bolsover Colliery Company, specifically for their use. Over 200 boys were immediately enrolled, providing a guard of honour, in uniform and carrying rifles, for its official opening in May 1909. By 1914, new cadet battalions had been raised in Nottingham by the Nottinghamshire Secondary Schools, the Boys' Brigade and the Church Lads' Brigade. Southwell was base for the 1st Cadet Battalion of the Church Lads' Brigade, with a further company based on Whitwell, Worksop Priory and Cuckney. Other cadet companies were raised in Walkeringham and at Welbeck, affiliated to the Sherwood Foresters' 8th Battalion.

Barracks

In 1839 land at High Oakham, Mansfield, was offered by the Duke of Portland for a barracks to accommodate regular cavalry who might respond to incidents of civil unrest. A tombstone in the grounds, dated 1843, marks the grave of a dog belonging to Captain Palmer of the 12th Lancers. Cavalry continued to be stationed there until 1854, when the Royal Scots Greys left for the Crimea. In 1894 the barracks had become the residence of the widow of a Mr Neale. High Oakham House remains in domestic occupation with a large, double-fronted Victorian house, adjoining cottages, presumably the original barrack buildings, in the yard to the rear, and a gateway with a square, pedimented guardhouse. High on one wall nearby is a metal plaque bearing the arms of Nottingham and the legend 'Notts and Derby' which would suggest a connection with the Sherwood Foresters post-1881. In 1840, the HQ of the northern counties regiments under the command of General Sir Charles Napier was in Nottingham's Wheeler Gate. The sixty-year lease on the Nottingham Cavalry Barracks expired in 1853, but was extended, eventually to be relinquished in 1861. Rooms were let out, and Blondin gave a demonstration in Barrack Yard in July 1861. The yard was used for parades by the Robin Hood Rifles until 1881, ten years after the buildings had been demolished. The site is now Pelham Crescent, in the Park Estate. In order to provide a new permanent depot for the Sherwood Foresters, the War Office bought 30 acres (12 has) of land on Hucknall Road, Nottingham. However, such was the public outcry that, as we have seen, the barracks went to Derby and in 1891 a prison was built on the

37 High Oakham Barracks, Mansfield, was built in 1839 as a base for cavalry who could be called out to aid the civil power; it remained in use as such until 1854; these are the stables behind the main block.

38 High Oakham Barracks: this badge, apparently that of the Sherwood Foresters after 1881, is attached to the wall behind the guardroom.

land instead. Possibly, the citizens of Nottingham thought they were getting a better class of neighbour. The depot of the 27th Infantry Brigade, of which the Foresters formed a part, was established in the newly built Glen Parva Barracks, Leicester, from 1880.

In 1855 a barracks was built in Newark's Albert Street for the militia. This consisted of a quadrangle of buildings around a drill-square. The main, south-east range was the armoury, with wings either side of a central gateway. On the entrance side onto Albert Street, there was housing for permanent staff with a detached residence for the adjutant, and canteens or messes for officers, NCOs and other ranks. Through the arch was a drill shed, cart-sheds and stabling for the officers' horses. The site was greatly expanded at least twice, for the use of the Nottinghamshire section of the Foresters' Special Reserve Battalion, the successor to the militia, and then for use by other units up until shortly before its demolition in 1974.

Volunteer drill halls

Once the individual corps of Rifle Volunteers were up and running, they could claim an annual grant from the War Office. The level of this grant was based on the number of 'effectives' in each unit. A man was deemed effective if he attended the regular parades and drills, was trained to march and to shoot, and diligently cared for his kit. Each unit

39 Nottingham Castle: the original orderly room of the Robin Hood Rifles, in use until 1893, is now used as a garden store.

was required to maintain an orderly room, where the administrative tasks were carried out, and an armoury, where arms and ammunition could be securely stored. Most units retained the services of a retired regular as a permanent staff instructor (PSI) and his accommodation might be provided by the corps. It also soon became evident that the provision of an indoor training space allowed round the year activities to be organised. Since much of the cost of the Volunteers was raised by public subscription and fundraising, some of these activities would be social. A band would be in great demand and would contribute to good public relations. Civic pride often meant that the provision of a drill hall became a municipal priority. The Robin Hoods' first orderly room was in the castle grounds and remained in use until 1893. It is still there as a garden store. The last race-meeting had been held at the Forest Racecourse in 1890 and the grandstand was offered to the Robin Hoods for a new orderly room and armoury, providing they left the castle. Designed by John Carr of York, the two-storey building measured 81ft (25m), with a large room on the upper floor, and offices beneath. The riding school of the Nottingham troop of yeomanry up against the castle gatehouse had become, in 1872, the Volunteers' drill hall, and remained as such until 1910. Other premises were also available for training. Bestwood Lodge had been built in 1862–65, designed by Teulon for the Tenth Duke of St Albans, who was Honorary Colonel-in-Chief of the Robin Hoods. A little later, a conservatory wing was built, and enlarged sometime after 1896, to become a drill hall. It is seven bays

40 Bestwood Lodge was built for the tenth Duke of St Albans who was Honorary Colonel of the Robin Hood Rifles; around 1896 he added a drill hall, seen on the left of this picture.

41 Albert Hall in East Retford held the stores of the Sherwood Rangers Yeomanry; a four-storey building opposite had an indoor range on the top floor, and further premises in adjacent South Street were also used.

42 Worksop: this purpose-built drill hall in Shaw Street was opened around 1900 for 'G' Company of the 4th Volunteer Battalion of the Sherwood Foresters.

long and now serves as one of the hotel's function rooms. There was a 25-yard range in the grounds. Sherwood Lodge, a large, brick-built eighteenth-century house with a pedimented front, the home of Colonel Seeley, was also used. It was demolished in 1974 for the new Police HQ, but the lodges of 1893 and 1903 survive. In East Retford, HQ of the Sherwood Rangers, the Albert Hall in Albert Road was used as the Yeomanry Stores with a four-storey building opposite incorporating a top-floor rifle range, and further premises in South Street, whilst West Retford Hall provided a social setting. In Worksop a number of public houses were used, but a dedicated drill hall was built in Shaw Street, sometime around the turn of the century. At Kimberley the Station Hotel was used from 1880, and in Bingham, a National School of the 1840s appears to have met every community need over the years. In Mansfield, a drill hall off Meetinghouse Lane was in use by 1892, and at Newark, the existing Assembly Rooms in Cartergate, now a carpet shop, was adapted as a drill hall, with a two-storey front-block containing an archway through to the hall behind.

However, after the establishment of the TF, it was clear that larger permanent premises were needed for all Nottinghamshire's volunteer units, starting with an imposing new drill hall on Derby Road, built in 1910–12 by Brewill, an architect serving as an officer in the Robin Hoods, and his partner Bailey with whom he had designed the Trent rifle-range some fifteen years earlier. The Derby Road drill hall has a front block nine bays wide and four storeys in height, with a lot of neo-Baroque detail. This accommodated the orderly rooms, the COs' offices, and the officers' and sergeants' messes, along with

43 This building on the corner of Fisher Lane has fulfilled many functions in Bingham, starting out as a school but also serving as a drill hall.

44 Newark's Cartergate drill hall, now a carpet shop.

a canteen and recreational facilities for the other ranks. The double-height hall, to the rear, was entered through a coach-arch in the façade, and surrounded by the armouries, tack-rooms and stores of the various units whose HQs it represented. The hall has now been replaced by flats, but a few single-storey out-buildings remain. Also from this period just preceding the outbreak of war was the equally elegant Sherwood House at Newark.

45 Nottingham: the impressive Derby Road drill hall was another of Brewill and Bailey's designs; it was built in 1910–12 for a number of Territorial Force units, including infantry, cavalry, field ambulance and service corps.

46 Newark: Sherwood House was built in 1910 and received additions in 1938 and 1956, remaining in use until 1996.

47 Arnold drill hall is another elegant building from just before the First World War, with rusticated quoins and a bowstring roof with glazed roof-lights.

48 Southwell drill hall was designed by Brewill and Bailey, opening in 1914; it, too, like Arnold and Sutton-in-Ashfield, has a bowstring roof.

A two-storey front block of eleven bays is entered through another Baroque Revival doorway with pillars and pediment. The new drill halls at Arnold, Sutton-in-Ashfield and Southwell all share the same distinctive feature, quite unusual for this building type, a bowstring roof. The land in Easthorpe (now Newark) Road, Southwell, was bought in 1912 for another building by Brewill and Bailey. The hall, measuring 60 by 30ft (18.5 by 9.25m), is fronted by a single-storey block containing an officers' room, a lecture room, the quartermaster's stores, and a small kitchen. Down one side

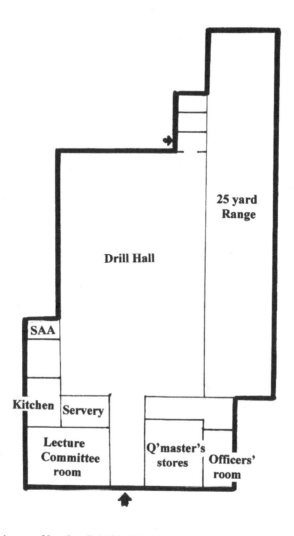

25 yard Range

Drill Hall

SAA

Kitchen **Servery**

Lecture Committee room

Q'master's stores

Officers' room

49 Plan of the layout of Southwell drill hall based on the architect's plans of 1912.

runs an indoor range, and there is a small-arms ammunition store on the opposite side of the hall. The Forest Town drill hall is another elegant Edwardian building with a hall measuring 60 by 36ft (18.5 by 11m), fitted out as a gymnasium for the use of the cadets of the Boys' Brigade.

A number of other premises were used in the early years of the twentieth century including numbers 24 and 34 Castle Gate in Newark, occupied by the 8th Battalion of the Sherwood Foresters, TF; in Nottingham, 26 Park Row, one of a terrace of four four-storey Regency houses used as ASC stores in 1910, and two years later as HQ of the Nottinghamshire and Derbyshire Mounted Brigade; and, also in Nottingham, 116 Raleigh Street, a large detached Victorian villa, with substantial outbuildings to the rear, in use as their Battery Office from 1910 by the Nottinghamshire RHA.

six

Nottinghamshire in the First World War

The army

The Nottinghamshire and Derbyshire Regiment, known as the Sherwood Foresters, fielded a total of thirty-three battalions during the First World War suffering over 11,000 casualties. Nottinghamshire's two yeomanry regiments which each recruited second- and third-line units, served in a number of theatres and roles along with the Nottinghamshire RHA.

Mobilisation and recruitment

On the outbreak of war, the 1st Battalion Sherwood Foresters was stationed in Bombay. At the beginning of September it sailed from India, landed at Plymouth a month later and joined the 24th Brigade, prior to sailing across to France, arriving on 5 November 1914. The 2nd Battalion had been based in Sheffield and had already gone to France early in September. The Territorial Force's 46th (1st North Midland) Division consisted of sixteen infantry battalions drawn from Leicestershire, Lincolnshire, Derbyshire and Nottinghamshire. One of its three brigades consisted of the 5th, 6th, 7th and 8th Battalions of the Sherwood Foresters. The 1/7th Sherwood Foresters, still popularly known as the Robin Hood Rifles, continued to recruit from Nottingham City with the 1/8th Battalion coming from the other Nottinghamshire towns, but centred at Newark-on-Trent. Nottingham's main Recruiting Office was in the Derby Road drill hall, with Newark's at Sherwood House. The Forest Town drill hall was one of many supplementary recruitment centres, and although no units were ever based there, a First World War machine gun stood on top of the porch for many years after the war's end.

As war broke out the 1/7th Battalion was on its annual summer camp at Hunmanby, near Filey, on the Yorkshire coast. On 3 August they were recalled to Nottingham and dispersed home, but the next day received the order to mobilise. The battalion assembled at the drill hall on Derby Road on 5 August and were billeted in the Mechanics' and the Victoria Halls with some men permitted to sleep at home to ease the pressure on space. Following a few days spent in the preparation of equipment and the organisation of stores, the battalion marched to Derby to join up with the rest of the Sherwood Foresters' Brigade prior to leaving by train for Luton (Bedfordshire) to join the division. This was centred on Luton Hoo House and the brigade was allocated billets in private houses in Harpenden (Hertfordshire). Following time spent constructing London's anti-invasion defences on the north-eastern edges of Braintree in Essex, the 46th was the first TF division to be sent to France, and it arrived in Le Havre in February 1915, and went straight into the trenches.

Immediately the four regular and the four TF battalions of the Sherwood Foresters had been mobilised, work began on raising second-line TF battalions. In September 1914, the 2/7th and 2/8th Battalions were raised in Nottingham and Newark-upon-Trent respectively, as part of the 59th (2nd North Midland) Division, which mirrored exactly the composition of the 46th Division. By March 1915, the recruitment of 3/7th and 3/8th TF Battalions was well under way. Alongside these efforts by the County Territorial Association there was the much-publicised direct appeal by Lord Kitchener for the cohorts which would make up his five New Armies (K1-5), and between August and October 1914, this produced a further six battalions (9th-14th) of the Sherwood Foresters. They spent around a year in training prior to being shipped to France. Added to these two initiatives was local enterprise. The Mayor of Nottingham and his Recruiting Committee raised the 15th Battalion in February 1915, and the 17th Battalion (the Welbeck Rangers) four months later. The 15th was a bantam battalion made up of recruits who failed to meet the army's minimum height requirement but were otherwise fit. They were gratefully accepted by the War Office which was struggling to find the necessary manpower to keep the field army topped up with reinforcements. Both these units made it to France in early 1916, a couple of months before the start of the Battle of the Somme, as did three similar battalions raised in Derby. Other battalions were raised, or put together through reorganisations throughout the rest of the war, including the 53rd (Young Soldier) Battalion raised as a training unit, and stationed at Clipstone in October 1918. The Nottingham University OTC sent some 1,600 cadets to the war, many of them as those infantry subalterns whose life expectation, once in the trenches, averaged just six weeks. Around 200 were killed in action or died of wounds, with a further 500 seriously wounded or suffering from life-threatening illness, injury or disease.

The deployment of local units

The Sherwood Foresters of the regular army and the TF

A total of eighteen battalions of the Sherwood Foresters served on the Western Front, most remaining there for the duration, but 11th Battalion also served on the Italian front from late 1917, returning to France in September 1918, and 9th Battalion served at Gallipoli. The 1st Battalion, having been thrown into the fray, un-acclimatised and straight off the boat from India, fought in France through the entire war, winning two VCs. The 2nd Battalion had, by the end of October 1914, fought in two major actions and had suffered casualties of thirty-three officers and 924 other ranks, more or less the equivalent of its entire strength. The two regular reserve battalions served on the north-east coast on anti-invasion duties as part of the Tyne Garrison for the whole war. The prime purpose of the second-line TF battalions was to train up and supply drafts for the first-line units. As this process eroded their manpower they drew on the third-line battalions. Eventually it was necessary to send what remained of them to France to be absorbed into the senior units. In February 1918 the War Office decided to reduce the number of battalions in a brigade from four to three, in order to maintain the number of divisions. The battalion dropped from the Sherwood Foresters' Brigade was distributed amongst the second-line battalions to produce one viable battalion, the second one being disbanded. The third-line TF and some of the other training reserve battalions remained in England, based at Thoresby Hall, Welbeck Abbey or Clipstone Camp, preparing new conscripts and sending them on as drafts. The 1/7th Battalion the Robin Hoods, and its second- and third-line units, between them lost sixty-five officers and nearly 1,000 other ranks during their four years on the Western Front, winning two Victoria Crosses, twenty Military Crosses and thirty-three Military Medals. The six New Army and the three privately raised battalions all served with distinction, mainly on the Western Front, the 16th Battalion winning a VC on the Menin Road Ridge. In all, Sherwood Foresters won nine VCs, including that of Captain Albert Ball of the RFC, who had belonged to the Robin Hoods. The 2/7th Battalion found itself in Dublin at Easter 1916, as part of the force despatched to put down the nationalist rising. They sustained heavy casualties as, untrained and ill-equipped, they made frontal charges against well-ensconced and experienced urban guerrillas in Dublin's city centre. In all, over 140,000 men served in the Sherwood Foresters, of whom almost 11,500 were killed in action, died from wounds or succumbed to sickness or injury.

The Nottinghamshire Yeomanry

There were still two yeomanry cavalry regiments in the county: the Sherwood Rangers based in Retford and the South Nottinghamshire Hussars based at Derby Road, Nottingham. Both started the war posted to Norfolk on anti-invasion duties, but by the summer of 1915 they had been shipped out to the Dardanelles where, without their horses, they fought as infantry alongside other British and Empire troops in a disastrous and ill-conceived campaign. The Rangers' troopship was torpedoed between Salonika and Egypt and the survivors were integrated into the Desert Mounted Corps, part of Allenby's successful forces expelling the Turks from the Holy Land. The Hussars shared a similar history for the first part of the war, but were then combined with the Warwickshire Yeomanry to become a battalion of the newly formed Machine Gun Corps (MGC). In transit from Alexandria, they too were torpedoed, the survivors eventually reaching France, as 100th Battalion MGC, in August 1918.

Both regiments raised second-line units which served as home defence troops and received bicycles instead of horses. Their third-line units were established as reserve cavalry regiments, the Rangers being based in Aldershot, and the Hussars at the Curragh, in Dublin. A number of photographs in the collection of Bassetlaw Museum show groups of Sherwood Rangers at West Retford House; one of these photographs, dated May 1915 however, is attributed to both West Retford House and West

Retford Hall. A photograph of officers outside West Retford House is attributed by the hotel to the RAF, so may be a legacy of a tradition linking it with RFC personnel from the nearby East Retford aerodrome.

The Territorial Artillery

The Nottinghamshire RHA was brigaded with the Berkshire and Honourable Artillery Company batteries and served in Egypt and Palestine, with a second-line unit formed in 1915, and posted, after its training, to India.

The Volunteer Training Corps

As the manpower shortage grew ever more acute, more ways of maximising resources were sought. In late 1916, barely, as we now know, halfway through the war, a royal proclamation was issued calling for volunteers for home-based military service from amongst those older than the usual recruit, or else in a reserved occupation. There are earlier references to such a force, but as the result of local initiative. Burton Joyce, for instance, had raised a company of the 'Citizens' Army' in 1915. In many places across the country such a force would not only include older volunteers, but also youngsters awaiting their call-up, giving them the opportunity to learn drill and marksmanship prior to mobilisation. However, the recruiting poster for the Nottinghamshire Volunteer Regiment, of February 1917, which survives in Nottinghamshire Archives (ref: CC/NP/25/10/16) specifically calls for physically fit men between the ages of 42–60, and emphasises that men employed in munitions production, including miners presumably, as government servants or as railway employees, were free to enlist. The poster was issued by the local Army Command, at Welbeck Abbey, and listed the new unit's key locations. RHQ and HQ of the 1st Battalion were in Thurland Street, Nottingham, whilst the 2nd and 3rd Battalions were located in the Bingham area, and around Hucknall and Arnold respectively. The 4th Battalion had companies in Retford, Worksop and Mansfield. Initially, the War Office was reluctant to issue more than GR armbands, hence the theme of the force's several nicknames, one, for instance, being 'Grandad's Relics'.

The purpose of those VTC units comprising older men was to carry out tasks which would release trained soldiers for front-line service. Duties included mounting guard on vulnerable points such as munitions factories, utilities or aerodromes, and key communications nodes such as road junctions, railway bridges, and river and canal crossings. This often involved night work, carried out after a long day in the mine or factory. Sometimes volunteers guarded their own place of work: mine, factory or railway depot for instance, so at least they were on familiar territory.

Training camps in Nottinghamshire

Amongst the twenty or so areas across the United Kingdom identified as assembly and training camps for elements of Kitchener's New Armies, two large areas in Nottinghamshire were selected. One was Clipstone Infantry Training Camp which

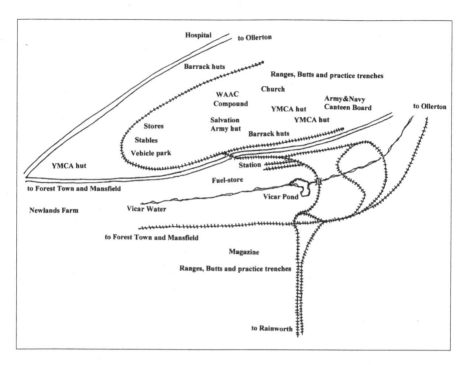

Hospital

to Ollerton

Barrack huts

Ranges, Butts and practice trenches

Church

WAAC
Compound

Army&Navy
Canteen Board

to Ollerton

YMCA hut

Stores

Salvation
Army hut

YMCA hut

Stables

Barrack huts

Vehicle park

YMCA hut

Station

to Forest Town and Mansfield

Fuel-store

Vicar Pond

Newlands Farm

Vicar Water

to Forest Town and Mansfield

Magazine

Ranges, Butts and practice trenches

to Rainworth

50 Plan of Clipstone Camp. (The rail layout includes the colliery's additions.)

was chosen as the initial base for the 33rd Division in the Fourth Army (K4), whose constituent units began to assemble there on 1 July 1915. A number of privately raised and themed battalions included five from the Royal Fusiliers: the 23rd and 24th Battalions recruited from sportsmen, and raised by Mrs Cunliffe-Owen; the 17th Battalion raised from amongst colonial expatriates by the British Empire Committee; the 22nd Battalion raised by the Mayor of Kensington; and the 18th Battalion recruited from the public schools. This last was one of four such units, the majority of whose members were shortly to be commissioned, and this original 98th Brigade was then replaced by two battalions of Worcesters, 9th Battalion Somerset Light Infantry, and 13th Battalion Sherwood Foresters. Additionally, the 17th Battalion Middlesex Regiment (1st Footballers) had been raised by W. Joynson-Hicks MP. To these were added battalions from other regiments, including the 16th (Church Lads' Brigade) Battalion Kings Royal Rifle Corps, the 13th Battalion Essex Regiment, raised by the Mayor of West Ham, and a second battalion of the Middlesex Regiment, 18th (1st Public Works Pioneers) Battalion recruited from municipal employees. The artillery of the Fourth Army's 33 Division also gathered for training at Clipstone. The division, by now almost 20,000 strong, soon moved south to Salisbury Plain to complete its training, and made its debut on the Western Front two weeks into the Battle of the Somme in July 1916.

Clipstone then provided a base for training and reserve units whose function it was to supply drafts to front-line units in order to replace battle casualties. From August 1915, the 21st Reserve Brigade, comprising depot battalions of the Prince of Wales's West

Yorkshire Regiment, was in residence, followed by the West Riding Reserve Brigade consisting of four third-line battalions of firstly the West Yorkshire Regiment from April 1916, next of the York & Lancaster Regiment from September 1916, and then, from October 1917, of the Duke of Wellington's West Riding Regiment. Other such training reserve brigades would include young soldier battalions from the Leicestershire Regiment and the Sherwood Foresters. Finally, in 1918, 208 Brigade of 69 (2 East Anglian) Division (Home Forces), consisting of battalions of Sherwood Foresters and the Leicestershire Regiment, was based at Clipstone, along with the ASC units which serviced the resident units. The camp, served by a railway line from Mansfield, consisted of long lines of timber huts, each holding thirty or forty men, with separate facilities for eating and washing. Alcohol-free canteens and reading-rooms were set up by organisations such as the YMCA and church missionary societies for the troops to use in their free time. Along with a post office, other shops were established, creating a self-contained 'tin town' for the troops' use. A timber church, seating 900 souls, was built after an appeal for funds by the Bishop of Southwell, and furnished by church groups within the diocese. After the camp closed, the church was dismantled to be re-erected in Kirkby-in-Ashfield. The drill hall at Forest Town was made available on three days each week for the recreational use of troops from the camp but, despite this provision and other attempts to keep soldiers out of the pubs, towns like Mansfield would still be invaded by uninhibited soldiers on their evenings off. It has been suggested that in order to allay the fears of Mansfield's citizens that the presence of licentious soldiery would destroy the town's reputation, the War Office ensured that Clipstone Camp's earliest residents would be wholesome young gentlemen from the public schools and clean-living sportsmen's battalions. Whatever the reservations, Mansfield doubtless still enjoyed the economic benefit of the troops' spending power on their excursions to the bright lights. After the war the long-planned Clipstone Colliery was built, opening in 1926.

51 Forest Town drill hall was built by the Bolsover Colliery Company for the use of the Boys' Brigade, then a quasi-military organisation.

52.West Retford House, now an hotel, was HQ of the 69th (2nd East Anglian) Infantry Division, and may also, possibly at a later date, have served as an officers' mess for East Retford aerodrome.

The second concentration of major training camps in Nottinghamshire was based in the Dukeries: Carburton Camp, Thoresby Park and Welbeck, along with other camps in the Retford area. TF battalions from the Bedfordshires and the Northamptonshires both passed through Carburton en route for Clipstone during 1917, and the Suffolks' 2/5th Battalion spent the summer of 1917 at Thoresby Park. However, the main uses of these camps was to house brigades of two Home Forces divisions, 185 Brigade of the 62 (2 West Riding) and elements of 206, 207 and 208 Brigades of the 69 (2 East Anglian), whose HQ was at West Retford House. A TF battalion of the York and Lancaster Regiment was stationed in Bulwell for the first six months of the war, ASC units were quartered in Retford later on and there was a RE Reserve Training Centre in Newark-on-Trent, one of two such camps relieving pressure on the REs' base at Chatham (Kent).

Along with others which sprung up near the camps, at least three in Clipstone alone, the long-established rifle ranges at Upton outside Southwell, at Epperstone and on the Trent, continued in use for the duration. Training facilities, such as the practice trenches in Babworth Woods outside Retford, sprang up all over the place.

The war in the air

There was an expectation at the beginning of the war that aerial activity would be confined to the battlefield with aircraft acting mainly in the reconnaissance role. However, the incursions of initially the Zeppelins and later on the Gotha four-engined bombers prompted the RFC to establish Home Defence squadrons based across the country and tasked with the interception and elimination of these aerial intruders carrying out bombing raids. Such raids against industrial targets including the steelworks of Rotherham and Sheffield brought enemy activity over Nottinghamshire, with bombs being offloaded over Retford. In the local area, the nearest of these squadrons were based outside the county, 38 Squadron at Melton Mowbray (Leicestershire) and 33 Squadron at Gainsborough (Lincolnshire). Although its HQ along with an air-strip for its CO's aircraft, was at The Lawn, on Summer Hill in Gainsborough, 33 Squadron flew its FE2 fighters from an operational base on the Nottinghamshire bank of the Trent, in the parish of Saundby and south of the A631, extending from the stream near the oil wells, as far as the railway line. This squadron also operated from East Retford aerodrome, a site now occupied by HMP Ranby, where some huts survive. These squadrons' operations required a much wider support network as, given the difficulty in synchronising interceptions with reports of airship or bomber sightings, it was imperative that fighters stayed in the air for as long as their fuel capacity would allow. This necessitated extra landing grounds right across the fighters' areas of operation so that they could quickly refuel and resume their patrols, and this network extended across Nottinghamshire. There were landing grounds at Wigsley, at Plungar and at Thurgarton, and those two latter locations were very close to sites which would later be selected for Second World War airfields. These landing grounds were provided with the very minimum of facilities: basically a hut for the small party of ground crew, and a fuel tank, kept topped-up for constant, if unpredictable, use. Those landing grounds specified for night-time use were given braziers which would be kept alight throughout the hours of darkness. Consequently, these very ephemeral sites have left no traces beyond the boundaries of the fields they occupied.

The second function of home airfields was training, supplying pilots for service on, mainly, the Western Front. Several squadrons used East Retford as a night-flying training station for both fighters and bombers, with an adjacent field designated as an area for bomb-dropping practice. Consideration for the local population prompted the daytime use of tinted goggles in order to simulate night-flight. In June 1918, No.199 (Night-training) Squadron was transferred to Harpswell (Lincolnshire) with its partner, No.200 Squadron, following in November. Both were disbanded there in June 1919. Nos 186 and 187 (Night-training) Squadrons also used East Retford until May 1919, after which 186 Squadron re-formed at Gosport (Hampshire) engaged in development work. Hucknall started out as a training station. With the planned introduction of the

53 East Retford: these huts, now used for training purposes by HMP Ranby, were originally built to accommodate RFC personnel from East Retford aerodrome, and then formed part of an army camp.

54 Hucknall: this pair of GS, or Belfast Truss (332/17 or 377/17), hangars were put up toward the end of the First World War to accommodate the four-engine, long-distance DH 0/400 bomber which was to have been the centrepiece of the newly formed RAF's Independent Bomber Force.

Handley Page 0/400 and the entry of the USA into the war there was a need for a vast training programme as the Allies sought to double the size of their air forces. To accommodate all these new training schools a large number of Training Depot Stations (TDS) were built across Britain and Ireland (numbered 1–62 and 201–211). Laid down in 1916, most were to become operational early in 1918. Hucknall, No.15 TDS, would appear to have trained pilots on the DH9 bomber, some 4,000 of which had been ordered in what would be the final year of the war and US personnel arrived for training early in 1918. With the birth of the RAF on 1 April 1918, two training squadrons were formed at Hucknall. The layout of a TDS was standard with three pairs of GS (Belfast Truss) hangars and a single Aircraft Repair Shed (ARS). The watch office was either a cabin mounted on the forward corner of a hangar, or else a single-storey hut adjacent to the flying-field, similar to those huts which served as workshops, messes, stores, barrack-rooms and training buildings. At Hucknall, two pairs of GS hangars (Grade II listed), and the ARS, remain in commercial use. Prior to Hucknall's selection as an aerodrome site, Papplewick Moor had been put forward as being suitable. On consideration, the ground there was judged too soft, but it was nevertheless designated as Hucknall's relief landing ground. Apart from the removal of some hedges, nothing was done to enhance this field which had no facilities at all.

Air defence

Nottingham fortunately underwent only a single Zeppelin raid, in September 1916. Retford was also bombed in September 1916, but by a Zeppelin which had become disorientated, mistaking the town for its true target which was Nottingham.

The city was given the protection of seven AA sites, first recorded in June 1917. These were located at Clifton, Bramcote, Wilford, Sneinton, Aspley, Wilsthorpe and Thrumpton. Five of these sites were equipped with 3in 20cwt AA guns, whilst the other two, Wilford and Sneinton, had 12-pounder 12cwt QF guns, a model designed for use either by the Royal Navy on board ship, or in coast defence batteries. These AA batteries usually consisted of a single gun, teamed with a searchlight. There would be an open gun-pit with a small brick ready-use magazine, a generator-house to power the searchlight, a store for the diesel needed by the generator, a crew shelter, ablutions and kitchen, the latter three being accommodated in timber hutting.

55 A 12-pounder naval gun, widely used as an anti-aircraft weapon; by 1917 one had been emplaced at each of the AA gun-sites at Wilford and Sneinton.

Munitions production

The insatiable demand for munitions, highlighted by the 'shells scandal' of May 1915 which brought down the government, forced existing manufacturers to re-focus their production, and encouraged new enterprise. Established firms quickly switched to producing materials for the munitions industry. Acetone was vital to the production of cordite, and by the beginning of the war, steps had been taken to establish plants to produce the acetate of lime from which acetone was derived. Acetate of lime was produced by the destructive distillation of wood and, unsurprisingly, the new plants were located in forests. The Worksop works of Anglo Shirley Aldred and Co. was part of this new home-grown industry, conveniently near to Sherwood Forest. As new sources of acetone were developed in the laboratories, then schoolchildren were sent into the woods to gather acorns and horse chestnuts. One way of packaging explosive was by infusing it into cotton, producing long cords of gun-cotton, hence 'cordite'. This was dependent on a plentiful supply of cotton-waste produced by works such as JC Ley & Sons' Canterbury Road Mills of Old Radford. Other firms had always made essential components for the war machine, a good example being Ransome & Marles in Newark-on-Trent whose ball-bearing manufactory had been established around 1900. Ransome's was one of many manufacturers who employed women to meet the increased demand for output while losing male employees to the armed services.

Firms usually catering for civilian consumers soon diverted their energies into war-production. By May 1915 fully a quarter of Nottingham's hosiery factories were engaged on fulfilling government contracts to supply the military. Boots, for instance, employed 900 women to make 90,000 gas-respirators per week, and in 1915 commenced the manufacture of pharmaceuticals on a commercial scale. At Raleigh's bicycle works the machinery was quickly adapted to new products. Those used to turning out Sturmey-Archer gears were put to producing fuses for shells, and the big sheet-steel presses made magazines for Lewis guns. The Raleigh workforce was increased from 2,000 to 5,000, mainly by the employment of women. Turney Bros' leather works switched their entire production into military clothing. Players produced the presentation boxes of cigarettes and tobacco which Princess Mary provided for every soldier at Christmas 1914. W.N. Nicholson's Trent Ironworks in Newark had produced agricultural machinery since 1840, and the need to increase agricultural production would have rendered their output even more vital than previously.

From the 1890s, Lyddite had been the explosive of choice for artillery shells, but the introduction of TNT in the early years of the twentieth century had necessitated the construction of new shell-filling factories. TNT on its own was very expensive but combining it with ammonium nitrate to produce a product called amatol provided a cheaper alternative. Four new National Filling Factories (NFF) were started in 1915, one of them being NFF No.6 at Chilwell. Linked to the Toton railway sidings by a gated military road, the factory was designed by Viscount Chetwynd using ideas drawn from other areas of industry. Combining TNT and ammonium nitrate presented a major problem. In a proportion of 20:80 parts the resultant substance was not sufficiently fluid to allow it to be poured into the shells. The best solution was to reduce the mix to a powdered form which could more easily be poured. Chetwynd applied technology from industries as diverse as mineral extraction, paint production and food processing, adapting existing machinery to render the amatol into a suitable consistency for pouring into shell-casings. Mills, seven storeys high, were used to replicate processes deriving from flour milling; materials were crushed using machines from coal mines and quarries; and a five-storey mixing house was built for combining the ingredients. The amatol in powder form was then packed into the shells using hydraulic pressure. Chilwell's major task was to fill 60-pounder and 6in howitzer shells with amatol and, by the end of the war, over 19 million shells, half of all those fired by the artillery, had been filled. The largest sections of the factory were the building where shell-casings were stored prior to filling, and the enormous Filled Shell Store. Here, 600,000 filled shells could be stored in a complex of sheds covering 9 acres (3.5 has), being moved around by seventy-two overhead cranes, and served by railway lines at each end of the building. As well as these shells, mines were filled for the Admiralty, and aerial bombs for the RFC and the RNAS. Though inherently dangerous, the munitions factories boasted a remarkable safety record but this was dependent on constant vigilance. The factories were designed to minimise the risks but any relaxation in following the prescribed procedures could end in disaster, and Chilwell was the plant where things went most wrong. On 1 July 1918, an enormous explosion occurred in the amatol mixing house, resulting in 134 deaths and 250 serious injuries, some workers being blown through the walls. Chetwynd refused to believe that the cause was other than sabotage and brought in the police to investigate, but nothing was ever proved. Twelve workers, men and women, were decorated for gallantry, and a monument in Nottingham cemetery provides a focus for an annual commemorative service on Remembrance Day.

If plants like Chilwell produced the filling, others were needed to provide the shell itself, and in 1915, a National Projectile Factory in Nottingham's Kings Meadows, a site already linked by railway to the Clifton Colliery, and able to draw on a pool of existing labour centred on the hosiery industry, was planned. Wm. Beardmore Ltd was a Clydeside ship-builder, heavily involved in providing capital ships and their armament for the Royal Navy. Cammell Laird and Co. were an amalgamation of a Birkenhead shipyard and a Sheffield engineering company, also heavily involved in the production of heavy armaments including warships and early armoured cars. Accounts differ, but it would appear that an invitation was extended to one, or both, of these concerns to build and, subsequently to manage, this factory. Production capacity was set at a weekly output of 2,000 of 9.2in and 6,000 of 6in shell-casings, and these targets were reached by September 1916, barely a year from the start of construction. The factory covered 13 acres (5 has) and consisted of corrugated-iron sheets over a steel frame, with a brick power-house at one corner. In 1917, shell production was complemented by a repair and refurbishment facility for 18-pounder field-guns, and the factory was re-designated a National Ordnance Factory. Following extensive preparatory work, production for the army of Mark XIX 6in Howitzers commenced in 1918, with a rate of eleven per week being attained by the end of the war.

Military hospitals

The high levels of casualties being brought home from, mainly, the Western Front, required an extensive expansion of the medical facilities available for their care. The Territorial Force No. 5 Northern General Hospital in Leicester was at the centre of a network of affiliated establishments including the Nottingham General Hospital, and the Bayley Hospital. Also affiliated were two of the county's VAD hospitals at Trent Bridge and Eastwood, staffed mainly by volunteers. Other RAMC out-stations were often set up by doctors who had previously served with the military, an example being Babworth Hall. The Nottingham County Asylum at Radcliffe on Trent was taken over by the War Office to receive soldiers suffering from what would now be called post-traumatic stress disorder but was then known as 'shell shock', or at worst 'lack of moral fibre'. Camps such as Clipstone and Welbeck Abbey had their own sickbays for dealing with their occupants' day-to-day accidents and sickness. Finally there were hospitals set up under the auspices of the Red Cross and staffed by volunteers, supported by local GPs. Examples of these are 'The Cedars' at Beeston and Arnott Hall. Soldiers domiciled in Nottinghamshire who needed artificial limbs were directed to the No. 2 Northern General Hospital in Leeds.

Prisoners of war

The arrangements for dealing with prisoners of war were often quite different in the First World War from those in force in the Second. The sort of POW camps which we would recognise by their serried ranks of huts, barbed-wire fences and armed guards in watchtowers, did exist, one such being set up in the Midland Agricultural and Dairy College at Sutton Bonington, where the captain of the *Emden*, a German cruiser captured while operating as a commerce raider, was held. Another agricultural college, Bulcote School, is listed as a camp so this may have been a similar set-up, and a camp for German POWs on the Babworth Estate near Retford is described as a 'compound camp' which would suggest some attention to security, but these would appear to have been very much in the minority. Apart from officers and their servants who were held separately and prevented by international treaty from being required to work, the majority of POWs were organised into small gangs, either providing working-parties for industry, or working on the land. Providing this work was not deemed to be contributing directly to the war effort, so no objections were raised by the POWs themselves or the Neutral Power, which had a right of inspection. However, POWs were employed in the construction of East Retford aerodrome. Some Allied POWs were starved and worked to death in Germany, the excuse being that the Allied blockade made food scarce for everyone. In Britain there were shortages of specific food items but nobody starved. A number of depots including Cuckney, Plumtree, Ranskill and Retford are listed as, presumably, the bases for working-parties. A few more specific locations are given as having POW work-gangs and these include Kelham Brickfields. The other major category is migratory gangs. These were based in a specific locality – Bunny, Gotham, Shelford, Walkeringham, Clayworth and Ruddington for example, and moved as necessary around the local farms carrying out work as required, replacing many of the indigenous agricultural labourers who had volunteered or been conscripted for the army.

56 Sutton Bonington Agricultural College, opened in 1913, was the site of a POW camp.

seven

Nottinghamshire
1918–39

Once the First World War was over, the country rapidly returned to peacetime working. One of the government's promises had been to provide 'homes for heroes', and one such scheme was designed by Barry Parker for Hawtonville in Newark-on-Trent, consisting of three-bedroomed 'parlour cottages', both semi-detached and in terraces of four. Nottingham Corporation also embarked on an extensive programme of public housing and sanitary improvements from 1919. Following a brief economic boom in the aftermath of the war, came the Depression, and with it, a consequent fall in public spending. However, by the early 1930s the need for rearmament was becoming apparent.

The RAF between the wars

At the end of the First World War the majority of airfields across the country were closed down, aircraft were scrapped wholesale and orders that had been placed for new ones were cancelled. Most of Nottinghamshire's airfields had been grass strips

57 Hawtonville, Newark-upon-Trent: homes for heroes designed in 1919 by Barry Parker.

with only minimal construction so they rapidly reverted to agriculture. Only at Hucknall was there any significant RAF activity. No.15 TDS had formed in April 1918 to train pilots on DH9s and Avro 504s and, early in 1919, the station became No.15 Training Squadron but by the end of the year this had been transferred away and the airfield went back to being farmland. However, unlike many such establishments, the hangars were left intact. Some civilian flying did continue through the 1920s as the Nottingham Flying (sometimes 'Aero') Club had acquired part of the former flying field. In 1928 the RAF returned, basing a day-bomber squadron of the Special Reserve there. Although the RAF had been fighting for its existence throughout the 1920s, an air-power policy had been agreed that would ensure parity with France. Essentially this provided a group of bomber stations in Wessex, and a screen of fighter airfields ringing London, leaving the Midlands pretty peripheral to this layout. The construction of these new Home Defence airfields did produce a range of building designs, and the rebirth of Hucknall is evidenced by some examples drawn from these designs: the guardhouse (1621/27), main stores (808/27), parachute store/armoury (815/27) and MT sheds (8147/27). The site was brought back to operational standards in 1927–28 and interestingly, on the Air Ministry plan of the airfield, the GS hangars, presumably from the TDS era and given a 1916 date in recent planning documentation, bear drawing numbers for a later design (1857/27) and the annotation 'Belfast Truss' suggesting that they were refurbished as part of the works carried out by Laings.

By the early 1930s it was apparent that war with Germany was becoming increasingly likely, and the RAF entered its Expansion Period which, anticipating attack across the North Sea, involved a re-orientation towards the east. In May 1936 Hucknall was set up as HQ of No.1 Group Bomber Command which consisted of light-bomber squadrons dispersed across the east Midlands. On the outbreak of war, this HQ was to be sent to

58 RAF Hucknall, the guardhouse (1621/27).

59 RAF Hucknall, main stores to a design dated 1927.

France to co-ordinate the RAF's light-bomber squadrons operating on the Continent. Late in 1938, Hucknall, already HQ of No.12 Group since May 1937, was officially reassigned to Fighter Command. Along with the Communications Flight, servicing the Group HQs, Hucknall, for a short while, accommodated a squadron of Hurricanes en route for Digby (Lincolnshire). It was envisaged that Fighter Command's Group HQs would be given protected premises either on established fighter stations or off-site. In 1938, No.12 Group selected a disused railway cutting in Watnall as a free-standing HQ consisting of three underground bunkers, one each for the Control Centre, the Filter Room and the Communications Centre. In line with the policy to co-locate the RAF command and control, the Observer Corps and the army's AA organisation, all these elements were gathered together, the HQ of the 2nd AA Division being nominally at RAF Hucknall. In 1934 Rolls-Royce had taken over some of the buildings at Hucknall, initially for engine test-flying. It was here that the early versions of the Merlin engine were put through their paces. The aircraft factory was served by No.1 Ferry Pilots Pool, delivering fighters and using a flight of six Avro Ansons to return the pilots back to base.

The real focus of the RAF's Expansion Programme was the provision of up-to-date airfields for the new aircraft which were beginning to appear from the factories. Newton was planned in 1936 and begun in 1938 as a standard airfield for light-bombers, the Fairey Battles, of No.1 Group. It was given the full range of buildings drawn from the suite of designs prepared by A. Bullock RIBA, the architect commissioned by the Air Ministry. These designs had been vetted by the Royal Fine Art Commission under the tutelage of Edwin Lutyens, and the Council for the Preservation of Rural England. Aware of the impact that several dozen new airfields would make on the landscape, it had been decided to adhere to a neo-Georgian style which might be seen to echo the country houses which were perceived as integral to the countryside. Much of Newton

60 RAF Watnall, the entrance to the underground bunker which held No.12 Group RAF Fighter Command's filter-room.

has now been demolished, but until recently it was presented as a virtually complete example of an Expansion Period airfield. Its watch office was the *moderne* 'villa' style (2328/39), which stood in front of five 'C' type hangars (8180/38), built in arcs to make them more difficult to bomb. The officers' mess is standard design with a central dining area and a projecting accommodation wing to each side (2290-2/34); the nine-bay, H-shaped barrack-blocks (1132/38); main stores (7064/37); the guardroom (469/38); the parachute store with its clerestory windows (175/36); station workshops (6957/37); the link trainer (12386/38); the institute/dining room with three port-hole windows in each forward-facing wing (8055/38); and the station HQ (1723/36); were all, along with the other buildings, completely typical of this narrow window of construction. As it was never to become an operational bomber station, it never received concrete runways.

Syerston, just up the road from Newton, having been planned in peacetime must be regarded as an Expansion Period airfield, but shows significant differences from, say, the earlier Newton. Whilst the watch office is the brick version of the 'villa' (5845/39) and the officers' mess (2290-2/34) is the same as Newton's, many of the structures must be classed as wartime utility. These include the two original hangars which were the less substantial 'J' type (5836/39), erected with some urgency just as hostilities were breaking out, and the water tower which consists of two Braithwaite tanks on a steel framework as opposed to that at Newton which is encased in brick. Dispersed communal sites such as that at Flintham Hall consist of hutting. Some work to modernise the airfield buildings was also carried out in the late 1930s at Hucknall, and whilst petrol-tanker sheds and pyrotechnic stores were necessarily of brick, much of it, especially accommodation for the increasing establishment, consisted of 'B' type timber hutting.

61 RAF Newton, the watch office (2328/39), the concrete version of the 'villa' type which included a meteorological office.

62 RAF Newton, one of its five 'C' type 'protected' hangars (5533/39) built in brick and concrete with a strengthened roof; the side windows were designed to dissipate damage from blast.

63 RAF Newton, the guardroom (469/38).

64 RAF Newton, the parachute store (175/36) with its clerestory windows.

65 RAF Syerston, officers' mess (2290-2/34) identical to that at Newton; this central block containing dining room, billiards room etc. and services was flanked by wings with quarters for thirty to fifty officers.

Training

Throughout the 1930s flying was gaining popularity as a recreational pastime, and this was evident at Bircotes where the Automobile Association listed a landing ground (SK658922). The Nottingham Aero Club had used Hucknall from its early days, and in 1931 the Nottingham Flying Club moved into the newly opened municipal aerodrome at Tollerton. By 1937 they were operating the Civil Air Guard scheme, anticipating the coming need for military pilots, and in June 1938 the RAF established No.27 ERFTS, run on their behalf by Nottingham Airport Ltd using civilian instructors. The airfield's facilities were improved and a Bellman hangar was built, together with

66 Tollerton aerodrome, the clubhouse of Nottingham Flying Club which moved there in 1931; by 1937 it was operating as part of the Civil Air Guard scheme.

training rooms, canteen and parachute stores. The school operated up to the outbreak of war when it was taken over by the RAF and combined with No. 30 ERFTS at Burnaston (Derbyshire), now the Toyota factory site.

The regular army and the TA

After the end of the First World War, the Sherwood Foresters soon reverted to their peacetime establishment of eight battalions: two of regulars, two of depot troops and reserves, two each of Derbyshire and Nottinghamshire Territorials. The regulars carried out their normal pattern of duties at home and abroad, with the 1st Battalion being posted to the West Indies in 1935, and then to Palestine, being stationed in Haifa in 1939.

The new Territorial Army (TA) was formed in 1920 from the old TF, but retained most of the original units. One of its new responsibilities was to be air defence, but there was little motivation and fewer resources to do much about this during the years of the Depression. The government also adhered to its Ten Year Rule which posited that as it would take at least ten years for a belligerent (meaning Germany) to re-arm, there was no need for the nation to incur unnecessary expenditure it could ill afford. This rolling timetable reached a low in 1932, at just about the time that hints of Germany's circumventions of the terms of the Versailles treaty were coming to light, but it was still some years before the AA defences received any significant attention. One way of generating new AA formations was to convert existing infantry units, and in 1936, the 7th Battalion the Sherwood Foresters, still based in Nottingham, became the 42nd (Robin Hoods) AA Battalion, RE as searchlight troops, transferring to the RA in 1939. Entirely new AA units were also raised including the 28th LAA Regiment RA, and the 27th LAA Regiment RA, both raised in 1939 in Nottingham and Newark-upon-Trent respectively, tapping in to the presence of trained operatives, particularly technicians and mechanics.

Just as in the previous emergency, a start was made on increasing the number of infantry battalions comprising each regiment. All TA units were required to provide a cadre of officers and NCOs who would form the nucleus around which a duplicate unit might be formed. The 9th Battalion of the Sherwood Foresters was cloned in 1939 from the 8th Battalion and based at Bulwell. Echoing the Volunteer Training Corps of the First World War and anticipating the Home Guard of the next, national defence companies were raised from 1936. No.45B Group was formed in Nottingham, later absorbed into the Sherwood Foresters as the 10th (Home Defence) Battalion in 1939.

The Sherwood Rangers, having finished the First World War as infantry serving in the Middle East, were reunited with their horses in 1920, and remained as horsed cavalry until 1940, one of only a very few such yeomanry units. The South Nottinghamshire Hussars had also served in the Middle East as infantry and then on the Western Front in the Machine Gun Corps, but in 1920 a further conversion to artillery took place. They became the 107th (South Notts Yeomanry) Brigade, RFA, later being designated 107 Field Regiment, RFA, and based at Derby Road, Nottingham. From this unit was cloned the 150th (South Notts Hussars) Field Regiment RA, TA. The Nottinghamshire RHA had been put into suspended animation in 1919, but was reconstituted as the Nottinghamshire battery of the 1st North Midland Brigade RFA with its HQ in Nottingham. In 1938 the brigade lost its Nottinghamshire and Leicestershire components being reduced to just its two Lincolnshire batteries and moving to Lincoln, but the 'RHA' designation transferred to the 107th (South Notts Hussars Yeomanry) Field Regiment.

In the early build-up to war, life for the regulars and the Territorials went on very much as before with the Robin Hoods spending their two weeks of summer camp at Filey in 1937, as usual, but by the beginning of 1939 developments were speeding up.

67 Newark-upon-Trent, Bowbridge RE Camp: huts incorporated into the primary school.

68 Blidworth drill hall, one of the first in a programme of building for rearmament.

69 Bulwell drill hall, built for the newly reorganised 107th (South Notts Hussars Yeomanry) Regiment, Royal Horse Artillery (TA).

The Militia Act required all fit young men to undergo six months' full-time training in a newly reconstituted militia. Hutted infantry camps were built, early in 1939, at Newark, where the Hawton Road camp on the golf course site had space for 500 trainees, Ollerton, Tuxford and Whatton-in-the-Vale. The REs had a further camp at Bowbridge in Newark. In addition, each AA unit of the TA was required to man the guns and searchlights continuously in a summer-long exercise known as the 'Couverture', with each complete unit serving for a month at a time.

Training for the Territorials had by now entered unfamiliar terrain. The AA units not only had new weapons to master, although only drill equipment was generally available at this time, but new methods of detecting incoming aircraft and of controlling fire had to be learned. Life for the infantry too was changing as mechanisation was brought in and new weaponry introduced. New drill halls were built to accommodate this kit and the specialist training rooms for practising with it. Starting with Rainworth in 1929, and Blidworth a year later, an extensive building programme was instigated

70 Newark-upon-Trent, Sherwood House, one of two later extensions to the drill hall.

71 Carlton drill hall, still home to the Sherwood Rangers squadron of a yeomanry regiment.

72 Beeston drill hall, now HQ of the East Midlands Universities OTC.

by the Nottinghamshire Territorial Association with a new drill hall opening in 1938 in Bulwell with extensive additions to Sutton-in-Ashfield and Sherwood House at Newark-upon-Trent, and at Carlton and Beeston the next year. Also produced in 1939 were plans for a new drill hall on Botany Avenue/Sutton Road, Mansfield, with an appearance very similar to others opening that year. Interestingly, to one side is a high entrance with sliding doors, suggesting a way of introducing bulky equipment into the interior. All the new drill halls, whether designed for infantry, field-guns, or AA artillery, are provided with plentiful garaging and workshop facilities. With the move of the putative university from Shakespeare Street to Highfields in 1928, an armoury for the NUOTC had been built, along with a rifle range, on the new site. In 1924 the Nottingham High School OTC finally got a new armoury and stores, and field days were sometimes spent exercising in Ramsdale Park, now a golf course.

Air defence

Whilst many of the successes of the First World War had been forgotten, there were, nevertheless, some lessons which remained in the planners' consciousness. The importance of integrating all the elements of air defence had resulted in the scheme known as Air Defence of Great Britain (ADGB), in effect, a nationwide expansion of the London Air Defence Area organisation. One element which could be maintained, at minimal cost moreover, was the function of observers in spotting and reporting the approach of hostile aircraft. By 1925, plans had been laid for the first posts in this new grid, but it would be fifteen years more before all parts of the country were included. As part of Stage 4 of the Air Ministry's expansion of the system, eight new ROC posts under No.6 Group in Derby were opened in Nottinghamshire in 1937–38. These posts would be staffed by rosters of volunteers with minimal training but eager to master the use of the basic equipment, notably the 'post instrument' which had been introduced in 1935, and to take on the challenge of aircraft recognition. Northern Area HQ had formed at Hucknall in 1935, prior to its move to Catterick, replaced alongside the 2nd AA Division's HQ, by the Midland HQ, which then moved to Grantham in 1938. In early August 1939, the whole system was tried out in an exercise involving 1,300 aircraft, the fifteen Chain Home RDF (radar) stations, the AA divisions and barrage balloons, the whole affair being monitored by scientists dubbing themselves the 'Lost Property Office' as they tracked aircraft which went unreported.

Munitions

The National Ordnance Factory, in Kings Meadows, Nottingham continued in operation after 1918, becoming one in a national network of Royal Ordnance Factories (ROF) in 1931. Run by Metropolitan Cammell Carriage and Wagon Co. Ltd, it built railway rolling stock for export. Once rearmament began in earnest, the works was given a £1 million plus refurbishment and, by 1938 was turning out numbers of the new 3.7in HAA guns, so desperately needed for the approaching conflict. In order to blend the factory into the surrounding streets of terrace houses, the roofs of the factory buildings were painted with stripes which continued the houses' roof-lines and the lines of the residential streets. The product of the ROFs was stored, ready for issue to units on mobilisation, in a parallel network of ordnance depots, centred on Central Ordnance Depots such as that at Chilwell. Many of these were run by the RAOC and, locally, these included two in Arnold, Bestwood and Redhill Lodges, and a third in Hucknall Lane, Bulwell, all served by dedicated railway branch lines or sidings.

In 1934, Rolls-Royce established a factory on the airfield at Hucknall, specifically for testing the engines, particularly the Merlin, which would power so many of the new breed of warplane. Another element of the military aircraft industry's support structure was the Civilian Repair Organisation, and Field Aircraft Services Ltd opened a CRO branch at Tollerton in 1938, adding the large factory hangar.

73 Tollerton aerodrome: the factory hangar, built in 1938, which was used throughout the Second World War by the Civilian Repair Organisation, run by Field Aircraft Services Ltd.

eight

Nottinghamshire in the Second World War

Nottinghamshire was one of those counties, distant from both the coast thus avoiding the emergency measures taken as a response to the threat of invasion, and from the enemy airfields expected to launch an aerial bombardment. Ironically that meant that the county was deemed safe enough to host munitions plants, and army and RAF training establishments, the very things which would rationalise it as a target for enemy bombers, particularly once they were able to operate from bases in Belgium and the Netherlands.

The deployment of local units

The sixteen battalions of the Sherwood Foresters enjoyed mixed fortunes during the war. The 1st Battalion began the war in Palestine but was soon redeployed to the defence of Egypt. The 2nd, 1/5th, 2/5th and 9th Battalions all fought with the BEF in France and were evacuated via Dunkirk and Cherbourg. The 8th Battalion fought in the Norwegian campaign then went to Northern Ireland, based at Dunady, as part of a training brigade. The 9th and 13th Battalions both became armoured car regiments, Nos 112 and 163 Regiments RAC, respectively. The 14th Battalion fought in the Middle East at El Alamein, and both the 2nd and 5th Battalions fought in Tunisia in 1943. The 12th Battalion was formed at Thoresby Park from whence it went to India, joining the 13th Battalion, both becoming training units, in jungle warfare and armoured cars respectively. The 1st Battalion was forced to surrender at Tobruk, as was the 1/5th Battalion at Singapore. The 70th (Young Soldier) Battalion became the 16th Battalion and then the 10th for a while. The 15th Battalion was disbanded in 1941. The 3rd and 4th Battalions kept the depot going in Derby, and staffed No.1 Young Soldiers Training Centre at Markeaton Park (Derbyshire). The Sherwood Rangers took their horses to the Middle East, became mechanised infantry and then coast artillery gunners for a short while, before being converted into an armoured unit in 1941. They served in the 8th Armoured Brigade with the 8th Army, at El Alamein, and then landed in Normandy in 1944 and fought through north-west Europe. The South Nottinghamshire Hussars served in the Western Desert as 107th Field Regiment RA

74 Thoresby Hall, base for the newly raised 12th Battalion Sherwood Foresters.

and then, along with its clone, 150th Field Regiment, took part in the Normandy landings. The former Sherwood Foresters' 6th and 7th Battalions both served in the UK as AA units, but the 7th went to Italy as 42nd S/L Regiment, to join 8th Army, and then rejoined the 6th Battalion, now 40th S/L Regiment, and served in north-west Europe, significantly against the VIs in Antwerp. Following service in the UK, the 27th LAA Regiment from Newark, fought in North Africa at the siege of Tobruk, whilst the 28th served at home for the duration.

Defence against invasion

In the summer of 1940 Nottinghamshire was out of the front line regarding invasion, but it would nevertheless play an important part in the country's anti-invasion defence plans. Much of the BEF's equipment had been left behind in France during the retreat to Dunkirk and this was especially true of artillery, armour and mechanised transport. This meant that Britain's defences against the expected invasion had to be based on static fortifications – hardened structures such as pillboxes and gun-emplacements and fieldworks consisting of weapons-pits, wire, minefields and AT obstacles. All these elements were present on the beaches, particularly those most suitable for amphibious landings. The major ports were already defended by heavy coast artillery batteries, and from 1940 the minor ones were given emergency batteries consisting of pairs of recycled naval guns from old cruisers. Together, these defences were known as the

'Coastal Crust' with the job of delaying enemy forces attempting to land. The planners envisaged the Royal Navy, dependent on the RAF to maintain dominance of the skies, sailing down from its harbours in Scotland to prevent the reinforcement and resupply of any enemy forces attempting to secure bridgeheads. Back from the coast, the next major line of defence was to be the GHQ Line, a continuous belt of anti-tank ditches, strengthened by hardened defences and fieldworks. It ran from the Bristol Channel in Somerset, followed the line of the Kennet and Avon Canal and the River Thames to Reading, thence below London to the River Medway. A spur ran south to Newhaven (Sussex) whilst the main line crossed the Hoo peninsular and the Thames east of London, and on up through Essex and Cambridgeshire to the River Welland, north-east of Peterborough, with a spur to the Wash at Kings Lynn (Norfolk). The line this far, planned to confront all of the most likely landing beaches to be reachable by German invasion forces with the limited naval support available and within range of air cover, was heavily fortified and had, naturally, been given the highest priority. Defences to the north of the River Welland and the Wash would be quite different.

The GHQ Line from the Welland to the Humber

The Reconnaissance Report of the RE officers surveying the Fourth Sector of the GHQ Line, running from Bourne (Lincolnshire) to Newark-on-Trent is far from clear in identifying an obvious line of defence, the terrain being a mixture of fenland, valleys, wooded hills and bare plateaux. This stretch would have to rely heavily on a combination of AT ditches, and the River Witham, in places forming a viable obstacle over some of the Line's proposed course, but the final stretch from Barkston Junction to Newark, following the LNER railway line from Grantham, running on alternate embankments and cuttings, would need 15 miles (24km) of continuous artificial AT ditch to be dug alongside the railway tracks. Whilst the planners were pondering the problems of where to draw the line, overall policy was beginning to change. While it was admitted that these defences were unlikely to have to face the full force of an invading army, it remained vital to secure a line of defences screening the industrial heartlands of England from deep penetrating raids by either amphibious or airborne forces. There was also a recognition that the resources of labour and materials would soon be giving out. At the same time, General Ironside, who had co-ordinated the emergency planning and formulated the only possible policy in the circumstances, was shortly to be promoted, to be replaced on 20 July, as C-in-C Home Forces, by General Brooke, who had decidedly different views. Brooke, with the benefit of several months' production from the munitions factories, felt that too much reliance was being placed on fixed, linear defences, and that forces should be mobile and flexible. The recommendations of the reconnaissance parties had been published in the middle of June, suggesting defensive measures in Sector 4 as already noted, and designating the course of the River Trent as far as the Humber as Sector 5. By the end of June, 44 (Home Counties) Infantry Division of I Corps, responsible within Northern Command for defending Sectors 5 and 6, had produced plans for the fortification of the Trent with pillboxes and anti-tank emplacements between Newark, Gainsborough and the Humber and, in Sector 6, of the River Ouse as far as Selby (Yorkshire). Within a week of these plans being formulated and still three weeks before Brooke's official takeover, 44 Division had been ordered to cease all work on hardened defences.

The defences of the River Trent

The orders preventing the construction of further pillboxes on the Trent was followed by the designation by I Corps of the Trent-Ouse Line as a Priority 1 Demolition Belt. An immediate survey of bridges on the Trent was begun by 209 Field Company RE, attached to 44 Division, and 213 Field Company RE (I Corps troops), to ensure that they could be blocked by AT obstacles and also prepared for demolition by the excavation within their piers of chambers for the appropriate explosive charges. Fortunately there were few crossings of the river: road and rail bridges at Newark, Dunham toll bridge, the railway bridges at Torksey and Fledborough, and road and rail bridges at Gainsborough and at Althorpe near Scunthorpe. A few weeks earlier, in May, German motorcycle troops had ridden across the weirs on the River Meuse to outflank the French defences of the Maginot Line. GHQ's Operation Instruction No. 3, distributed from 15 June 1940 and headed 'GHQ Policy for Home Defence' had drawn attention, in Paragraph 22, to the use of canals as AT obstacles and the necessity to guard locks as possible crossing-points. The Trent was tidal up-river to Cromwell Lock, below Newark, and this location, along with other similar ones, was included in the list of vulnerable points to be guarded. By August 1941, the defence of the river had been entrusted to Trent Force, with HQ at Markeaton Park, Derby. For administrative purposes, the river was divided into three stretches: from the Humber to Gainsborough was known as the Left Bank with Keadby Bridge and Gainsborough as

75 Newark-upon-Trent, Borough Buildings, Balderton Gate: HQ of the 11th Battalion, Nottinghamshire Home Guard, and Sector HQ for the army's North Midlands District and for Trent Force.

points to be defended; from Torksey up to Newark, known as the Right Bank, focusing on the railway viaduct at Fledborough, Torksey, Dunham, Newark and Gunthorpe; and the Nottingham Sector, above Gunthorpe. In the event of an enemy attack, it was the task of Trent Force to secure the crossings, blocking them against enemy movements but only in the last resort, probably after a major landing on the Lincolnshire coast, would the bridges be blown. Gainsborough was organised as an anti-tank island bridge-head, with all-round defences, manned by Lincolnshire Home Guard's 11th Battalion and the staff and trainees of the RAOC depot on Corringham Road. The other crossing-points were allocated local Home Guard garrisons supported by a few regular units. Guns of the 2nd Reserve Field Regiment RA were dug in to cover these points, firing on fixed lines but, as the colonel commanding Trent Force pointed out, they were 4.5in howitzers of First World War vintage and not noted as anti-tank weapons. To complicate matters, sectors of the North Midlands Area of Northern Command did not necessarily correspond with those of Trent Force, only at Newark were the two HQs co-located at Borough Buildings, Balderton Gate. Those Home Guard units in a position to support the defence of the Trent crossings were generally based some way from the river, at Retford, for instance, with other regular units such as the 9th Reserve AA Regiment at Ranby Camp. The onus was thus on the Trent River Patrol to make first contact and to hold their ground.

The Trent River Patrol

There were a number of water-borne Home Guard units across Britain, including those on the Upper Thames, the Norfolk Broads, Lake Windermere and the canals around Birmingham and Edinburgh. The Trent River Patrol (TRP) was formed to patrol the 100 mile-long (160km) River Trent from Sawley, just to the west of the Derbyshire border marked by the confluence with the River Erewash, through to the Humber Estuary, the final stretch north of Gainsborough being in Lincolnshire. The TRP constituted the 14th Battalion of the Nottinghamshire Home Guard with its administrative HQ at 31 Derby Road, later 47 Loughborough Road, Nottingham. A number of premises were requisitioned for use as havens for the patrol boats including the rowing club near Trent Bridge, and other similar boathouses along the river. Water-borne patrols carried out their duties, all the time liaising with shore-based units along the river such as that ensconced in the stand at Colwick racecourse. The TRP was initiated when, at a meeting at the Anchor Hotel, Gunthorpe, owners of small motor cruisers, based on the river, were invited to join a riverine Home Guard unit. Of those asked, three-quarters volunteered, and many owners continued to skipper the boats themselves or, if on active service elsewhere, lent their boats for the duration. One owner even portaged his boat from the Norfolk Broads to serve on the Trent. The TRP's stated task was to mount nightly patrols up and down the river, with a particular focus on vulnerable points: bridges, ferries, locks and weirs. Training was held at the weekend and there were ranges set up at convenient points along the river. Boats, flying the Blue Ensign and a blue and white pennant, were armed with machine guns, and their crews carried rifles and grenades. Most boats carried Lewis guns but the *Cygnet* was one of those armed with a

Vickers 0.303in medium machine gun. The Trent was an important AT barrier and its bridges were mined for speedy demolition, so it was important that such arrangements were continually monitored, the most efficient way being by boat. Maintaining communications was a secondary role for the TRP which became adept at firing telephone lines across the river using rockets. Their own system for communicating with colleagues on the bank was equally eccentric. It was based on the use of a revolving semaphore disc, on which arm or flag positions, highlighted in white paint, could be dialled for display to the recipients of the, hopefully brief, message. Uniform was the standard army battledress but photographs of members carrying out albeit suitably nautical activities, doing things with ropes, show it worn with jaunty naval caps. Some of the TRP's boats may well have been built by Hoylecraft of Nottingham, whose *Miss Margate* had been one of the little ships at Dunkirk.

The river was divided into equal stretches which became the responsibility of the battalion's eight companies, with four (A-D) covering Nottingham itself, and the others (E-H) the rest of the river downstream to the Humber. These latter four companies based, respectively, at Gunthorpe, Farndon Ferry, Gainsborough and Keadby Lock were responsible not only for dusk-to-dawn patrolling, seven days a week, but also for the point defence of the crossings. In addition, observing GHQ's strictures about locks, they included these Nottinghamshire VPs in their list of defended localities: Hazelford Lock and Ferry, the locks at Stoke and Cromwell and the bridges at Muskham, Kelham, Gunthorpe and Torksey. In August 1941, when

76 Cromwell Lock (SK808612): the spigot mortar mounting with the Home Guard's explosives and inflammables store in the background.

77 Fledborough railway viaduct (SK816715): sockets for the AT rails which were used to block access to the bridge over the Trent; similar sockets may be seen on the railway bridge at Torksey (SK837792).

Trent Force Memorandum No.1 was issued, the combined strength of E-H Companies was 476 men with 261 rifles and 23 light machine guns, sailing thirty assorted motorboats capable of speeds of between 6 and 14 knots. Little evidence of fixed defences remains. At least one of two known pillboxes at Kelham has been up-ended in the river; at Cromwell Lock there is a spigot mortar pedestal and an ammunition store; and on the Lincolnshire side of both Fledborough (SK816715) and Torksey (SK837792) railway bridges are the concrete sockets into which AT rails were inserted. Sparseness of such evidence would suggest that the moratorium on the construction of hardened defences after July 1940 was rigorously observed.

Contingency anti-invasion plans

In the event of a raid, it was assumed that local forces would hold their positions and mop up the intruders. If, however, the area was facing a full-scale invasion from the Humber estuary or the Lincolnshire coast, then limited reserves were available behind the GHQ Line, poised to respond to such an emergency. The North Midland Area of Northern Command was divided into three sectors: Nottingham with HQ at 7 Clinton Terrace, Derby Road; Newark with an operational HQ in Caunton; and Retford with HQ at Ranby Camp. These controlled regular units but in no great force. From July 1940, 132 Brigade, one of three infantry brigades of 44 Division, held the Line from Gainsborough to the Althorpe bridges and on up to the River Ouse at Goole, with one battalion held in reserve at Blaxton north of Misson. This meant that a maximum of around 2,000 men held a front of over 25 miles (40km). Even supplemented by several battalions of home guardsmen, this provided but scant coverage. The GHQ Mobile Reserve consisted of the best-equipped and most mobile units, split into two forces, one concentrated in the south to counter the likely invasion beaches from Dorset to Kent, and the other in the east Midlands to cover East Anglia. This latter force, consisting of an armoured division with only light tanks, an infantry division (the 43rd), and artillery, was moved from Lincolnshire to Northamptonshire in July 1940. It would deploy at short notice to wherever an invasion occurred, and all possible destinations were denoted by a series of boys' names as code words. On the receipt of 'Horace', an armoured brigade would be despatched to Goole and the Humber to attack enemy armoured columns striking inland. Until these reinforcements arrived, the meagre forces available would have to hold the Trent crossings. By early 1941 many of these units from the GHQ Mobile Reserve had been sent abroad to shore up the defences of Egypt and the Western Desert, and a solitary armoured reconnaissance brigade, armed with 300 Beaverette armoured cars carrying Bren guns and Boys AT rifles, was stationed in Daventry (Northamptonshire). By May 1941, 44 Division had been moved south for training prior to a move to North Africa, and had not been replaced, leaving the Line in the hands of a few reserve and training formations and the Home Guard. Throughout 1941, the Lincolnshire coast was guarded by the lower establishment Lincolnshire Division, and after its disbandment in December 1941, by the re-formed 48th Infantry (Reserve) Division, another second-line formation, until 1945. However, the German failure to invade by winter 1940/1, and the invasion of Russia in summer 1941, more or less removed the threat of an invasion of Britain, but the Chiefs-of-Staff invasion committee, second-guessing the enemy's intentions, continued to meet well into 1942, and even then the danger was not held entirely to have evaporated.

Vulnerable points (VPs)

A wide variety of locations were designated as VPs including utilities – telephone exchanges, power stations, water- and gasworks; factories and mines; and road- and rail-junctions; as well as military installations such as airfields, AA and searchlight sites, and depots. Factories and utilities often raised their own Home Guard units and airfields had their own garrisons, but many VPs were simply given night-time sentries or included in the rounds of Home Guard patrols. Although Nottinghamshire was not included in the regular patrol itineraries of the armoured trains, there were occasions when they were seen in the county, one train providing the centrepiece of a War Weapons Week in Mansfield in autumn 1940.

Searchlight sites

Early in the war, searchlight sites were regarded as permanent fixtures, 10,400 yards apart across the countryside. They constituted one of those straws to be grasped in the summer of 1940 when invasion was imminently expected, with orders going out from S/L Brigade HQs that sites should be surrounded with barbed wire and weapons pits, and that as many as possible should be given a pillbox. Thus, utilising the personnel manning the site, they would constitute ready-made resistance points acting as rallying places for retreating troops and local home guardsmen. Many such isolated pillboxes still stand across Nottinghamshire, making no sense in the modern landscape, and perpetuating the myth that they were built willy-nilly to no plan or purpose. Good examples of these S/L site pillboxes remain at Hose Lodge Farm (SK718308), at Vimy Ridge Farm (SK668311), at Costock Grange (SK576208), and Trowell Moor (SK504403). A further pillbox at Gotham (SK523302) still exhibits damage sustained when an enemy bomber attempted to extinguish the searchlight. All these pillboxes

78 Hose Lodge Farm (SK718308), a DFW3/22 pillbox defending a searchlight site; similar pillboxes were built at intervals of 3 miles (5km) across the county.

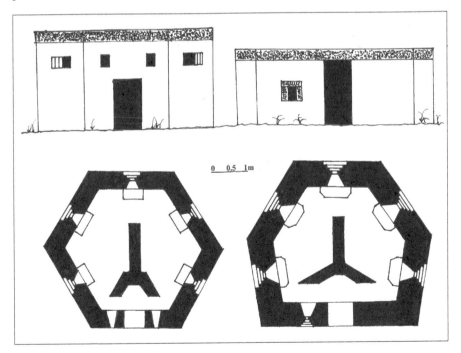

79 Pillboxes: type DFW3/22 (left) and DFW3/24 (right); these hexagonal, splinter-proof pillboxes are the models most commonly found in the county – primarily on airfields, at searchlight-sites, and defending vulnerable points.

were the basic DFW3/22, a regularly hexagonal structure with loopholes for rifles in five faces and an entrance flanked by one or two pistol loops in the sixth face. Walls were 15in (40cm) thick, proof against bullets and splinters but not sustained bursts of automatic fire. A Y-shaped anti-ricochet wall supported a concrete roof, 6in (15cm) or more in thickness. In-built wooden shelves below each loophole provided a rest for the rifleman's elbow. Following the changes to the searchlight layout, sites were given AA light machine guns on either regulation or extemporised mountings but always in a sandbagged sunken pit, built to the standardised design of the archaeologist Lieutenant Colonel (later Sir) Mortimer Wheeler, the CO of a S/L regiment. S/L Battery HQs used requisitioned premises, No.402 Battery, for instance, being based at Wiverton Hall in 1942.

Airfield defences

From the very start, airfields were given garrisons, usually from a unit stationed nearby, but a need to set priorities soon became apparent as demand exceeded supply. In September 1940, the Air Ministry invited Major-General Taylor, Director of Fortifications and Works at the War Office to frame a suggested policy. Taylor set a number of criteria, generally based on location, which would determine the level of provision. Airfields within 20 miles (32km) of designated ports came into Class I. Class IIA contained airfields which were important in counter-attacking invasion forces. Airfields within 5 miles (8km) of important inland VPs, such as centres of munitions production, became Class IIB. Interestingly, although the Aircraft Storage Units together constituted Class IIC, their Satellite Landing Grounds such as Grove Park received no automatic protection at all. Class III swept up the remainder. In Nottinghamshire, Newton, Syerston, Hucknall and Tollerton were all Class IIA airfields, soon to be joined by Balderton and Winthorpe, leaving Worksop in Class III, and Gamston, Langar, Ossington and Wigsley too late to be included. Most, however, would receive pillboxes and other defences in significant quantity. Only Class I airfields qualified for the Pickett-Hamilton disappearing forts, but the level of fortification suggested for all Class II airfields was quite formidable. Taylor laid down a complement of fifteen to twenty-four pillboxes, some facing inward to the landing ground and others facing outwards to the field, and supported by fieldworks and wire, with three armoured vehicles for mobile defence. AA defence posts would be integrated into the ground defences. Garrisons should consist of 225 regular soldiers, supplemented by another 125 or so RAF personnel, trained to use the balance of the 350 rifles issued to each airfield. Light machine guns were at a premium and were allocated at the level of one per pillbox and two per AFV. By 1941, armoured units were re-arming with new tanks so their old light tanks would be passed down for airfield defence, but in the meantime it was a question of make do and mend. The Armadillo was a flatbed truck carrying an open chamber made of boxes filled with shingle. Loopholes with sliding shutters were provided in the sides and a Lewis gun on a mounting pointed skywards from the middle of the floor. These were mass-produced in the factories and issued to the grateful defenders of Britain's airfields.

In 1941, whilst the threat of a general invasion had all but disappeared, the experience of the German attack on Crete, spearheaded by paratroops dropping on the airfields, caused a deal of unease. If we could land commandos to steal the Germans' radar equipment then they could do the same to us, and the obvious place to land was an airfield. Unknown to the British Chiefs of Staff was the fact that General Student's paratroops had sustained such crippling casualties on Crete that any more such adventures were forbidden them. So the defences of British airfields had to be improved and maintained, and the RAF Regiment was formed for the specific role of safeguarding the RAF's airfields against surprise attack. The War Office had put out a suite of designs for defence works, some of which had been built on airfields, mainly the DFW3/22. The Air Ministry developed its own designs for airfield pillboxes and laid down strictures about their use. The wall-thickness of the DFW3/22 would be increased to 42in (1.07m) as all pillboxes should be at least shell-proof. The number of loopholes would be reduced, reportedly, to minimise the possibility of grenade or flame-thrower assault. A specialist Battle HQ (11008/41) was designed to provide the ground defence commander with a protected vantage point from which to direct operations. This was an underground blockhouse housing a PBX, a room for runners, and a shelter, entered down a ladder accessed via a hatch, and topped with a thick concrete cupola over a lateral observation slit giving 360 degrees of visibility. This was a great improvement on some of the one-offs built previously. Hucknall's BHQ, built to a local design (TG1), was a tall, four-storey tower, originally linked by tunnel to an underground shelter, with more Stanton shelters nearby. This may have represented a balance of visibility and vulnerability, but the new design, if sited well, achieved the one without the risk suggested by the other. There is an example of the standard design BHQ at Ossington (SK740652).

Some of the pillboxes found on Nottinghamshire airfields are found nowhere else, which would suggest the work of a local Air Ministry works officer, or even a RAF Regiment officer, or warrant officer, with building experience. Tollerton retains the most interesting defence works of any British airfield. Around the perimeter are a total of seventeen pillboxes, of which seven were the Air Ministry version of the DFW3/24, hexagonal with a loophole in each of five faces, and an entrance flanked by pistol-loops in the longer sixth face. The rest were of a design found only here at Tollerton (9) and at Newton (2). It is almost square with all

80 RAF Hucknall (SK519475), unique Battle HQ, once apparently part of a complex of underground bunkers.

81 RAF Ossington (SK740652), a surviving example of the standard Battle HQ (11008/41).

four corners chamfered to produce faces long enough for a machine-gun loophole. The entrance is in the middle of one side entered from either end of a low porch which runs the length of the entrance face. The number and positioning of the loopholes depends on the orientation of the pillbox, its neighbours and its fields of fire. With eight possible faces to be loopholed, the maximum in any one pillbox is five, and the minimum is two. There is an H-shaped anti-ricochet wall with shelf supports on the returns, and on the outside of the wall opposite the entrance is a brick box with a concrete roof which could have contained tools or suchlike. The examples at Tollerton appear to be built on sound foundations but one of Newton's has a crack right through it. Also at Tollerton is a very unusual defence post built *inside* the large hangar used by Fields. Only two other examples of similar structures have been recorded, both in hangars used by MAP, one at Manchester Airport and another at Byley (Cheshire). At Newton is a single example of what appears to be an adaptation of a design found only on the Lincolnshire coast, consisting of two square chambers linked by an open walled space with an AA machine-gun mounting. The only other known example on an airfield was at Eglinton in Northern Ireland. At Hucknall there are two different non-standard pillboxes, one of them almost a regular hexagon with two blank walls, one of which contained a low entrance under a pentice porch (SK528464) like those at Tollerton and Newton. The other has three faces with loopholes, two short blank walls and a long rear wall with steps down into the firing chamber and an open court with offset entrance protected by blast walls (SK526463). Two of Newton's seven pillboxes are rectangular but split into two compartments at different levels.

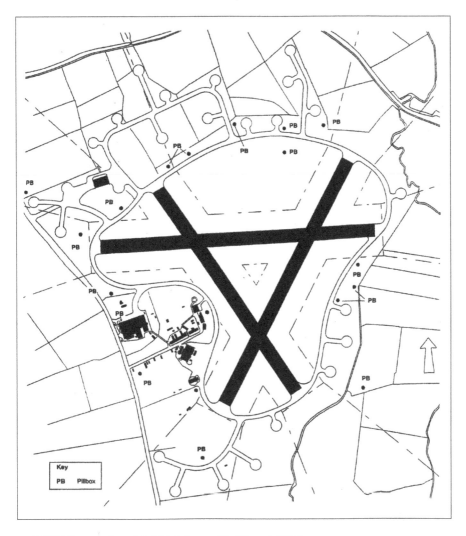

82 RAF Tollerton, plan of airfield defences. (Paul Francis/AiG)

In addition to hardened defences and fieldworks, airfields were protected by camouflage. At Tollerton, the scheme, set out by the Directorate of Camouflage in 1942, consisted of the painting of hedges across the flying-field, and the texturing of runways and perimeter tracks with bitumen and chippings to reduce glare from above. The earliest airfield defences followed a linear model, but after the RAF Regiment was formed, the format changed to a series of defended localities (DLs), dotted around the airfield, to avoid a situation where if the line was breached all would be lost. DLs were usually wired areas containing weapons pits, trenches, machine-gun posts and, sometimes, existing pillboxes, some being constructed around AA defences. These DLs were manned by a mixture of RAF Regiment personnel, home guardsmen, and RAF drivers, cooks, clerks and groundcrew.

83 RAF Tollerton, a type DFW3/24 pillbox.

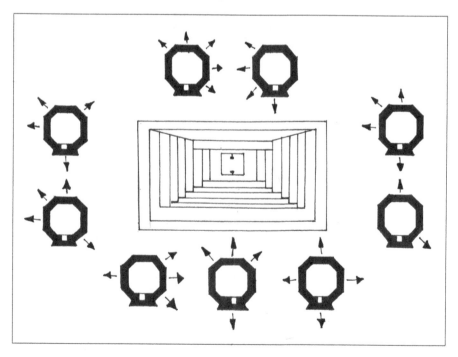

84 RAF Tollerton: nine examples of a locally designed pillbox with four long sides, four shorter ones, and a protected entrance–tunnel, survive at Tollerton; most have loopholes, fitted with Turnbull mounts, in only half of the available faces; this chart shows the full range of configurations.

85 RAF Tollerton, one of nine surviving pillboxes to a local design; this one has four loopholes – one in each of its long sides.

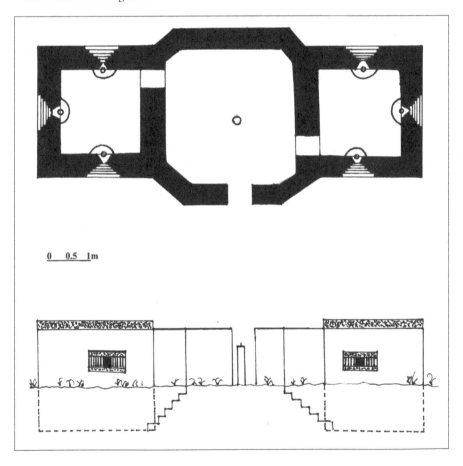

0   0.5   1m

86 RAF Newton (SK691413): pillbox to local design consisting of two square-covered chambers, each with three loopholes, linked by an open court holding an AA light machine gun on a fixed mounting; each loophole has a semi-circular shelf and is fitted with a simple mounting for a Lewis gun on a monopod. (Plan and elevation.)

Other VPs

Another category of hardened defences was those constructed to protect important transport links, both road and rail. A pillbox stands at a T-junction, for instance, at Underwood (SK483506), and the road and rail crossings of the River Soar between Stanford-on-Soar and Loughborough (Leicestershire) are covered by a spigot mortar (SK544216). Two pillboxes have been recorded at Orston, guarding the S/L site but also the rail-crossing. The pillbox at Arnold Lodge, Woodborough, may have had the protection of the S/L site as its primary purpose, but it is sited so as to cover the

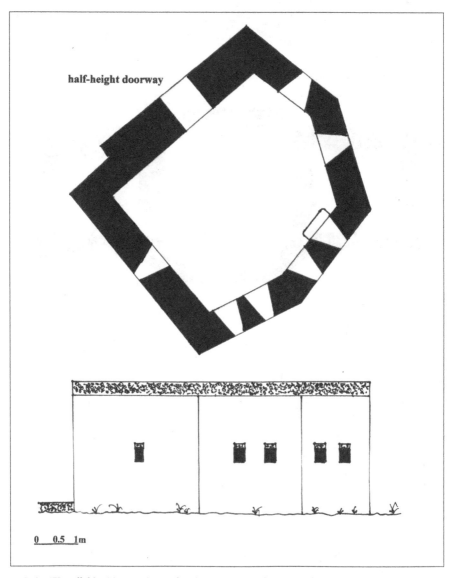

87 RAF Watnall: blockhouse, formerly adjoining a guardroom, at the entrance to 12 Group RAF Fighter Command Filter Room; plan and elevation.

adjacent road junction as well (SK606467). Similarly, a pillbox attached to a S/L site in Bingham guarded the main road in and out of town. At Stanton-on-the-Wolds, a machine-gun post was established on the top of a water-tower, and this would have commanded both the main railway line and main road. Many pillboxes and AT blocks were of necessity sited in inconvenient places, that being, of course, the whole point, so those obstacles blocking Trent Bridge were demolished as soon as possible, the *Nottingham Evening Post* reporting their destruction on 15 August 1945.

The 12 Group RAF Fighter Command Filter Room at Watnall was probably the most sensitive site in the county and it was provided with close-defence pillboxes. Attached to the guardhouse was an irregularly shaped blockhouse (SK506454) with seven loopholes whilst, up on the former railway embankment, overlooking the rear approach to the bunker, was a hexagonal pillbox with six loopholes (SK507455).

Royal Ordnance Factories were given their own individual type of defence post. This was a small guard-post, roughly 8ft (2.4m) square, with a long horizontal slit in each face, for fire-watching, observation and general security as much as weapons ports. The entrance was contained in a low porch. One such remains at Ranskill (SK692841). Nottingham Castle was requisitioned by the army during the war and a small, rectangular, loopholed guard-post was built next to the Robin Hoods'Victorian orderly room (SK569395), to cover access through the gatehouse.

88 Ranskill (SK692841): defence post of a standard type found at Royal Ordnance factories. (Photo: Trent & Peak Archaeological Trust via Margaret Sibley)

89 Nottingham Castle, Second World War loopholed concrete defence post, end-on to the Robin Hoods' orderly room; it would have covered the outer gate of the castle from inside (SK 569395).

The Home Guard

In May 1940, the Local Defence Volunteers was launched to help defend the country against the expected invasion. Within a few weeks, 9,000 men had enlisted in Nottinghamshire. These were all men in reserved occupations on the land, down the mines, on the railways or in the munitions factories, with some young lads awaiting their call-up. Crammed into a working week of six long days were guard duties, patrols, drills, parades and exercises. The Home Guard, as the LDV was soon known, gradually became a highly trained, well-equipped force, the complete antithesis of their portrayal on TV. Nottinghamshire's Territorial Association under the authority of the Lord Lieutenant raised fourteen battalions of the Home Guard. Twelve of these were attached to particular localities, five of them in the environs of Nottingham itself, and others in centres of population such as Mansfield, Worksop, Newark and Retford. There was a further battalion recruited from GPO employees, scattered across the county, and there was the Trent River Patrol, whom we have already met. Together they totalled around 15,000 men, all proudly wearing the cap-badge of the Sherwood Foresters. Later in the war there were AA units, manning rocket batteries, and in January 1944 the North Midland Home Guard Transport Column was formed. Its HQ, along with two MT companies, was in Nottingham, and five other MT companies were spread between Lincoln, Derby and Leicester. The NUOTC joined the Home Guard en masse and were given training responsibilities within the Nottinghamshire force.

Home Guard weapons and sub-artillery

In the period up to 1942 when invasion was still a possibility, arms and equipment were in short supply. This was especially true of AT weapons, so much improvisation took place, and a range of what was known as sub-artillery was developed specifically for Home Guard use. One of these weapons was the Blacker Bombard or spigot mortar, which became available in 1941. It would be stored in the dry, probably in one of the Home Guard's ammunition stores, and then fitted onto its permanent base for use. This consisted of a cylindrical concrete drum, embedded in which was a steel frame called a 'spider' with a stainless-steel pintle on top, protruding from the domed top of the drum, onto which the mortar was fitted. The drum was sunk in a pit lined with ready-use lockers to store the bombs. The mortar fired a 14lb (6.5kg) anti-personnel bomb, or a 20lb (9kg) anti-tank one. The ideal range was around 150 yards so cool heads were required. At Cromwell Lock there survives both the spigot mortar mounting and an explosives and inflammables store (SK808612). Some spigot mortars were deployed on portable field mountings made of tubular legs with spade-grips. Another scratch weapon was the Northover Projector. This was a length of drainpipe, mounted on a tripod, which was designed to fire self-igniting phosphorous (SIP) grenades, but at a pinch could project Molotov cocktails. SIPs, also known as AW bombs, standing for Albright & Wilson, who manufactured them, were also issued to groups of guardsmen designated as bomb parties, positioned to throw the grenades at passing enemy vehicles from behind cover. A number of other ambush weapons were attempted such as the flame fougasse which was a cluster of oil drums filled with inflammables and ignited by a grenade. Any enemy troops or vehicles caught in such an ambush would be showered with burning oil. There were mines on wheeled trolleys, flying mines, cup-dischargers that could fire grenades from a standard rifle and sticky bombs, designed to adhere to enemy vehicles. The idea of all these was to hit tanks, preferably whilst they were stationary, so they were often employed in conjunction with roadblocks. In early 1941, Captain the Viscount Hanworth, a Cambridge-trained mechanical scientist and qualified RAFVR pilot, was posted to Northern Command's North Midland District HQ in Nottingham as 2i/c of 213 Field Company RE. Part of his role was to train both the Home Guard and regular troops in the techniques of anti-tank warfare. He invented the Hanworth Torpedo which, using explosives in the form of AT mines, could be blasted the few feet (1m) from the verge, at great speed, into the tracks of a passing tank. As the nose of an advancing tank came level with a marker, two of these torpedoes would be remotely fired simultaneously by a hidden home guardsman with a bell-push, and the resulting explosion was devastating. Hanworth carried out practical demonstrations, such as one at Retford in May 1942 for specialist tank-trapping Home Guard officers, continuing until 1943 when many of these extemporised weapons were withdrawn. McNaughton or Canadian pipe-mines were laid under airfield runways to facilitate quick destruction if enemy aircraft were to land, and some of these, too, found their way into the hands of the Home Guard.

Local Defence Plans

By early 1941, urban centres like Nottingham had quite complex defence plans, put together by the municipal, military, medical and civil defence authorities through the Invasion Committee, composed of representatives of all concerned bodies, statutory and voluntary. These plans covered every eventuality from First Aid to Emergency Feeding, from bombs to billeting, from refugees to rat-catching, but the original purpose had been to lay out clear plans for defence against enemy attack. The plan set down the troops and weapons available; the defended localities; and their garrisons; the procedures for closing roadblocks, disabling abandoned vehicles and destroying fuel stocks; the chain of command and the channels of communication; and finally, if it were to come to it, the area selected for the last-ditch stand, or 'Keep'. The garrison of Nottingham consisted of five battalions of the Home Guard plus some regular units, and its defensive perimeter was quite extensive. Villages also, were required to produce defence plans and some of these have survived (Nottinghamshire Archives reference DD MM 3.1.3.1-16). Many of these villages were held by, often weak, platoons – at Colston Bassett just twenty men, and at Upper Broughton and Hickling, only twenty-four, whilst at several villages the garrison strength hovers around the forty-ish mark. At Farnsfield, actually west of the village itself on the A614 (SK628570), the defenders were split into three groups, one clustering around HQ in the White Post Inn at the crossroads, another where the Ollerton road crosses the railway, and a third at a farm on the Nottingham road, a total of sixty-four men. At Newark-on-Trent the castle and the adjacent bridge and rail-crossing provided the major focus for the defence of the town but three other outlying positions were held in strength: Devon Bridge on the Farndon Road, the Lincoln Road bridges on the Fosse Way, and the Highfield and Barnby rail-crossings astride London Road and Barnby Gate/Road. Together, the numbers available to hold these four DLs came to 206 men. These crossings would be blocked on receipt of the code '20' whilst all other road and rail blocks around the town were activated by '13'. These garrisons were under orders to remain in place, whatever the circumstances. Of those places for which plans survive, Lockwell Crossing (SK629585) was one of the most strongly held, with a garrison of 120 men with its HQ at Cottage Farm where a reserve-force of thirty men was held. This vital crossroads was ringed by OPs and two of the roads, from Newark on the east, and from Ollerton to the north, were blocked by barricades and bomb posts, a feature common to all of the defences. Given the circumstances under which these amateur forces were operating, these tactics reflect the two most obvious imperatives: spot the enemy before he arrives, and delay his onward progress. Firepower was generally limited to rifles, a single light machine gun for each platoon, and perhaps a Northover Projector as at Newark's LNER station or at Kelham. Roadblocks were usually accompanied by bomb posts which could have meant any of the AT devices mentioned above. Church towers provided many of the vantage-points occupied by OPs, and company and platoon HQs tended to use public buildings like village halls and inns. If nowhere else was available then a cottage or, as at Gringley-on-the-Hill, a room over a shop had to do. Village platoons were usually deployed around a fairly tight nucleus but particularly vulnerable locations would either have their own protection, as with the 'special squad' which guarded the bridge over the

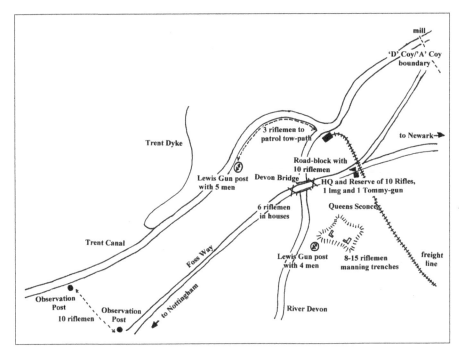

90 Plan of Home Guard defensive deployments at Devon Bridge, Newark-upon-Trent, manned by a sixty-strong platoon of D Company, 11th Battalion. This is one of nine such Defended Localities controlling movement into and around the town with special attention being paid to road, rail and water routes.

Idle north of Misterton, or were incorporated in a regular patrol scheme. In the event of an invasion, isolated platoons would have been in danger of losing out on the big picture. The villages around Kelham therefore set up a Main Communication Centre at South Muskham with a group of runners whose job it was to maintain regular physical contact with HQ in Newark, Trent Force, neighbouring platoons and OPs.

As the war progressed, so Home Guard tactics evolved. The DL had superseded the continuous defended perimeter by 1941, but attempts were made to inject some mobility into Home Guard capability. Mobile columns were formed at Radcliffe on Trent, at Cropwell Butler, based on The Elms and The Grove, and at Bingham. Toward the end of the war, these columns would comprise lorry-borne infantry and small armoured reconnaissance vehicles, but early versions used any available road-worthy vehicle, whilst Bingham's column started out on bicycles.

Air defence

Although Nottinghamshire was spared much of the intensity of bombing-raids experienced by many cities, there were nevertheless raids which proved devastating for parts of Nottingham and Newark-upon-Trent. It was, therefore, vital to maintain effective AA defences and PAD systems throughout the war, to protect transport links, vital industries, the operational and training activities of the armed services, and the morale of the civilian population.

Anti-aircraft defences

Throughout the war AA weaponry was scarce and, at times, the personnel to operate it were even scarcer. The experience of the First World War had demonstrated the supreme importance of integrating all the elements of Air Defence Great Britain (ADGB): the fighters and the guns, the balloons and the searchlights, the observers and the technological detection systems, and the reporting, command and control systems.

HAA guns

At the outbreak of war, the HQ of the 2nd AA Division was at Hucknall airfield as laid down in the policy to co-locate all command and control elements of ADGB. On 23 August 1939, 78 HAA Regiment was ordered to deploy all available guns from the AA practice camp at Weybourne (Norfolk), and four First World War 3in 20cwt guns were accordingly despatched to the Central Ordnance depot at Chilwell via the local HAA unit covering the Nottingham & Derby GDA, 68 HAA Regiment at its drill hall. On 26 August, Hucknall ordered passive air defence (PAD) measures to be taken on all searchlight (S/L) sites. The 2 September saw thirty-two Lewis guns, for the defence of airfields and industrial targets, being despatched to Nottingham from Norwich, RHQ of 78 HAA Regiment, followed a fortnight later by personnel to relieve the holding unit. Once these minimal deployments had been made, the Phoney War took the pressure off, but after Dunkirk, the beginnings of the Blitz and the Battle of Britain once more emphasised the paucity of Britain's AA defences. One of the biggest problems was the scarcity of modern LAA weapons given the multiplicity of potential targets – military, industrial, commercial and communications. In May 1940, for instance, the 345/78 LAA Battery was moved from RAF Duxford (Cambridgeshire) to Nottingham, thus stripping a vulnerable fighter airfield to protect a no-less-exposed industrial target. It would appear that 345 Battery was equipped only with AALMGs as in July 1940 the 2nd AA Division had only a single modern LAA gun in the whole county, deployed at Hucknall. The HAA guns of the Nottingham & Derby GDA were controlled from the AAOR at Elvaston. There were a total of twenty-nine allocated gun-sites, numbered DNH1-29, with eighteen out of the first twenty-one on the list given alphabetic designations as well. So, for instance, site DNH15 at Clifton was also referred to as 'T', and it is by letters that the sites are identified in War Diaries and brigade orders.

By September, there were a total of forty HAA guns available for the defence of Derby and a further sixteen for Nottingham. The War Diaries of 50 AA Brigade reveal a constant movement of guns between areas, GDAs and individual gun-sites. On 30 September, eight 3in guns were sent from Clifton (DNH15 'T'), Wilford Cemetery (DNH16 'U'), Colwick Wood ('W') and Bulwell Common (DNH21 'Z') to 4th AA Division covering Liverpool and the north-west region, and on 1 October, four further 3in guns were sent from Elvaston (Derbyshire) and Bulwell Common to

Birkenhead, opposite Liverpool Docks. Two days later a further four from Clifton and Wilford Cemetery went to Wellington (Shropshire). These movements would suggest that Nottingham's original sixteen older-pattern guns had been quickly moved on and that the arrival in Nottingham on 27 September of four modern 3.7in guns straight from the ordnance factory (could it have been Kings Meadows?) for mounting at Sunrise Hill (DNH20 'Y') being joined there ten days later by GL radar from Grantham, had signalled real improvements to Nottingham's AA defences. On 29 November, a pair of 3.7in mobiles was transferred from Mapperley (DNH19 'X') to Adbolton. It would appear that more sites were prepared, and maybe even constructed, than were ever permanently used. Out of the twenty-nine sites, only eight are known to have had guns on them by the time the defences were consolidated. In Nottingham, these were Robins Wood (DNH14 'S'), near the government offices in Chalfont Drive; Clifton (DNH15 or 'T') just north of the church; Adbolton (DNH17), now a caravan park; and Sunrise Hill (DNH20) in Bestwood. Each had four 3.7in static guns but Robins Wood was equipped with four mobiles. The first two sites were manned from June 1940 by 68 HAA Regiment, and all four from May 1942 by 144 (Mixed) HAA Regiment which included women from the ATS operating the Mark II GL Radar. This had been installed at all the sites except Sunrise Hill which had an earlier model and had also been moved to an alternative location close by its original site. According to the available records, site DNH28 at Arnold Lodge whose remains lie near the farm, was never armed, but local memories include windows rattling when the guns were fired. Similarly, all but four of the Derby sites are listed as 'unarmed' in June 1942.

LAA guns

The provision of LAA weaponry for the defence of Nottingham (vulnerable point No.240) against low-flying aircraft, was only slightly less complicated. Three troops of the local 28th LAA Regiment manned four positions either side of the Trent in Wilford and Meadows, another near Trent Bridge cricket ground, and a fourth in Rylands, to the east of Beeston. Between them they mustered eight static 40mm Bofors guns and fifty-odd Lewis guns. At least one of these Lewis guns was mounted on the Kop Stand at Notts County's Meadow Lane ground in June 1941 when part of the main stand was destroyed by a bomb. Further troops of 28th Regiment manned LAA defences at RAF Newton, with eighteen Lewis guns and at Newark, where Ransome & Marles' ball-bearing factory was so vital to the aircraft industry, with four Bofors and eighteen Lewis guns. RAF Syerston was defended by twelve more Lewis guns with a single Bofors gun being emplaced, on a temporary basis, in January 1941. By the middle of 1941, more Bofors guns were becoming available and four went to RAF Newton on 25 May. Airfields often salvaged aircraft cannon from wrecks and mounted them on jeeps or on static mountings, integrating them into the ground defences. At Syerston a Quadruple Vickers, more often seen on warships, was mounted. Factories sometimes managed to acquire some exotic weaponry, but this could simply raise problems of obtaining the appropriate ammunition. By 1941, many factories were forming their own Home Guard LAA units, usually as independent troops, notionally parented by their local Home Guard battalion. Both Ransome & Marles Bearing Co. and Worthing-Simpson Ltd in Newark-upon-Trent retained such units, three in all, parented by the 11th Battalion, Nottinghamshire Home Guard. Two further troops were raised at the ROF Ranskill.

The air attacks on Nottingham commenced in May 1941 when in one night ninety-five aircraft bombed Nottingham. There were a further ten bombing raids on the city but no more, fortunately, of such ferocity and by June 1942 much of the city's AA defences were largely in suspension. Units continued their movements in and out of the city, backwards and forwards to other target areas, to the AA practice camps, particularly Stiffkey (Norfolk), and for periods based in the militia camps at Whatton, Tuxford and Hawton Road, Newark. No. 511 S/L Battery, for instance, moved into Whatton camp in May 1941, was joined there by No. 567/30 Battery in August, and moved out in January 1941. In December 1941, a troop of 111th LAA Regiment was sent from its post at Boots in Beeston to the militia camp at Hawton Road, Newark, for training.

The searchlights

The searchlight units led an even more itinerant existence, in many ways similar to the AA gunners, but mainly because the policy governing their deployment kept changing. Early in the war, single searchlights were placed in permanent positions in grids covering much of the country, where each light was roughly 3 miles (5km) away from its neighbour in any direction. Such patterns in Nottinghamshire can be discerned, for instance, along the line: Bradmore, Stanton-on-the-Wolds, Vimy Ridge, Hose Lodge and Stathern, this last site in Leicestershire. This system was intended to illuminate large areas of sky to enable fighters to find enemy bombers before the days of airborne radar. Some searchlights had been co-located with AA guns, the normal arrangement in the First World War, but in February 1941, 50 Brigade ordered that searchlights be withdrawn from gun-sites, possibly to make them available for the various experiments taking place. The first trial saw the lights clustered, often in threes, but a number of alternative groupings were tried. One such trial had begun in October 1940, run by 30th S/L Regiment on eight sites in the area between Doncaster and Scunthorpe. Each site was given a 150cm projector with a sound locator and five regular 90cm projectors, producing an extremely bright concentration of light. Three of these sites, manned by 315 S/L Battery, were in Nottinghamshire, at Beckingham (Sandy Furze Farm), Blyth and Cottam. From the evidence of the plan of such a site between Mansfield and Kirkby-in-Ashfield, it can be seen that these cluster sites with three or more lights had become quite significant impositions on the landscape. The lights were grouped together, backed by a command post and then all the other necessary structures for sustaining a community of some fifty souls were ranged either side of the approach road. These included sleeping huts, offices and accommodation, some of it tented, for officers and NCOs, canteen, cookhouse and ration store, training facilities, generators and fuel store, and all the usual offices. If, as was usual, there was an ATS presence on the site, then many of these buildings needed to be duplicated. Most sites were mixed by 1941 and, based on the experience of a trial held over five months at Newark militia camp, some, initially in the Midlands would, by early 1942, be run entirely by the ATS. After the experiments in clustering, which may have been less than definitive, there was a return to deploying searchlights singly, but in defined belts. The general principle was that specific belts of searchlights catered for fighter activity, these being kept quite separate from those belts where the AA guns were operating. A list of S/L sites plotted from the memory of an engineer whose job it was to maintain them would appear to indicate a belt running north/south in between Nottingham and Derby, possibly to work with the AA guns emplaced on each side.

ZAA and the Home Guard

As much of the ROFs' output was destined for the armies fighting abroad, there were never enough AA guns. A long-term solution was provided by the invention of the 3in Un-rotated (Rocket) Projectile (UP), more widely referred to as ZAA, and firing the equivalent of a 3.7in HE shell. The projectors, which entered production in 1940, were mounted on concrete pads, 8ft (2.4m) square and 5in (8cm) thick, in groups of sixty-four. The earliest projectors could fire only a single rocket, but a twin-barrelled version was quickly built, becoming the most commonly used, and then, eventually, types with four, nine and even twenty launch rails were developed. Although it was known that AA weapons could never produce the density of fire to effect a meaningful barrage, salvoes of shot were often enough to put bombers off their aim. The Z-batteries could produce a curtain of fire which at low level would certainly deter dive-bombers even if they were usually unable actually to shoot them down. One of the first five ZAA troops to be assembled was deployed, with thirty-two projectors, at Chilwell COD in early 1941. By this time the Home Guard was taking on many new responsibilities, and it was soon realised that ZAA was a perfect task for them. The 9th AA Regiment, Home Guard was formed in Derby with three batteries in Derby and three in Nottingham, totalling 384 projectors firing salvoes of 768 rockets. Apart from a tiny nucleus of regulars, these batteries were manned entirely by home guardsmen who had full-time jobs in the day, so could only put in one night's duty in every eight, meaning that each battery equipped with twin-barrelled projectors had to recruit over 1,400 personnel, and in competition with all the other organisations seeking labour. The attraction, especially in areas that had undergone bombing raids, of being able to retaliate meant that there was, in fact, no shortage of recruits. When the 20-barrelled projectors came into use, the complement of a battery could be halved. Training took place on the Rocket Firing Range at Sutton-on-Sea (Lincolnshire). The HAA site on the racecourse at Colwick (DNH18) is listed in May 1942 as being guarded, rather than manned, by 181 Battery of 15 ZAA Regiment.

Although the worst of the bombing was over by the end of 1942, there was still a need for AA protection. Newark retained AA cover throughout the war, with units undergoing constant training. In December 1943, for instance, 287/134 LAA Battery was posted from Newark (VP 256) to No.11 AA Practice Camp, Stiffkey (Norfolk), returning to Newark in February 1944. The strategy for dealing with the onslaught of the V1s or 'Doodlebugs' involved moving every available AA gun onto the coast in order to intercept them before they could do any damage. In late 1944, 144(M) HAA Regiment, last seen in Nottingham, had taken its guns to sites in Holmpton, on the Holderness coast, east of Hull, part of the 'Diver Fringe'. This was the northern-most sector of the anti-V1 defences, made necessary by the migration of the V1 launch-sites into Holland, as those in northern France were overrun by the Allied invasion forces. The AA defences shot down hundreds of V1s, four times the RAF's bag, and only one solitary rocket made it to Nottinghamshire.

AA sites

The HAA sites made quite significant footprints in the landscape. The guns themselves were mounted on square, iron hold-fasts set in octagonal pits with concrete-block walls, about 4ft (1.3m) high, containing built-in ready-use magazines for shells and fuses. Each battery had four pits in an arc, to the rear of which stood a concrete command post, more magazines and crew shelters. The GL radar was next door to the guns. Behind the battery itself was the camp containing accommodation huts, canteen, offices, workshops and garages, often surrounded by a wire fence with a guardroom controlling access. Given the nature of Nottingham's urban expansion there are, unsurprisingly, few remains. The Adbolton site retains a magazine and the access road which curved around the arc of gun-pits. The site at Elvaston, over the Derbyshire border, still retained its gun-pits a few years ago.

LAA sites, on the other hand, left behind very little in the way of evidence. Many of the Bofors guns were mobile, needing no permanent emplacement. Static guns sat on a simple holdfast set in a concrete slab. Most of the mountings for Lewis guns, and even the heavier 20mm Oerlikons, Hispano-Suiza and Polstens, consisted of tubular curved steel poles, Stork or Motley mounts, which sat in sockets secured in the base of a sewer-pipe section or a sandbagged pit. Some accommodation at S/L or LAA sites was in tents, but even if huts were provided they would have been removable. The only structural reminder of the LAA defences is a tower in the council depot's yard in Newark. This is a rectangular box with sturdy reinforced concrete pillars and struts on the inside, very necessary to withstand the resultant forces when the 40mm Bofors LAA gun mounted on the roof fired a burst at a low-flying aircraft. It appears to have been sited to protect the railway station and the RAF MU.

Balloons

Barrage balloons were deployed mainly over cities in order to deter enemy aircraft from flying low enough to be accurate with their bomb-aiming. Balloon Centre No.7, at Crewton, Alvaston (Derbyshire), manned by No.918 Squadron RAF covered the Nottingham/Derby GDA. By 1942 the Women's Auxiliary Air Force (WAAF) provided most of the personnel for RAF Balloon Command.

The Royal Observer Corps in Nottinghamshire in the Second World War

The war opened with most of the pre-war ROC network in place, with only two sites at East Markham and Walkeringham/Wiseton being added during the course of the war after 1941, and the Blyth post being re-sited into Nottinghamshire. Nine of these posts were within 6 Group, administered from Derby, whilst two of the others were in 11 Group (Lincoln) with Walkeringham in 10 Group (York). In line with the policy of co-locating the ROC with the fighter-direction system, the Midland HQ of ROC was moved from Grantham to Watnall in 1942, to operate alongside the Filter Room of 12 Group RAF Fighter Command. The basic role of the observer posts was to spot incoming aircraft, gauge their direction and the speed at which they were travelling using a rudimentary plotting instrument, and communicate this information to the central control as quickly as possible by telephone. During the period when invasion was still a possibility, ROC posts were issued with coloured flares to be launched as a means of instant communication: red flares for invasion forces spotted on land, and green flares for enemy forces landing from the sea. As the sky began to fill with friendly rather than hostile aircraft, then the ROC was involved in attempts to help Allied aircraft return safely from missions. 'Granite' was the code name for a very simple safety procedure. A number of posts, located near high ground, were equipped with red flares which they would light when the cloud-base was below the 1,000ft (300m) contour. If posts saw aircraft in danger of flying into a hillside they could light flares on their own initiative. Posts on the east of the Pennines equipped with Granite included Blyth, Edwinstowe, Farnsfield and Hucknall. Much of the ROC's success depended on observers' ability to recognise the dozens of aircraft types flying in British skies. Clubs were formed to practise aircraft recognition and often it was schoolboys who proved most enthusiastic and most adept, many spending their evenings up church towers searching the skies for the latest model. Eventually all observers, still volunteers giving up their spare time, sat proficiency tests, in which the successful recognition of fifty aircraft silhouettes accounted for a significant number of marks. So skilled were ROC personnel that some 800 of them, uniformed as temporary petty officers, were taken on board ships involved in the D-Day landings to prevent the trigger-happy AA gunners shooting down too many Allied aircraft.

Passive air defence in the Second World War

Bombing decoys in Nottinghamshire

By 1939 most established airfields had been provided with decoys. There were two types. Those designated 'K' were for daylight use, and were given dummy aircraft built by the technicians of Shepperton Studios. Night-time, or 'Q' sites were provided with lights. These were operated electrically by a small party of RAF personnel, working from a concrete bunker. The drill was that, as the sound of approaching enemy bombers was heard, the lights were switched off, but only after there had been an opportunity for the enemy to spot them. Some lights simulated landing lights and another, mounted on the roof of the bunker, stood in for the light by which an aircraft on the ground might navigate its way to a hangar. Such decoys had been provided for Newton at Cotgrave and Tithby, for Syerston at Kneeton and for Ossington at Upton.

The ability of bombers to pinpoint specific targets, especially at night, in the early years of the war, was yet to be developed. Bomber pilots, therefore, tended to look for places where other bombers had already bombed, and this behaviour provided a means of defence against the bombing of civilian or industrial targets. Most cities were given Special Fires sites (coded SF or 'Starfish') on open land at some plausible distance from the city itself. Grids of braziers filled with suitable combustible material, were laid out on the ground. These could be set alight as the bombers approached, to suggest that the raid had started and this was where to drop the bombs.

Specialist targets, however, came to receive more sophisticated treatment. Such targets as the COD at Chilwell, the mine at Gedling or Toton railway marshalling yards, employed different tricks of lighting to simulate the glows and sparks from a locomotive's firebox, doors slowly closing, and the subdued lighting which enabled night-working to proceed. The efficiency of these techniques would be gauged in an unexpected way. On the night of the big raid on Nottingham, the 8/9 May 1941, the little village of Plungar on the border with Leicestershire was inexplicably bombed. This attack could only be explained by deduction. German pilots had spotted the decoy fire set at the Cropwell Butler Starfish site and assumed that it represented the Rolls-Royce works at Derby. Taking bearings from this, they reckoned they had located Nottingham, their secondary target for the night, and released their bombs. The shock experienced by the villagers of Plungar had at least diverted some of the misery from the citizens of Nottingham. These decoys were kept in operation from August 1941 until May 1943. Although it is always difficult to evaluate the effect of preventative measures, some conclusion may be drawn from the fact that across the country there were over 800 instances of bombs being dropped on decoy sites.

ARP and Civil Defence

Nottingham was the HQ of both the North Midland Civil Defence area (Region 3), which included Derbyshire, Leicestershire and Rutland, Lincolnshire and Northamptonshire, and of the NFS Fire Force Area 8, comprising Nottinghamshire.

The chief constable also served as head of the ARP organisation. Nottingham was the first authority to organise ARP and fire guard work on the basis of sectors linked to the NFS. Aware of the extent to which so many of the city's services would be reliant on volunteers, the city council issued a handbook not merely detailing emergency procedures and sources of support for the victims of enemy action, but also emphasising the opportunities open to the volunteer whether in the AFS, the Home Guard, the WVS or the various bodies trained to render first aid, alongside information concerning compulsory paid activities such as fire-watching. Public air-raid shelters

91 Beeston: an air-raid shelter on the Boots site. (Courtesy of Boots Archives)

to accommodate around 36,000 persons were provided mainly near the city centre, and these included tunnels cut into the rock below Nottingham Castle. This was based on a general formula that allowed the provision of public shelters for 10 per cent of the population. In normal circumstances the bulk of the population would be at work where shelters had to be provided by firms with more than fifty employees, or at home where the householder would have installed an Anderson shelter in the garden, a Morrison shelter in a downstairs room, or made alternative arrangements, such as taking steps to strengthen a cellar. The council estimated that after the application of a means test, 65 per cent of the city's population would be eligible for free domestic shelters. Nottingham prided itself on the quality of its fire service, soon to be comple-mented by well-trained volunteer auxiliaries, but realised that threats of the widespread dropping of incendiary bombs across large areas of the country made a nationally organised fire-fighting force essential in order to realise the benefits of co-ordinated response and equitable deployment of resources. A large concrete shelter survives at Boots in Beeston, with smaller, brick-built ones on Mansfield Road, Nottingham.

The biggest attack came on 8/9 May 1941 when ninety-five bombers dropped 137 tons of HE and nearly 200 incendiaries, killing or wounding several hundred people, destroying hundreds of houses and businesses, and rendering whole streets uninhab-itable. Nottingham, Newark, Worksop, Retford and Eastwood were all disturbed by several hundred alerts. Newark suffered eight attacks during the Second World War, including the deadly one on 7 March 1943, when ten bombs were dropped on

Ransome & Marles' ball-bearing factory. Five bombs exploded, killing twenty-nine men and twelve women, and injuring a further 165 workers, some of whom were treated in the factory's own, only recently rediscovered, underground hospital.

The air war

For much of the war the focus of Nottinghamshire's airfields remained training. At different times this emphasis shifted under the pressure of circumstances, an expected invasion, for instance, or specific projects such as the airborne operations of Overlord (D-Day), or Market Garden (Arnhem). As well as the RAF, many units of other Allied nations such as the Poles, the Canadians and the USA were stationed in the county.

The first nine months of the war were taken up with the completion of construction projects already begun, and the commencement of new ones. Alongside this activity went the continuous effort to train pilots and aircrew, with Polish trainee pilots being gathered together at Hucknall. Tollerton was initially assigned to Bomber Command as a scatter field for the dispersal of aircraft. After Dunkirk, the HQ of No.1 Group RAF Bomber Command re-formed at Hucknall, with airfields in south Yorkshire and north Lincolnshire under command, flying mainly Wellingtons. In July 1941 the HQ moved to Bawtry Hall in order to be more centrally placed amongst 1 Group's airfields, and Bircotes was opened to house its communications flight.

Meanwhile, the preparations for bringing new airfields into being were coming to fruition, and Newton, Syerston and Winthorpe all opened before the end of 1940. These three encapsulate the span of airfield structures of the time: Newton as an example of the fully developed, top-of-the-range Expansion Period airfield; Syerston as the compromise model with elements of both the deluxe and the economy designs; and Winthorpe as the out-and-out utilitarian, bargain-basement model. Over the next two years more airfields of the utilitarian type came on stream: Balderton, Ossington and Orston in 1941; Langar, Gamston and Wigsley in 1942; and finally Worksop in late 1943. Ossington was designed from the start as a heavy bomber field and was built with three concrete runways, but most started as grass fields. Balderton's four grass runways were waterlogged for a couple of months either side of Christmas 1941 forcing the resident squadron to move out, and it soon became obvious that concrete runways were vital for uninterrupted use on bomber fields. The work involved necessitated significant closure periods in turn. Winthorpe closed for ten months during 1942, and Balderton for even longer the next year, whilst a runway of 2,000 yards and two of 1,400 yards were laid at each. Although many of these airfields were notionally assigned for use by OTUs, there were also considerable periods of operational use by bomber squadrons. The Canadians flew over 1,200 sorties in nine months from Balderton, for instance, and both Syerston and Langar were home to bomber squadrons of the Main Force for at least a year, within Nos 5 and 7 Groups, whilst Wigsley and Winthorpe both acted as satellites for Swinderby (Lincolnshire). Some airfield sites were identified but never built. Flying Training Command earmarked Snarestone Willoughby in Leicestershire as a base for a (Pilot) Advanced Flying Unit with a satellite at Farnsfield, and although the project had reached the stage of warning notices being sent out to the landowners, neither site was taken up, being rejected in the Air Ministry's review of December 1942.

Wartime airfields

The new airfields constituted the construction industry's greatest achievement of the war, taking up a third of all available labour. In 1942 a new airfield was opened every three days. It had taken just over six months from the first cut to the first take-off, with a further year to complete all the hard surfaces and buildings. At each site, some 400,000 tons of soil would have been excavated, 4.5 million bricks laid and 10 miles of roadway built, to provide the base for the 2,000+ personnel needed to keep two squadrons of bombers in action. The increasing weight of the heavy bombers meant that the thickness of the concrete laid in runways and hard-standings also had to be increased, putting further strain on the construction effort. Rubble was brought in by train from the country's blitzed cities.

These new utility airfields of the war years could not have been more different from those of the elegant Expansion Period with their high production values. Instead of the *moderne* villa, the wartime watch offices were built of 'temporary brick' (tb) meaning walls of a single brick's thickness, supported by buttresses and stuccoed.

92 RAF Langar: the watch office (13079/41) was a type 'A' for bomber satellite airfields.

93 RAF Gamston: this watch office (13726/41) was another bomber satellite type.

94 RAF Wigsley: the unique three-storey watch office.

At first these watch offices were designed for the airfield's specific function, Langar's and Balderton's, for instance being a type 'A' for bomber satellites (13079/41), and Gamston's a different bomber satellite type (13726/41). Winthorpe, for some reason, was given the tower designed for night-fighter stations (12096/41). All of these types were later merged into a general-purpose tower (343/43) one of which was built at Worksop. There appears to be no obvious reason why Wigsley was given its unique and distinctive three-storey watch office.

With so many new airfields to be built, the speedy construction of hangars became a priority, and the most common new type was the T2. This was a transportable construction consisting of cladding on a prefabricated steel frame. The B1 hangar, distinguishable by the steeper pitch of its roof, was provided as a workshop for civilian MAP employees to carry out first-line repair to damaged aircraft. Although the earliest satellite stations such as Balderton commenced operations without hangars at all, bomber airfields had a standard allocation of one B1 and up to four T2s as at Gamston and Ossington, for instance, but two was more common, as at Wigsley. Some were given extra hangars for particular purposes such as glider storage at Langar and Balderton, for which they were each provided with an additional two T2s. Hucknall and Tollerton both had a mix of hangar types because of the repair, construction and development work that was being carried on there. Tollerton had an 'R' type hangar, and Hucknall had several large MAP sheds, similar to the one built at Tollerton pre-war, and a timber-framed Blister hangar. Orston was a satellite for Newton, and as such was used by a range of smaller training aircraft which could be accommodated, when necessary, in its nine Blister hangars. Bircotes, a grass field, primarily used by the communications flight servicing No. 1 Group RAF Bomber Command HQ at Bawtry Hall (South Yorkshire), doubled for short periods of time as a satellite for various OTUs, and was given one T2, one B1 and a canvas Bessoneau hangar of First World War design.

95 RAF Langar: a re-clad T2 hangar, probably one provided for glider-storage and later used by AVRO.

Whereas the Expansion Period airfields had been planned as small townships with all the buildings grouped together around a parade ground and a neat chequerboard of roads, the watchword for the new airfields was dispersal. Hangars and hard-standings were dotted around the perimeter; the technical site with workshops and stores was in one area, the administrative site with its operations block and offices in another; the various communal sites with accommodation, messes and ablutions were scattered outside the perimeter track. All this was intended to reduce the impact of aerial attack, following the severe damage sustained by Fighter Command's nucleated airfields during the Battle of Britain. The bicycle quickly became an essential item of equipment.

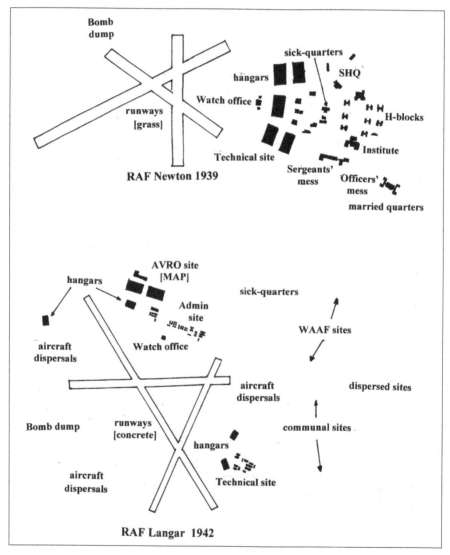

96 Comparative plans of RAF Newton and RAF Langar; the first, a nucleated Expansion Period airfield, the second, to a dispersed Second World War plan.

Apart from generator houses and stores for bomb-sights, pyrotechnics, inflammables and munitions, everything else was constructed in tb or prefabricated hutting. Just as in the 1930s, a central suite of designs was drawn up for the contractors to work from. Gamston provides good examples of many of these buildings. Pairs of Romney huts, often linked by a tb annexe, were used for the main stores (5539/42) and the station workshop (5851/42). One of the few structures on the technical site designed for one specific purpose was the parachute store (10825/42). Near to the watch office stands the usual fire tender house (12563/40) and night-flying equipment store (12411/41). The squadron offices are in a Nissen hut, as are the camouflage stores and the

97 RAF Gamston: the parachute store (10825/42).

98 RAF Gamston: a fine example of a double Air Ministry Laboratory Bombing Teacher (6301/42); the trainee bomb-aimer lay on the upper floor with an image of the target projected onto the floor below, whilst a 'pilot' simulated the movement of the aircraft. A single AML Bombing Teacher (816/43) stands nearby.

99 Coddington House, RAF Winthorpe's early officers' mess, now a private residence.

photographic block (4781/42). Other buildings such as the gas respirator store (12049/42) are of tb construction. The synthetic training site has a single and a double Link trainer (4188/42) for training pilots in instrument flying, and a single (6301/42) and a double AML bombing teacher (816/43 or 6301/42). On the upper floor was a device with a rotating lamp and mirror which projected a simulated landscape onto the ground floor, enabling the bomb-aimer, prostrate on a platform overlooking the image, to be trained to hit a target more accurately, synchronising his bomb-release mechanism with flying speed, ceiling height, and the speed and direction of the wind. In order to reduce the amount of building needed, existing structures were requisitioned. Coddington Hall, for instance, first served as the officers' mess at Winthorpe, later becoming officers' quarters. West Retford House is reported as having been in RAF occupation.

Flying training

Nottinghamshire's airfields were perceived as being sufficiently out of the front line as to be safe for training activities. Both Tollerton and Hucknall were well established as pre-war training stations, and both continued as such in tandem with the production and repair of aircraft, sponsored by MAP. Tollerton provided a RLG (Relief Landing Ground) for Newton, and Hucknall was the home of successive basic flying training units. It reopened the First World War RLG at Papplewick Moor, but inter-war building made use difficult, so the Tiger Moths of No.25 FTS were confined to dummy landings. The facilities at Newton, although never upgraded to hard runways, were considered good enough to host advanced flying training, and later on, Beam Approach Training, formerly known, clearly disconcertingly, as blind approach flying. Orston served mainly as another RLG for Newton, but its 1,200-yard grass strip was often unusable after heavy rain. Balderton, designed as a bomber station with grass runways, opened in June 1941 as a satellite of 25 FTS at Finningley (Yorkshire), but after three hard runways had been laid in 1943, it became a Heavy Conversion Unit flying Lancasters and Halifaxes. Although Ossington had been built as a heavy bomber field with hard runways from the start, it was transferred to Flying Training Command as soon as it opened in late 1941 as No.14 (Pilots) Advanced Flying Unit, soon becoming No.14 SFTS. Equipped with well over 100 aircraft, use was made of Gamston and Langar as RLGs. This school was succeeded by No.82 OTU, and then in 1945, by No.6 Lancaster Finishing School, joining No.5 which, throughout 1944, had been at Syerston. Worksop opened in late 1943.

The United States Army Air Force

Two of Nottinghamshire's airfields were used briefly by the Americans. Balderton (Station 482) was passed to the US IXth AAF Troop Carrier Command in January 1944. W. & C. French, the contractors who had earlier laid the hard runways, came back to add extra hard-standings and additional accommodation raising the capacity to 2,413 persons. The Americans stayed only until April, but were back in September, taking part in the Arnhem operation with fifty glider tows and a further thirty aircraft carrying paratroopers, bound for Nijmegen. Langar (Station 490) was loaned to the US IXth AAF Troop Carrier Command for its support and repair units in late 1943. Initially, a RAF Bomber Command Substitution Unit liaising with the US command structure and advising the newly arrived USAAF transport units on Procedures, Flying Control, Signals, Codes and Intelligence, was set up. Before long, US IXth AAF flying units had arrived to undergo glider-towing training prior to the D-Day landings, converting to the Horsa gliders. The airfield was also used at this time for constructing Hadrian gliders for issue to troop-carrying units. As they completed this initial training, units moved to airfields in the south-west, and new units moved in. A return to RAF control was delayed until after the Arnhem operations in September 1944. Three groups of aircraft, totalling nearly 200 C-47s, half of them towing gliders, flew from Langar to take part in the drop on the Nijmegen area, delivering 2,000 men of the US 82nd Airborne Division.

The Polish Air Force

Much of the training of Polish airmen took place in Nottinghamshire. No.18 (Polish) OTU formed in March 1940 at Hucknall to train bomber crews, followed by No.1 (Polish) FTS from January 1941, which split with its advanced squadron becoming No.16 (P) SFTS and moving to Newton. No.25 (Polish) SFTS then arrived in July 1941 at Hucknall from Peterborough (Cambridgeshire). Worksop opened in late 1943 as a satellite of No.18 OTU based at Finningley (Yorkshire), training Polish crews on Wellingtons for Bomber Command.

Satellite Landing Grounds

As new aircraft were released from the factories, it was essential that there were safe havens for their storage. The extensive network of Aircraft Storage Units (ASU), mainly located in the western half of the country, was supplemented by several dozen Satellite Landing Grounds (SLG). These were small, well-camouflaged airfields with a landing-strip, minimal buildings and dispersed aircraft-standings, often under tree-cover, where they could be secured by being tied down to cylindrical concrete blocks. No.51 Maintenance Unit at Lichfield (Staffordshire) established two SLGs in Nottinghamshire: No.35 SLG at Blidworth opening in August 1941, and No.38 SLG at Grove Park, opening a year later. Blidworth, with a grass strip 820 yards long, was assessed with a capacity of fifty-two fighters. Grove Park, whose strip extended to 900 yards, was expected to accommodate from 50–100 aircraft. Administered by MAP, there are few records of actual use but stories of Lysanders flying covert missions out of Grove Park probably have a simpler explanation. Grove Hall was occupied by the army who may have flown Army Co-operation aircraft off the adjacent, very convenient airstrip. SLGs had few substantial structures. There was usually a standard bungalow-type watch office, a tractor shed, a fuel store and, if the pilots, many of them women of the Air Transport Auxiliary, were lucky, somewhere for them to await their lift home. Blidworth's guardhouse has been put to domestic use. At Grove Park, the big house has gone and the only evidence remaining consists of concrete hard-standings and scatterings of the concrete blocks used for anchoring the aircraft down.

RAF Maintenance Units (MUs)

Supporting the RAF's operations were a number of ancillary units. Some were concerned with the supply of replacement aircraft, running the ASUs and SLGs. Some were responsible for maintaining a supply of bombs and small-arms ammunition, holding sufficient stocks securely at the various points along the supply chain. Others collected wrecked aircraft to repair those least badly damaged, to harvest spares and to recycle scarce materials. No.4 Salvage Centre, initially based in the LMS railway yards and station at Newark, but soon to occupy a site on Lincoln Road, now the Yorke Drive estate, became No.58 MU Salvage and Repair Depot in 1940 with sub-units at Newton, Skellingthorpe (Lincolnshire) and Honington (Suffolk). Two dozen salvage gangs, predominantly composed of RAF personnel, roamed the countryside collecting crashed and damaged aircraft and returning them to Newark by road, on Queen Mary low-loaders, for repair or cannibalisation. Haygarth House outside Retford, now stables, was HQ of the Air Ministry Works Department's No.5 Area. In Budby Road, Cuckney, was a RAF Maintenance and Supply Depot, the concrete bases of some of whose huts are still traceable in the woods.

100 Blidworth (SK 573530), the guardhouse of this Satellite Landing-ground (SLG) for the storage of new aircraft prior to their issue to operational airfields.

Camps and depots

The army ordnance depots at Chilwell, Arnold and Clumber Park, along with those of the RAF at Basford and Newark, were to play an important part in the logistical side of keeping fighting units effective. Chilwell, at the heart of a widespread network of ordnance depots stretching over the entire country, was the national HQ for the supply of all tanks and other vehicles. The big house at Clumber had been demolished in 1938 and the park was taken over as an ordnance store with 60,000 tons of shells and SAA, including heavy naval shells, stacked along the estate's roads; it was serviced by the Royal Pioneer Corps, later on in the war, surprisingly, supplemented by POW labour. Saxondale, near Bingham was a RE depot, used particularly for the storage of prefabricated hut sections. The Command Ordnance Depot on the Lincoln road out of Newark where, mainly, AA equipment, guns and RADAR were stored, maintained and serviced, was run by the RAOC, and after 1941, by REME as well. The US Army established a Stores Depot at Boughton, served by a WD Siding on the Lincoln to Shirebrook railway line. Information gleaned locally suggests that the bomb dumps in the woods at Bircotes were served by a dedicated narrow-gauge railway, possibly coming from the ROF at Ranskill via the main Retford-Doncaster line which passes within a mile of both the ROF and Bircotes airfield, a little way north of Bawtry.

As in the previous war, stately homes were the target of numerous agencies looking for space to train troops, store national treasures, accommodate displaced schools and evacuees and hide munitions. Thoresby Hall and Holme Pierrepont Halls were both homes to battalions of the Sherwood Foresters at different times; East Markham Hall was a base for the Lovat Scouts, a Scottish yeomanry regiment, still with their horses in 1939 prior to being posted as the garrison of the Faroe Islands; Wollaton Park was the assembly point for 7th Battalion the Norfolk Regiment; Winthorpe Hall was a RASC depot; Flintham Hall provided overspill accommodation for RAF Syerston; and Welbeck Abbey was a training camp. Rufford Abbey, used for training purposes by armoured units, suffered such damage

101 Boughton: Romney huts at this US Army stores depot.

102 Winthorpe Hall, location of a Royal Army Service Corps depot.

that it underwent a 'controlled demolition' after the war, leaving much of the structure roofless. The militia camps continued to be useful, Newark's Hawton Road Camp becoming an AA training centre. It then became the base for 21st Independent Parachute Company, which trained there as a combat engineer unit, clearing, marking out and establishing drop zones for glider-borne assault troops who followed on. The company fought at Arnhem. Bowbridge Camp had a long tradition as a RE depot, and a Royal Engineers Training Battalion, with its HQ at The Friary, occupied the camp. Here sappers were trained to build Bailey Bridges, using structural parts fabricated at Blagg and Johnson Ltd. From 1942, a RE OCTU prepared sapper officers for duties, attending lectures at Newark Technical College. Practice bridges were thrown across the Trent, and the defensive qualities of concrete were explored. The Albert Street militia barracks housed a Mechanical Equipment Training Wing using heavy plant, and other buildings such as Northgate House and Barnby Road School were also used. Preparations for the Normandy landings saw the 2nd Armoured Division at Barnby Moor camp, Ranskill, and tank-training was carried out at Church Warsop. A reference to the Life Guards having a HQ in the Old England Hotel at Sutton-on-Trent may relate to the presence of the Guards Armoured Division in training prior to D-Day. The arrival of the US Army made further demands on camps. Elements of the 82nd Airborne Division were based at the former militia camp at Whatton, and in Wollaton Park, prior to their drop on Normandy in June 1944. The US military police, nicknamed 'Snowdrops' because of their white helmets, had a camp at East Retford, possibly at Ranby. Forest Town had a further concentration of Nissen huts for the Bevin Boys, lads conscripted to work in the coal mines.

Prisoner-of-War (POW) Camps

Being an inland county, Nottinghamshire provided suitable locations for secure POW camps. These took a number of different forms. Carburton Camp is described as being

103 Wollaton Park, the last surviving hut from the army camp, later a POW camp.

a collection of huts with a double barbed-wire fence, with a raised watchtower at each corner, pretty well the paradigm which everyone would recognise. Many were set up in the grounds of stately homes as at Tollerton or Wollaton Park. Only towards the latter stages of the war did large numbers of POWs need accommodation, and it was at that stage that camps vacated by troops taking part in the invasion of Europe were brought into use. This would include Boughton depot and Ranby Camp for instance. Although most POWs were put to work on the land, as at the Woodborough Road Camp, now Podders scrapyard, there were other tasks they could carry out. German POWs from Wollaton Park were, on several occasions, employed to shift snow from Notts County's Meadow Lane ground. Many POWs were held until up to two years after the war had ended, so redundant camps such as one of the communal sites at RAF Langar were utilised. Although the camps were seen as being temporary, a number of remains may be seen. A hut at Wollaton Park is now a sports pavilion, and more huts may be seen at Caunton and Nether Headon, whilst at Proteus Camp and HMPs Whatton and Ranby, huts have been repaired and remain in use.

Munitions production

The Royal Ordnance Factories

There were three Royal Ordnance Factories in Nottinghamshire. One of them, at Ranskill, was concerned with the production of cordite, whilst another, Ruddington, was a filling plant, loading explosives into shells, mines and bombs. The third one, at Kings Meadow Road, Nottingham, was important for the manufacture of ordnance. By 1945, over 19,000 gun-barrels, or 'tubes', had been produced in a variety of calibres. The South Shop was added in 1941 exclusively for the production of 40mm Bofors LAA guns for the Royal Navy. As well as this, from 1944 the factory carried out conversions of US M4 Sherman Mark V tanks into Mark VC Fireflies, armed with the lethal 17-pounder gun, and arguably the most powerful tank used by British armoured units in the war.

Fuel supply and PLUTO

The heavy demands for fuel in the east of England for, particularly, the Allied bomber effort, outpaced the ability of the railway to meet these needs. With the opening of a second front in the offing, it became even more urgent that this particular problem was solved. The answer lay underground, in a pipeline running from Stanlow on the Wirral, across the country to a terminal at Misterton. From here the fuel was piped on down to Sandy in Bedfordshire, with spurs stretching eastwards into Norfolk and Suffolk to feed the bombers. Ultimately, this pipeline became a key arm of the *Pipe Line Under The Ocean*, popularly known as PLUTO, which crossed the Channel in two places to keep the Normandy invasion rolling forward. The Misterton depot still functions as part of Britain's strategic fuel management system, and structures dating from the Second World War are still visible.

Nellie – a secret (but not very useful) weapon

Clumber Park was to provide the setting for one of the more anachronistic projects of the Second World War. This went under the code name 'Nellie', from the Naval Land Equipments branch of the Admiralty, subsequently transferred to the Ministry of Supply, and charged with the development of a trench-cutting machine. In 1939, Winston Churchill was First Lord of the Admiralty and one of his pet projects was to commission a machine which could extend the Maginot Line from its northern and vulnerable terminus on the Belgian border, now rendered even more exposed by Belgium's neutrality. The project was passed to Ruston-Bucyrus of Lincoln, a company specialising in mechanical excavators for the civil engineering industry. A test rig was constructed, put through its paces on a site at Skellingthorpe near Lincoln, and adjudged successfully to have met its brief. Next, a pilot machine was constructed at the Anchor Street works of Ruston-Bucyrus in Lincoln, and given its field trials in August 1941 at Clumber

104 Misterton: buildings from the Second World War phase of this fuel depot which formed part of the PLUTO system.

Park, delivered there by an army low-loader, specially ordered from Chilwell COD. The convoy, unable to use the cast-iron Dunham Bridge over the Trent, was forced to detour to Newark, progressing from there up the Great North Road to Clumber Park. Here, a RE company was camped out in the Park with mobile workshops in trucks, and messes in Nissen huts. The civilians from the Ministry of Supply stayed in a hut next to the Normanton Inn, on the Blyth road, later moving into the Park. In the presence of members of the General Staff, Nellie duly dug her trench to the required dimensions – 7ft 6in (2.3m) wide, and 5ft (1.5m) deep, disposing of the spoil to form two banks of equal height either side of the trench. Powered by a pair of 600hp engines, the machine moved forward at a speed of around 0.5mph (800m), many of its features being derived from the First World War tanks built by the Ruston element of the new company. The test site lay in the area of Clumber known as South Lawn, on the opposite side of the lake from the house site. In November a special demonstration was laid on for Churchill and his staff which included Sir Alan Brooke. Nellie again performed creditably, impressing her audience, but the whole *raison d'etre* for the project had been overtaken by events, resources were scarce and its continuation could not be justified, although Nellie was handed over to the army in February 1942. More trials were held in more challenging terrain in Bedfordshire, and despite the white elephant dimension, four examples of each of the two different types were completed. Only in May 1943 was the project declared officially dead and, by 1950, all the machines had been scrapped.

Ministry of Aircraft Production (MAP) plants

Three major sites were run by firms who were part of the aeronautical industry, but placed under the control of MAP, headed by Lord Beaverbrook. AVRoe (AVRO), whose Lancaster bombers were built mainly in Manchester, ran a network of workshops for repairs to aircraft which were too complex to be carried out on the airfield. One of these, from 1942, was at Langar, on the opposite side of the road to the bomber airfield, where parts from Lancaster wrecks salvaged at Bracebridge Heath outside Lincoln were cannibalised to get damaged bombers back into the air. An extensive complex of hangars and workshops was built, much of it still visible today. Hucknall had been set up in 1934 by Rolls-Royce as an engine test establishment where much of the development of the Merlin engine was carried out. From 1940, there was an Experimental Unit repairing Spitfires and Hurricanes. As work towards the development of the jet-engined Meteor progressed, the grass airfield proved inadequate, and the Meteor Flight Trials Unit transferred to Balderton in 1943 then to Church Broughton (Derbyshire). Another CRO was run by Field Aircraft Services, at Tollerton, repairing mainly Lancasters, but basically any Bomber Command aircraft that was brought in, flown in and out by ATA pilots. The Handley Page Harrow was an updated version of an earlier tri-plane, introduced as a heavy bomber in 1936. By the beginning of the war it had been largely replaced by the Hampden and the Wellington, but retained a future in a different guise. One of Field's specialisms was converting Harrows into 'Sparrows'. Named for its distinctive new nose fairings, the Sparrow was a transport aircraft which could carry twenty troops or, in the ambulance version, twelve stretchers.

105 Langar, a hangar on the aircraft repair site run by AVRO for MAP repairing damaged Lancaster bombers.

The Eakring oilfield

As well as the friendly invasion by the GIs and airmen of the US Army, there was the less-publicised arrival in Nottinghamshire of forty-four US roughnecks. They came from Oklahoma on a year's contract to help exploit the oilfields round Eakring, which had been discovered in 1939, and had gone into production but were nowhere near realising their potential. In 1942 Britain was down to two months' supply of oil. In normal times 5 million barrels were held, but with the destruction of 1 million barrels by bombing, and the number of tankers being sunk by U-boats in the Atlantic, this figure had fallen to just 2 million. High-grade oil, suitable for use in Rolls-Royce aero engines, was coming out of Dukes Wood and the other local fields, but in insufficient volume, and so the Americans with their more efficient practices, general expertise and specialist equipment were recruited. When they arrived at Dukes Wood there were already ninety-seven wells in operation, but the Americans added a further 106. By skating their four rigs on rafts rather than dismantling them, and by using their drill-bits to destruction, the Americans worked five times faster than the British crews had managed. They once drilled down over 1,000ft (300m) in a morning, and completed most wells within a week. The oil was put on tanker-trains in sidings at Bilsthorpe and sent to Pumpherston Refinery near Edinburgh. As part of the attempt to keep the whole operation secret, the Americans were billeted in the theological seminary of the Society of the Sacred Mission, living alongside the Anglican monks in Kelham Hall. Despite the glaring differences between the two groups' way of life, no problems appear to have arisen. By the war's end over 3 million barrels had been produced by the oilfields at Eakring, Dukes Wood, Kelham Hills and Caunton, with 1.4 million barrels from Dukes Wood alone. Only in 1944 was any of this made public, although over 1,000 locals, as well as Italian POWs, had been involved in the operation.

Local industries

Boots in Beeston became the largest plant in the world producing penicillin, and Ransome & Marles of Newark produced the ball bearings needed for everything from aero-engines to tank-turrets. Most companies could find a wartime need they could fulfil, an example being Turney Bros who switched their production of their heavier 'Levant' leather, previously used for upmarket footwear, to army boots.

The Barlock Typewriter Company in Nottingham switched its production to sears for Lee-Enfield 0.303in rifles, with further parts made by other Nottingham engineering workshops. Parts for Lancaster bombers were made in Mansfield, and Raleigh Cycles converted to manufacturing jerrycans for storing and transporting fuel.

106 A preserved 'donkey' in Dukes Wood.

107 Kelham Hall, home of the US wranglers who pumped the oil in Dukes Wood and on other local wells.

nine

The Cold War
and Beyond

By 1948 the state of armed truce which had existed since the end of the war was developing into the period of Cold War which was to last until almost the end of the century. This was characterised by an arms race between the USSR and the Western powers, but held in check by the notion of Mutually-Assured Destruction (MAD), which held that the initiator of nuclear war would not survive the retaliation. Such was the density and spread of nuclear weapons that even a pre-emptive strike – getting your retaliation in first – would provide no sure-fire guarantee of avoiding annihilation.

The RAF in the Cold War

In 1945 the RAF had too many aircraft, too many airfields, too many bombs and too many personnel, and its priority was to reduce the numbers of all of these as quickly as possible. Lancasters were flown into Tollerton for scrapping. Those airfields which had never developed much beyond landing grounds such as Blidworth, Orston and Papplewick Moor were closed immediately, though Grove Park was safeguarded, being seen as potentially useful in the future. Bircotes became a storage unit for MT under No.250 MU, and Balderton was taken over by No.254 MU as No.1 Equipment Disposal Depot, and then as a sub-site of No.93 MU for explosives storage, with 10 kilotons of munitions, including 4,000lb bombs, being stored along the runways from 1948–55. Gamston became No.9 Air Crew Holding Unit, whose task was to dispose of personnel surplus to requirement. This involved the repatriation of hundreds of Commonwealth aircrew and, at one point, there were almost 2,000 Royal Australian Air Force personnel awaiting flights home. One way of solving the pilot surplus was retraining, and at Ossington, No.6 Lancaster Finishing School was run by the RAF and BOAC together, as a joint venture to train pilots for the new Lancastrian civil airliner, and to convert Lancaster pilots to fly the Avro York transport aircraft. This initiative continued well into 1946.

Training in the Cold War

Those Nottinghamshire airfields which stayed active after 1945 tended to be concerned with training. Newton, although 12 Group RAF Fighter Command's HQ, was handicapped by its lack of hard runways, so its major activity was ground-based training. Flying training, however, continued uninterrupted at Syerston, and included the training of Fleet Air Arm pilots from 1948 for two years, using Tollerton as a RLG. It became the first FTS, anywhere in the world, to train novice pilots on jet aircraft. After a break of two years at both Worksop and Gamston, flying training resumed in the early 1950s, continuing until 1957. Both Hucknall and Worksop were home to units of the RAuxAF until it was disbanded in 1957. Hucknall's Spitfires had been moved to Wymeswold (Leicestershire) in 1949, prior to the squadron's conversion to Meteors. Also at Hucknall was a LAA squadron of the RAuxAF Regiment, and an Air Observation Post squadron, operating light aircraft as spotters for artillery units. The HQ of the county's RAuxAF units was Upnah House in Balmoral Road, now used by Nottingham High School for Girls. Syerston has remained the major national focus for RAF glider-training since 1975 when the Central School was established there.

Newton's training role embraced a whole range of non-flying activities ranging from handling dogs to handling missiles. A school of technical training, at Newton from 1958–74, embraced electrical and instrument ground training, and guided-weapons courses which had moved there from Yatesbury and Melksham (Wiltshire). In 1973 the RAF School of Education, and the RAF School of Management Training arrived and, twenty years later, the RAF Department of Training merged with the RAF School of Education, staying at Newton until 1995. Winthorpe, from 1952–58, was home to the Central Servicing Development Establishment of Maintenance Command, whose role was to determine the most efficient and effective methods of servicing all the different types of aircraft on strength, and disseminate those findings throughout the RAF.

Airfield improvement

Nottinghamshire's airfields received very little attention in the period after the end of the war. Hucknall, from whence Rolls-Royce had been forced to move its test-flying of Meteors to Balderton back in 1943, redeployed its RAuxAF squadron, soon itself to be flying Meteors, to Wymeswold in 1949. Eventually, a new concrete runway, 6,850ft (2,100m) in length, was laid at Hucknall in 1955. Worksop's new role as an advanced flying training school demanded some new facilities, especially as it was providing cover while Finningley was being rebuilt as a V-bomber base. Two new T2 hangars were built, along with an adjacent pair of Aircraft Servicing Platforms (ASP).

Logistical support for air operations

To support the operations of the RAF's sharp end during the Second World War, an enormous logistical tail had been developed, and the requirements of the Cold War proved no less demanding. No.42 Group RAF, much of it based on the munitions dumps of Norton Disney (Lincolnshire), was responsible for the supply of nuclear weapons and fuel to Bomber Command 1953–58. Part of this group was No.93 MU with its HQ at Newton and explosives storage operations at Balderton. Hucknall was HQ of No.53 (Maintenance) Group from 1947–56. The most significant changes came at Langar. This became a RCAF supply base providing logistical support for the 1st Canadian Air Force which was serving with NATO forces on the Continent, centred on Metz (Lorraine). This commitment necessitated the building of warehousing and an air-freight terminal on Langar airfield. Spare parts were stocked not only for the F-86 Sabre fighters of the Canadians, but also for those flown by the Greek and Turkish Air Forces, as well as for other types of aircraft flying with the Belgian Air Force. In 1961 the arrival of larger transport aircraft meant that direct flights from Canada could carry sufficient cargo direct to the advanced base in France without offloading at Langar. Winthorpe was allocated to the USAF as an emergency hospital in 1956–58 but the offer was never taken up.

The army: camps, depots and TA Centres

The Regular Army

The successor unit of the Sherwood Foresters was the Worcestershire and Sherwood Foresters Regiment, formed in 1970, but itself subsequently subsumed as the Mercian Regiment's 2nd Battalion, currently (2013) in a light infantry role based in Belfast with 14 Mechanized Brigade. The Foresters' regimental depot at Normanton Barracks, Derby, had closed in 1963 but was used by the city council for storage until 1984 when it was demolished and the site developed for leisure use. In 1950, Ranby Camp became home to No.19 (Tank Transporter) Company, RASC who stayed there until 1969. Bestwood Lodge was given additional buildings, opened in 1956, and served first as HQ 49 Infantry Brigade, and then as a base for the Royal Army Pay Corps. The buildings now form part of the Nottinghamshire Fire and Rescue Service HQ. There was a REME Command Depot on London Road, Newark-on-Trent, its site now a motor-caravan dealership. A number of engineer and MOD quartermaster units are based at Chetwynd Barracks, Chilwell, but its main user is the Reinforcements Training and Mobilisation Centre. This runs a two-week 'training package' for, mainly, army reservists and TA personnel, as an induction exercise prior to serving overseas with the regular army. Civilian contractors and MOD civil servants may also be included in the training. There is also a two-day course for those serving with the UN.

108 Bestwood Lodge, barrack buildings opened in 1956 on this site, previously used by the military as a mobilisation depot, now Nottinghamshire's Fire and Rescue service HQ.

109 Chetwynd Barracks: the guardroom.

The Territorial Army

One legacy of conscription and large numbers of reservists with experience from the Second World War and Korea was the size of the TA in the early 1950s. An official handbook issued around 1949 by the Nottinghamshire Territorial and Auxiliary Forces Association lists twelve operational units, two of them including WRAC detachments, the University OTC, and three county battalions of the ACF. When the TA had been reconstituted in 1947, the Sherwood Rangers were equipped as an armoured regiment with Comet tanks; the South Notts Hussars were formed into two separate regiments of artillery, one (307th) with Ram 25-pounder guns, and the other (350th) with 7.2in howitzers as self-propelled and heavy artillery respectively; the 8th Battalion Sherwood Foresters was re-formed as a motorized battalion, to provide the infantry element of an armoured brigade. Of the AA units which had been formed before the outbreak of war, the Robin Hoods, formerly the 7th Battalion of the Foresters, were equipped with LAA guns alongside their searchlights as the 577th LAA/SL Regiment, and the former 28th LAA Regiment became the 528th (Notts) LAA Regiment. One new addition was the 48th Counter Bombardment Troop which consisted of specialists whose battle-field task was to analyse intelligence reports in order that appropriate targets might be selected for the available field artillery units. There were also two signals units and, on the logistical side, units representing the RASC, REME and RAOC.

By contrast, in 2013, 'C' Company of the 4th (TA) Battalion of the Mercian Regiment, with its HQ in Wolverhampton (west Midlands), is based in Mansfield. Elements of No.73 Engineer Regiment, RE (TA), with its Regimental HQ at Wigman Road, Bilborough, are dispersed across a number of TACs in the county, and carries out an air support role preparing landing grounds. Cavendish Road, Carlton, is the base for 'S' (Sherwood Rangers Yeomanry) Squadron of the Royal Yeomanry, fulfilling a very specialist role as a Chemical, Biological, Nuclear and Radiological Reconnaissance unit carried in armoured vehicles. No.307 (South Notts Hussars) Regiment RA is based at Bulwell, and there are medics at Beeston and at Triumph Road, Lenton, and Royal Naval and Royal Marine Reserves at HMS Sherwood in Chalfont Drive. In 1954, the NUOTC moved to the Beeston TAC, where it remains as the East Midlands Universities OTC.

TA Centres

The majority of the TACs were in premises which had long been used by volunteer forces, with the Sherwood Rangers' tanks based in the old militia barracks in Albert Street, Newark, and the REME/RAOC unit based at Cromwell Camp, the Central Ordnance Depot in Baskin Lane, Chilwell. In 1948, a new TAC in the form of a hutted camp, with houses only for permanent staff, was proposed on Sutton Road for Mansfield and was in use the next year. Most of the TA units were officially headquartered at Nottingham's Derby Road TAC, with the County TAFA, later RFCA, and the Counter Bombardment Troop, across the road in Clinton Terrace. One new TAC was immediately scheduled post-war for construction in Triumph Road, Lenton, duly opening in 1953, and followed in the next four years by similar builds in Wigman Road, Bilborough, and Hallcroft Road, East Retford. The old RE Bowbridge Camp in Newark continued in use by a company of the Sherwood Foresters whose Battalion HQ remained in Sherwood Avenue. The last quarter of the twentieth century saw three new TACs being built in Nottinghamshire. In Worksop, the old Scofton House was rebuilt to be reopened on 29 June 1974 by Princess Anne; Mansfield finally got its new premises in Bath Street after the old drill hall, demolished

110 Wigman Road, Bilborough: the HQ of a TA engineer regiment.

111 Worksop, Scofton House TAC, opened by the Princess Royal in 1974.

112 Mansfield, Bath Street TAC, opened in 1982 and now home to a company of the Mercian Regiment's 4th Battalion and a detachment of 73 Engineer Regiment.

113 Swiney Way, Chilwell: the TAC.

in the early 1960s, was replaced by a new TAC being opened by Denis Thatcher in 1982; and Foresters' House, in Swiney Way next to the Chilwell COD and Chetwynd Barracks, built in a style very similar to the Mansfield model. In 1990 the TAC in Triumph Road was given an anti-blast screen as a defence against terrorism. The wall stands 6ft 6in (2m) high, and is 9in (23cm) thick, with double-thickness brick piers.

Preparing to defend against nuclear war

In the context of MAD as a physical and psychological deterrent, it was still necessary to formulate contingency plans for if it all went wrong. So there were attempts in Britain to convince the population that taking a few simple measures, disseminated as a process known as 'Protect and Survive', would enable many of them to weather the nuclear storm, but realistically the best that could be done was to try to ensure that key elements of the governmental, military and communications infrastructure might remain safe.

The Royal Observer Corps and ROTOR

The air defence organisation perfected during the Second World War was continued into the Cold War period until it was realised that many of the components were unable to cope with the changing circumstances of modern warfare. The ROTOR system had been set up to target incursions by hostile aircraft into UK airspace. It consisted of radar-guided HAA guns, the GCI radars controlling the RAF's fighters and, to complement these, the visual spotting network of the ROC, for whom a new post was added to the system at Collingham in 1948–49. Observers had hitherto made do with rudimentary instruments mounted on often unstable platforms, but by 1955, over 400 new purpose-built structures had been provided nationwide. These standard posts stood either at ground level, or were raised up on 6ft (1.8m) high concrete legs. The post consisted of a box, constructed of prefabricated concrete panels, measuring 10ft (3m) by 6ft 8in (2m), one half being open, and the other half roofed over, allowing plotting instruments to be used. However, it soon became apparent that the high speeds attained by jet aircraft made visual spotting no longer viable. The Nottingham/Derby GDA had been based at Elvaston outside Derby but, in 1955, AA Command was stood down and, at the same time, a new role for the ROC was in the process of formulation. Observers would henceforth be part of a new organisation, UKWMO, to track and record the impact of nuclear explosions and the consequent spread of radioactive fallout. It was also realised that the ROC posts were too exposed for their new role, and that a less vulnerable structure was needed. The solution was an underground post, not dissimilar to the spotting post, but with roughly twice the space, and sunk 15ft (4.5m) underground. Entry was through a hatch and down a shaft by ladder. Each post was crewed by three men or women who were provided with minimal sanitation, sleeping and feeding facilities. Power came via a car battery, and the main water source was captured rainwater. At the same time, the Group HQs were deemed to be vulnerable, but only from 1959 were new protected premises built. The Watnall HQ was moved to Grantham in 1953 when the Midland Area had been temporarily disbanded, eventually finishing up in a new protected HQ at Fiskerton (Lincolnshire) in 1976. Many of the county's established ROC sites were unsuitable for conversion to underground ones so, over a period of several years, a number were re-sited. These included Blyth, Dunham-on-Trent and Walkeringham which was renamed Wiseton. In all, there were, by 1964, thirteen underground posts operational in Nottinghamshire, split between Groups based on Coventry (No.8), Lincoln (No.15) and Leeds (No.18).

114 Burton Joyce, the 1960s ROC post, showing the hatch and the external instruments.

A reorganisation of the ROC in 1968 led to the closure of some posts including Collingham, Cotgrave, East Retford and Ollerton. The remainder closed when the ROC was stood down in 1991. Some, such as the Farnsfield post, were demolished. Although there appear to be no traces left of the aircraft-spotting posts, all apparently having been destroyed, the superstructures of several underground posts can be seen at Blyth, Collingham and Burton Joyce for instance. That at Kelham Hills was on the market in 2003 with an asking price of £3,000.

The Bloodhound surface-to-air guided weapon (SAGW) system

With the dissolution, in 1955, of AA Command in recognition of the fact that HAA guns would not be able to deal with the developing delivery systems of atomic weapons, an alternative was sought. Two SAGW systems had been in the pipeline since the late 1940s and they came to fruition in 1958. *Red Shoes* was taken on by the army in a mobile form known as Thunderbird, and *Red Duster* was developed by the RAF as Bloodhound. The ROTOR system had been founded on three extensive Gun-Defended Areas (GDAs), but Bloodhound was to be much more point-specific in its coverage. As a stop-gap until an effective ICBM (Inter-Continental Ballistic Missile) was available to NATO, the THOR missile system was installed in Britain. This was only an IRBM (Intermediate-Range Ballistic Missile), with a range of around 3,000 miles (4,800km) so, in order to be capable of reaching targets in western Russia, it had to be based in Europe. Twenty THOR sites, each equipped

with three missiles were, from 1958–63, located down the east side of Britain, under joint British and American control. These sites dovetailed with the V-bomber airfields, and so an integrated air defence system was thus required to defend this chain of twenty-nine operational bases. Bloodhound became available from 1958, but only in limited numbers, and just ten sites were selected for its deployment. These were inevitably a compromise, with the greater priority being given to the V-bomber bases. RAF Finningley was the furthest north of these, and was given its own Bloodhound base, with the expectation that collateral protection would also be afforded to the five Yorkshire THOR sites, two of which, Breighton and Carnaby, also had Bloodhounds co-located with their THORs.

115 Misson: a Bloodhound missile.

The location of Finningley's Bloodhound site was Misson (SK705975), unlike its fellows, not an airfield site but a former bombing range. Each Bloodhound site had an identical layout, approached by a guardhouse and administrative buildings and the gabled missile-assembly shed which was the only large structure on the site. The arming and fuelling of missiles took place in separate buildings designed to minimise the risk of accidental ignition. The missiles themselves were laid out in two fire units of sixteen, side-by-side. Each of the two fire units was backed by its own launch control post, works services building and hard-standing for the Type 83 *Yellow River* or *Stingray* target illuminating radar (TIR). Each missile stood on a holdfast connected by cable ducting to the control post, routed through a cable termination pillar. Long-range target information came from the Type 82 *Orange Yeoman* control radar at RAF Lindholme (Yorkshire). Misson was in operation for only three years from 1960, manned by 94 Squadron. The removal of THOR coupled with the accelerating obsolescence of Bloodhound, forced the closure of the sites.

Support for the personnel manning the Bloodhound sites was provided from Newton by No.9 School of Technical Training, from 1958 until 1974, and the RAF's Guided Weapons Course, which had arrived at Newton from Yatesbury (Wiltshire) in 1959.

Cold War communications

It was assumed that the effects of a nuclear strike would include the disruption of telephonic communication, so the Home Office, responsible for ensuring that the country did not collapse into anarchy, established a network of radio stations across the country. These would allow regional commissioners to stay in contact with each other, and to co-ordinate the deployment of the police and military in maintaining public order. These radio stations were code-named 'Hilltop', one in Nottinghamshire being at Robin Hood's Hills (SK513551) near Kirkby-in-Ashfield.

As part of the early warning system being put in place in the late 1950s, a network of microwave towers was developed, the best known of which is the Post Office Tower in London's Tottenham Court Road. The system was code-named 'Backbone' and its main spine

116 Kirkby-in-Ashfield, Robin Hood's Hills, the aerial of the former Home Office 'Hilltop' radio site (SK513552).

117 The Microwave Tower at Farleys (SK706703).

ran from Stokenchurch (Buckinghamshire) close to the main command centres, up the centre of England to the east coast of Scotland above Edinburgh. A number of parallel relays were installed as back-up, one of which ran from Morborne Hill near Peterborough, through Lincolnshire and Nottinghamshire to Tinshill near York. The microwave tower at Farleys (SK706703), west of Tuxford and the highest point in the county, provides the relay link between similar towers at Carlton Scroop, to the south, and Upton to the north. All the towers obviously contained the same standard components, but were all individually designed, that at Farleys having four circular platforms to carry the distinctive horn-shaped aerials which characterise these installations.

In the event of nuclear war it would also be vital to maintain secure road-routes for the movement of troops and supplies. These Essential Service Routes would be barred to civilian traffic and controlled by police and armed TA units. In Nottinghamshire these designated routes included the M1, A1 and A46, and the east-west routes across the county linking Nottingham and Mansfield to the M1 and the A1 (A612, A615, A617, A616, A6075 etc.), and through to Lincoln and Gainsborough (A57 and A620). In addition to these roads, the army designated a Military Road Route System which ensured access to the major military bases and the strategic military ports and airports. Included in this system, unsurprisingly, were the M1 and the A1. Private motorists were not completely barred from the roads – only from those roads which went anywhere.

Bunkers

Across Britain, central and local government, public utilities and military installations were given protection against nuclear attack in the form of underground bunkers, and a number of these were provided in Nottinghamshire. Once it was realised that the USSR enjoyed a nuclear capability, it was recognised that an exchange of atomic weapons would inevitably result in the complete obliteration of London. A network of alternative Regional Seats of Government was therefore set up, Nottingham becoming the centre of Region 3 comprising Derbyshire, Leicestershire, Rutland, Lincolnshire, and Northamptonshire. Each of the twelve mainland Regions was assigned a commissioner who would operate utilising surviving civil servants from the adjacent offices to administer emergency supplies, with military and police personnel to enforce a state of emergency under Martial Law. All food and water supplies, energy sources, channels of communication and transport would be tightly controlled, personal movement restricted, and objectors, non-conformers and looters summarily shot. The original Nottingham War Room, in Chalfont Drive, was opened some time in the early 1950s. Located within a wartime dispersal estate of temporary government offices, it had one storey underground containing plant room, segregated dormitory accommodation, canteen, water tank and telephone exchange. The other floor, at ground level, comprised offices and the Perspex-sided control cabins which overlooked the central, double-height map room, kept constantly up-to-date to display the current state of play. There were air filtration systems, designed to keep out radioactive dust, and a thick reinforced-concrete roof.

Within a short time these war rooms were deemed inadequate to sustain life for the increasingly long recovery periods envisaged as necessary after the detonation of ever more powerful atomic weapons. The solution was either to extend existing buildings or to construct new ones, in order to provide more space for longer terms of regional government, to include more functions and to house more personnel. These new expanded establishments would be known as Regional Seats of Government (RSG). Alongside the emergency services, the commissioner's staff would henceforth include scientific advisers; representatives of government departments including health, Home Office, agriculture, justice, civil defence and information; a BBC studio and staff to communicate advice and orders to the local population in different media; and HQ staff for each of the individual armed services. Nottingham was one of three war rooms chosen for expansion rather than replacement. Unfortunately there was no available space in which greatly to extend the footprint of the building, so the original war room was encased in a new structure which sat on top, becoming a third level, cantilevered out to overhang the sides, and supported on concrete pilotis. A further, more

118 Nottingham, Chalfont Drive, the upper storeys of the War Room and the Regional Seat of Government (RSG).

119 Mansfield, the Severn Trent Water HQ on Great Central Road, containing an emergency underground bunker.

decorative, feature was textured concrete panels on the upper level. The Nottingham RSG remained in use until around 1970 when alternative accommodation was found for a new organisational structure. A site visit by members of Subterranea Britannica in 2002 revealed a good state of preservation with many features such as the pneumatic message handling system, better remembered from 1960s department stores, still intact. Also *in situ* was the Beeston Robin Hood oil-fired boiler.

Alongside central government's plans for the continuation of life after the bomb, local government and public utilities were also required to make such provision. However, although Nottinghamshire County Council had a small emergency centre underneath a 1960s extension to County Hall in West Bridgford, their main stand-by facility was shared with Severn Trent Water, whose emergency control centre was under their headquarters in Mansfield. The Thatcher government was still financing local authority nuclear bunkers into the late 1980s, and Mansfield District Council made use of this largesse to incorporate an emergency control centre under its new Civic Centre on Chesterfield Road in 1990.

MAFF Buffer Depots

In order to stockpile non-perishable food-stuffs, cooking equipment and utensils, for the use of communal feeding-stations in an emergency, the Ministry of Agriculture, Fisheries and Food (MAFF) and the Ministry of Supply, together established a network of Buffer Depots. These were usually near transport nodes such as that at Gamston Airfield (No.87) by the Great North Road, and Coxmoor Road (No.336T) at Sutton-in-Ashfield, where an existing cold-store next to the railway may represent that depot. The rail links to the former ROF Ruddington made it especially suitable, and also kept the premises in commission for future eventualities. Depot No.336 at Main Road, Smalley Gate, though assigned to Nottinghamshire, may lie just over the Derbyshire border.

120 Sutton-in-Ashfield, Coxmoor Road, emergency government cold-store.

Munitions

Aviation

A number of aeronautical concerns continued to operate in the county. AVRO's Langar workshops serviced a wide range of aircraft including Shackletons, Yorks, Meteors and Vulcans, finally closing in 1968. The wartime sheds were used with an additional Repair Shop 6, and the T2 hangar on the airfield side of the road. Most of these sheds still stand, in use by a number of commercial companies. Truman Aviation at Tollerton has maintained both flying and repair facilities up to the present time, using the wartime MAP hangar. Rolls-Royce retain a presence on Hucknall airfield, in 1971 for instance, testing the 'flying bedstead', with its two Nene engines, there.

Ordnance

For five years after the end of the war, ROF Nottingham on Kings Meadows took whatever work it could find, even acting as a sub-contractor for Raleigh cycles, but from 1950, a new rearmament drive brought military contracts. Second only to Woolwich Arsenal in tube production, ROF Nottingham manufactured 20-pounder guns for the Centurion tank. Within a few years, production had broadened out to include AA fire-control equipment, armoured trucks, and Bloodhound missile launchers. For the next thirty years, the factory was heavily involved in producing weapons and armoured vehicles including 81mm mortars, 105mm light guns for the artillery, and the 165mm demolition gun mounted on the Centurion AVRE used by assault engineers. With the closure of ROF Leeds and the Enfield Royal Small Arms Factory, the range of work increased even more. The disused South Shop was converted into the Nottingham Small Arms Facility with a proof and test range, and a dedicated building, known as the Pattern Room, was erected to house the MOD Small Arms Museum. The ROF closed in 2001, its manufacturing facility being taken over by BAe in Barrow-in-Furness, and the contents of the Pattern Room going to the Royal Armouries in Leeds. The site is now covered by housing.

Appendix 1

Prehistoric Camps

Arnold, Cockpit Hill, Ramsdale Park, rectangular earthwork with two ditches   SK596485
Burton Joyce, Burton Lodge Camp   SK634446
East Retford, Castle Hill Camp   SK740804
Farnsfield, Combs Farm Camp   SK631551
Farnsfield, Camp Hill   SK669580
Gringley-on-the-Hill: Beacon Hill Camp   SK742908
Oxton Camp, Oldox (Old Works) Camp on Robin Hood Hill,
    3 acres (1.2ha), univallate on west but three banks and ditches on south-east;
    entrances on NW and SE; 20ft (6m) high barrow outside   SK634532
Shireoaks, Scratta Wood, Iron Age/Romano-British settlement with bank and ditch   SK544803
Styrrup, Crow Wood, Iron Age defended settlement   SK608910
Woodborough/Calverton, Fox Wood, earthworks, small oval hill fort bivallate,
    defences well preserved on N and W   SK613484

Appendix 2

Castles, Fortified Manors and Moated Sites

Earthwork Castles

Annesley, motte and bailey	SK509518
Aslockton, Cranmer's Mount, motte and bailey	SK743402
Bothamshall, Castle Hill, ring-work	SK671732
Cuckney, Castle Hill, motte and bailey in churchyard	SK566714
Darlton, Kingshaugh House, hunting lodge fortified 1193–94	SK765735
East Bridgford, Cuttle Hill, motte	SK690433
East Retford, Grove, Castle Hill, camp refortified in Civil War	SK742804
Egmanton, Gaddick Hill, motte and bailey	SK735690
Gringley, Beacon Hill, prehistoric camp, possible motte	SK742908
Haughton, motte and bailey later adapted as duck decoy	SK684731
Kirby-in-Ashfield, Castle Hill, possible castle earthworks	SK491558
Laxton, motte and two baileys	SK720676
Lowdham, motte	SK664468
Southwell Minster, surrounded by ditch and defended in 1142	SK702538
Thurgarton, Castle Hill, possible motte on confused site	SK693490
Worksop, Castle Hill, large ring-work and bailey	SK593798

Masonry Castles

Greasley	SK490470
Newark-on-Trent	SK796541
Nottingham	SK568395
Wiverton, gatehouse of C15	SK713363

Moated Sites/Fortified Houses

Bilborough, moated site destroyed *c.*1950	SK520418
Clifton Hall, tower-house, lost in later mansion	SK540348
Clipstone, King John's Palace, hunting-lodge	SK607645
Clipstone Peel (Beeston Lodge), hunting-lodge	SK570640
Halloughton, Manor Farm, tower-house	SK690517
Hawton, moated site, refortified in Civil War	SK785513
Hodsock, gatehouse and moat, *c.*1500	SK612853
Holme Pierrepont, gatehouse, *c.*1510	SK626393
Kingshaugh, hunting lodge	SK765735
Kinoulton, moat	SK673294
Linby Hall, tower-house in later hall	SK534512
Norwell, moated sites	SK775617, 770618, 744628

Sibthorpe moated site   SK767452
Stoke Bardolph, site of stone house   SK647415
Strelley Hall, tower-house in later hall   SK504422
Wellow, Jordan's Castle, moated site   SK679666
Worksop, Gateford Hall, moat   SK569815

Ecclesiastical Fortifications

Aspley, hunting lodge of Lenton Priory, with tower, destroyed   SK540414
Beauvale Priory, three-storey tower-house and gatehouse range   SK493489
Lenton Priory, gatehouse stood until C19   SK552388
Southwell, palace of archbishops of York   SK702537
Worksop Priory gatehouse   SK590789

Appendix 3

Civil War
Fortifications

East Retford, Castle Hill Camp: refortified prehistoric earthwork	SK740804
Felley Priory, a Royalist outpost in 1643	SK483513
Newstead Abbey, a Royalist garrison during 1643	SK542537
Norwell Manor, an outlier Royalist garrison for Newark in 1645	SK776617
Shelford House, a Royalist outpost of Newark, 1642–44	SK673434
Staunton Hall, taken from Royalists in 1645	SK805433
Thurgarton Priory, Royalist outpost of Newark 1642–44	SK692492
Welbeck Abbey held in turn by both sides	SK565743
Wiverton Hall, Royalist outpost of Newark 1642–44	SK713364

Newark-on-Trent

ROYALIST defence works

Queen's Sconce	SK790530
Sconce at Muskham Bridge	SK786562
Raised battery at Crankley Lane	SK789558
Work at Crankley Point	SK801561
Town bank in gardens of the Friary	SK803541

PARLIAMENTARIAN siege-works

Colonel Gray's sconce	SK802560
Scots redoubt	SK795547
Sandhills sconce	SK786538
Stoke Lodge sconce	SK787544
Crankley Point redoubt	SK800560
Edinburgh, HQ of Scots	SK783550

PARLIAMENTARIAN village defences

BALDERTON, traces of banks and stream course	SK816516 and 822517
CODDINGTON, fragments of two angles	SK833540 and 833543
FARNDON, fragment of angle bastion	SK770516
WINTHORPE, defence line inferred from stream course	SK812568
HAWTON, rectangular redoubt in medieval moated site	SK785513

Appendix 4

Army Barracks, Camps, Depots and Ranges

Pre-First World War

Burton Joyce: rifle range, 1907
Collingham: rifle range between railway and Green Lane, by 1910
Epperstone: rifle range, by 1910
Mansfield Barracks, High Oakham House, 1839–54
Mapperley Old Coppice range, Querneby-Woodborough Roads, 1860–90
Nottingham Cavalry Barracks, 1792
Trent: rifle range, 1895
Upton, Southwell, rifle range, by 1910

First World War

Babworth Woods, practice trenches

Bulwell, 62 Division, 187 Brigade 2/4th Battalion York and Lancaster Regiment 1914

Carburton Camp, Rough Breck: 69 Division, 207 Brigade, 2/5th Battalion, Bedfordshire Regiment and 2/4 Battalion, Northants Regiment, May 1917, then to Clipstone, November 1917

Clipstone Infantry Training Camp:

33 Division (K4) with 98, 99 and 100 Infantry Brigades: five battalions of Royal Fusiliers, two of Middlesex Regiment, one each of Essex Regiment, Somerset Light Infantry and Kings Own Royal Lancaster Regiment and Kings Royal Rifle Brigade, 1915

21 Reserve Brigade: four Training Reserve battalions, 1915–16

West Riding Reserve Brigade: four battalions Prince of Wales West Yorkshire Regiment, 1916–17

West Riding Reserve Brigade: two battalions York and Lancaster Regiment, 1916–17

West Riding Reserve Brigade: four battalions Duke of Wellington's West Riding Regiment, 1917

2 Reserve Brigade, 1917 and 1 Training Reserve Brigade, 1918

69 Division, 207 Brigade including 52nd Battalions of Leicestershire and Notts and Derby Regiments, 1918

26 Reserve Park Army Service Corps, 1914

No.3 Coy ASC Train 69 (East Anglian) Division (Home Forces)

Newark-on-Trent: Royal Engineers Reserve Training Centre

Retford: 69 (East Anglian) Division (Home Forces), Nos 1 & 3 Coys ASC Train; 62 Division, 185 Brigade: 2/5th Battalion Prince of Wales West Yorkshire Regiment, November 1915

Thoresby Park: 62 Division, 185 Brigade: 2/5th Battalion, Suffolk Regiment, 2/5th Battalion Prince of Wales West Yorkshire Regiment, 1915 and 51st Battalion, 1918

Welbeck Abbey: 69 Division, 206 Brigade: 51st Battalion, Northumberland Fusiliers 1917; 207 Brigade: 51st Battalion Leicestershire Regiment; 208 Brigade: 52nd Battalions Notts and Derby Regiment and King's Own Yorkshire Light Infantry, 1918

West Retford House (now Hotel): HQ 69 (East Anglian) Division 1917–18

The Nottinghamshire Volunteer Regiment (VTC)

Nottingham, Thurland Chambers, Thurland Street: RHQ & HQ 1st Battalion

Nottingham, 15 Long Row: HQ 2nd Battalion with companies at Bingham, Elton and Radcliffe on Trent

Nottingham, 19 Trinity Square: HQ 3rd Battalion with companies based on the Drill Hall, Arnold and the Market House, Hucknall

Worksop, 16 Potter Street: HQ 4th Battalion

Retford, Exchange Street: HQ A Company, 4th Battalion

Worksop, 40 Overend Street: B Company, 4th Battalion

Mansfield, Red Lion Hotel: C Company, 4th Battalion

Stanton-on-the-Hill, The Limes: D Company, 4th Battalion

Sutton-in-Ashfield, Low Street: D Company, 4th Battalion

Militia Camps 1938-39

Newark-on-Trent, Bowbridge RE militia camp

Newark-on-Trent, Hawton Road militia camp

Ollerton militia camp

Ranby militia camp

Rufford Abbey militia camp

Tuxford, Ollerton Road, militia camp

Whatton-in-the-Vale, militia camp

Camps, Barracks and Depots: Second World War

Arnold, Bestwood and Redhill Lodges, RAOC Mobilisation Depots

Arnold, Bestwood Lodge: HQ Northern District, Northern Command, 1939–45

Bingham, Bingham Road, Saxondale RE Stores, military hut storage depot

Bottesford, No.17 Army Fuel Depot and RASC camp

Boughton, US Army 1961st Engineer Depot Company stores

Bramcote Hills Park: ATS training camp for Chilwell COD

Bulwell, Hucknall Lane: RAOC Mobilisation Depot

Chilwell, Central Ordnance Depot, Tanks and Vehicles HQ

Clumber Park, Royal Ordnance Depot (Harriecroft sidings), Ollerton/Checker House, off Retford-Sheffield railway line

East Markham Hall, HQ Lovat Scouts, 1939

Flintham Hall, army camp

Holme Pierrepont Hall, 70th (Young Soldiers) Battalion Sherwood Foresters

Kneeton army camp, satellite of Hawton Road Camp

Mansfield (Woodhouse), Grove House: RASC canteen

Morton Hall, billets for *inter alia* US Army officers serving at Ranby Camp

Newark-on-Trent, Bowbridge Camp, RE Training Battalion and OCTU

Newark-on-Trent, Hawton Road Camp, AA training then airborne forces

Newark-on-Trent, Lincoln Road, REME Command depot

New Ollerton, Proteus Camp

Ranby Camp, 9th Reserve AA Regiment; Rifle Brigade Holding Battalion and No.96 Primary (infantry) Training Centre; possible US Army Military Police base

Ranskill, Barnby Moor, camp for 2nd Armoured Division (after mid-1942)

Rufford Abbey army camp

Thoresby Hall, 12th Battalion, Sherwood Foresters, 1940

Warsop, tank-training area

Welbeck Abbey, training camp for Guards Armoured Division, 1943

Whatton, Airborne Forces camp

Winthorpe Hall, RASC Depot
Wollaton Park, mustering area for 7th Battalion, Norfolk Regiment, 1939;
      508 Parachute Infantry Regt, 82nd Airborne Division, US Army, 1944
Woodthorpe House/Grange, requisitioned by War Office

Camps, Barracks and Depots Post-1945

Bestwood Lodge: HQ 49 Infantry Brigade, then Army Pay Corps depot until 1973
Chilwell: Central Ordnance Depot
Chilwell, Chetwynd Barracks, in current use (2014)
New Ollerton, Proteus Camp, in use until 2002
Ranby Camp: No.19 (Tank Transporter) Company, RASC, 1950–69

Appendix 5

Rifle Volunteer, Yeomanry, Militia, Territorial Force, Territorial Army and RAuxAF Drill Halls

Arnold
*Arnott Hill Road, *Drill Hall*, *c*.1914; two-storey front block and hall with bowstring roof; indoor-range behind; occupied by TA until 1980s, now in commercial use; in 1914, drill station B Squadron South Notts Hussars; base F Coy, 8 Battalion, Notts & Derby Regiment; in 1949, base for one battery 528 (Notts) LAA (Mobile) Regiment RA, TA
*Redhill Lodge; in 1949, base 3504 (County of Nottingham) Fighter Control Unit
Beeston
*Broadgate, *Drill Hall*; 1939 square, two-storey block, with garages etc. to rear; in use by EM Universities OTC; in 1949, base for one battery. 577 LAA/SL Regiment (The Robin Hoods-Foresters); HQ + Squadron 5 AA Group (Mixed) Signal Office Squadron, Royal Corps of Signals
Bestwood Village
*Bestwood Lodge, 1862–65 by Teulon; *Drill Hall* added to side of main house for use by the Rifle Volunteers; seven bays, single-storey, with stepped gable; now a hotel; 25-yard rifle range in the Park, 1914
Bilborough
*Wigman Road, *TAC*; 1957, T-shaped, two-storey, *moderne* block, with garages etc.; in 2013, RHQ 73 Regiment RE + REME Light Aid Detachment
Bingham
*Corner of Fisher Lane and Long Acre, built 1840 as a National School; in 1892, officer + 30 men of E Coy 4th Volunteer Battalion Notts & Derby Regiment; in 1914, base for A Squadron South Notts Hussars; drill station for E Coy, 8 Battalion, Notts & Derby Regiment
Blidworth
*New Road, *Drill Hall*, 1930, T-shaped, brick-built, gabled hall with range across rear; foundation stone; in use by ACF
Bulwell
*Bulwell Hall (demolished 1958) used by NUOTC *c*.1914; park used for training
*Hucknall Lane, *TAC*; 1938; two-storey main block plus garages etc. to Ludford Road; in 1949, base for one battery 307 South Notts Hussars Yeomanry, Field Regt RA, TA; base for one battery 350 (South Notts Hussars Yeomanry) Heavy Regiment RA, TA; base for one company 307 (Northern Command) Battalion WRAC, TA
Burton Joyce
Rifle-range opened 1907; company of 'Citizen Volunteer Army' photographed 1915
Carlton
*Station Road, drill hall and 30-yard range in use 1912; possibly building on corner of Conway Road, lately RBL social club; in 1914, base E Coy, 8 Battalion, Notts & Derby Regiment, and drill station for A Squadron, South Notts Hussars

*Cavendish Drive; *TAC*, 1939; two-storey square plan + wings; in use; in 1949, base for one squadron The Notts (Sherwood Rangers Yeomanry) RAC; base for one battery 577 LAA/ SL Regt (The Robin Hoods-Foresters); HQ + one company 905 AA Command (Mixed) Transport Company RASC, TA; in 2013 'S' (Sherwood Rangers) Squadron, The Royal Yeomanry

Chilwell

*Swiney Way, Foresters' House, *TAC*, 1990s; in use

*Cromwell Camp, Central Ordnance Depot; in use by TA in 1949; in 1949, HQ + RAOC Stores Section Workshop attached 9 Armoured Workshops REME + RAOC Section; in 2013, 73 Regiment RE, 350 Field Squadron RE, 170 Engineer Group

Collingham

Stores and 30-yard range in use 1910

Epperstone

30-yard range in use from at least 1887, and still in use 1910

Forest Town

Built in 1908 by the Bolsover/Mansfield Colliery Company for the Boys' Brigade; was a Recruiting Office in WWI and a British Restaurant and army cadets' base in WWII

Gedling

Drill hall reported, 1910

Kimberley

No dedicated building; probable venue at Station Hotel (*c*.1880) with indoor range at Brewery; both used by Rifle Club *c*.1907, and by Home Guard WWII; volunteers arrived by train to drill at Swingate Colliery – site now Kimberley Primary School; in 1912, base for F Coy, 8 Battalion, Notts & Derby Regiment

Mansfield

*Westgate/Meeting House Lane, drill hall in use 1892 until at least 1920; demolished for redevelopment; Yeomanry Store and drill hall, Infantry Store and drill hall, 30-yard range and stores all in use 1910; in 1892, base for 4 Notts (Volunteer) Battalion, Notts & Derby Regiment; in 1914, base for B Squadron Sherwood Rangers, and D Coy, 8 Battalion, Notts & Derby Regiment

*Botany Road/Sutton Road, *TAC*, in use 1949; staff house + Cadet Centre on site; plans of 1948 show proposed huts & sheds with permanent building only for PSI; in 1949, base for one squadron, Nottinghamshire (Sherwood Rangers Yeomanry) RAC, TA; base for one battery 577 LAA/SL Regt (Robin Hoods-Foresters) RA, TA

*High Oakham House, barracks built 1839 in use to 1854; Foresters badge suggests use by Notts & Derby Regiment between 1881 and 1894 when in domestic use

*Bath Street, drill hall, 1923 (plans of 1939 show Beeston-type buildings, presumably never built) demolished for replacement *TAC*, opened 1982 by Denis Thatcher; in 1949, base for one company 307 (Northern Command) Battalion WRAC, TA; HQ 3 Notts. Battalion ACF; in 2013, 73 Engineer Regiment and one company of 4th Battalion, Mercian Regiment, TA

Newark-on-Trent

*60 Carter Gate, Beaumont Cross, *Drill Hall*, in use up to 1912; built as Assembly Rooms; hall to street, arched entrance, hipped roof, seven bays deep; now carpet shop, previously Salvation Army Hall; in 1892, HQ + B and C Coys, 4 Notts Volunteer Battalion, Notts & Derby Regiment

*Albert Street, Militia Stores, built *c*.1855; later depot of Notts section of 4 Battalion Notts & Derby Regiment (Special Reserve) in 1912; extensive additional buildings shown on 25in OS Map 1914, still in use 1949, demolished 1974; in 1949, HQ + one squadron, Nottinghamshire (Sherwood Rangers Yeomanry) RAC, TA

*24 *Castle Gate*, now offices of architectural practice; 19C building with blocked coach-arch; in 1912 and 1914, HQ 8 Battalion, Notts & Derby Regiment, TF

*34 *Castlegate*, listed as drill hall; in 1912, base for B Coy, 8 Battalion, Notts & Derby Regiment, TF

*Sherwood House, Sherwood Avenue, *Drill Hall*, 1914 for 8 Battalion, Notts & Derby
    Regiment; neo-Georgian two-storey block with elaborate detailing in stone; to rear,
    garages and additions of 1938 and 1956; in use until 1996; now architectural and
    engineering consultancy; in 1914, base for A Squadron, The Sherwood Rangers; in 1949
    HQ 8 (Motor) Battalion, Notts & Derby Regiment, TA
*Bowbridge Road, Bowbridge Camp, TAC in 1949; huts etc. remain as part of Junior School;
    in 1949, base for one company 8 (Motor) Battalion, Notts & Derby Regiment, TA; base
    for one company 307 (Northern Command) Battalion, WRAC;
*Lincoln Road, REME Command Depot, WWII–1970s (motor-caravan dealership)
Nottingham
*Castle Road, Infantry HQ, stores and drill hall, Yeomanry riding-school of 1798 used from
    1872 by Robin Hood Rifle Volunteers; large stone-built hall with castellated round tower
    attached; demolished 1926; (a riding school was still in TA use in 1933)
*168–174 Derby Road, *Drill Hall*, built 1910–12 by Brewill & Bailey; large four-storey
    brick block with neo-Baroque detail; most of the ancillary buildings and the hall
    itself have gone; at the rear is a brick building possibly former stabling; in 1914, HQ
    + C Squadron South Notts Hussars; HQ & A-H Coys, 7 Battalion, Notts & Derby
    Regiment; ASC Divisional Transport & Supply Column, Notts and Derby Mounted
    Brigade; Notts and Derby Mounted Brigade Field Ambulance, RAMC, TF; in 1938,
    base for 107 (South Notts Hussars Yeomanry) Field Regt RHA, TA; in 1949, HQ +
    one Battery 307 (South Notts Hussars Yeomanry) Field Regt RA, TA; HQ 577 LAA/
    SL Regiment (Robin Hoods-Foresters) RA, TA; HQ + one Battery 350 (South Notts
    Hussars Yeomanry) Heavy Regiment RA, TA; HQ 528 (Notts) LAA (Mobile) Regiment
    RA, TA; HQ + one Squadron 21 (North Midland) Corps Signal Regiment TA; base
    for one company 8 (Motor) Battalion, Notts & Derby Regiment; HQ + 1 Company
    307 (Northern Command) Battalion WRAC, TA
*5–6 Clinton Terrace, Derby Road, five-storey regency house; possibly Territorial Association
    Offices from 1908; in 1949, HQ + one Troop, 48 Counter-Bombardment Regiment RA, TA
*7 Clinton Terrace, Derby Road, HQ North Midland District, Northern Command
* Nottingham Castle, *Orderly Room* of Robin Hoods, in use from after 1859 until 1893;
    now used as gardener's store; single storey, stone-built, with pitched roof;
*Forest Racecourse Grandstand used as Orderly Room & Armoury from 1893–1910
26 Park Row, third of terrace of four four-storey Regency houses; no outbuildings; in 1910,
    ASC stores; in 1912 HQ of Notts and Derby Mounted Brigade
116 Raleigh Street, large detached Victorian villa, with substantial outbuildings to rear;
    Nottinghamshire RHA Battery Office in 1910 and 1912; now flats; in 1914, HQ
    Nottinghamshire RHA and Ammunition Column
Upnah House, 22 Balmoral Road, TAC in 1949; stone-built double-fronted Victorian house;
    halls added to rear post-1914; described in 1949 as having canteens, messes, lecture
    rooms, indoor games facilities and space for dances and socials; now Nottingham Girls'
    School junior department with 2007 additions to sports hall of 1997; in 1949, 2504
    (County of Nottingham) LAA Squadron, RAuxAF
*Triumph Road, *TAC*, 1953, two-storey block + garages; in use as East Midlands HQ of
    RFCA; anti-bomb screen added 1990s
*Coppice New Road (now Ransom Rd), Mapperley, rifle range; lodge, originally with
    RHR monogram over porch
*Trent (800 yard) Rifle Range; lodge with ammunition store, built 1895, by Major Brewill,
    local architect and adjutant 2 Battalion; still inhabited and called * *Trent Rifle Lodge*; another
    lodge to south of Range by lock, formerly lock-keeper's cottage; now Yacht Club-house
*Bilbie Walk (off Shakespeare Street) premises used by NUOTC *c.*1914
*University Park, OTC premises 1928–54
Radcliffe on Trent
Stores and range in use 1910

Rainworth
Drill Hall built 1929, destroyed by fire 2004, and rebuilt as Village Hall
Retford
In 1910, Yeomanry stores, Infantry drill hall, stores and 300-yard range. A photograph of
   May 1915 shows a group of Rangers officers outside West Retford Hall/House
*Ashley Place, London Road, in use 1892; in 1892, A Coy, 4 Volunteer Battalion, Notts
   & Derby Regiment; in 1936, base C Squadron Sherwood Rangers; in 1949, base one
   Squadron Nottinghamshire (Sherwood Rangers Yeomanry) RAC, TA; base one Coy
   8 (Motor) Battalion, Notts & Derby Regiment
*34 Albert Road, Albert Hall, *Yeomanry Stores*, pre-1912; small mission-like T-shaped hall;
   four-storey building opposite with range on top floor; in 1908, Kelly's lists 34 Victoria
   (*sic*) Road as HQ TF including HQ Notts & Derby Mounted Brigade and 8 Battalion,
   Notts & Derby Regiment; in 1912, HQ Sherwood Rangers; in 1914, HQ and base
   D Squadron Sherwood Rangers
*South Street, premises used by Sherwood Rangers
*West Retford Hall used by Sherwood Rangers tempus WWI
*Storcroft Road, drill hall, in use 1912; no trace, possible site occupied by 1970s bungalows;
   possibly same site as Ashley Place; in 1912, base for A Coy, 8 Battalion, Notts & Derby
   Regiment; in 1914, base A Coy, 8 Battalion, Notts & Derby Regiment
*Hallcroft Road, ex-*TAC* and current *ACF* centre, 1956; front-block and yard with extensive
   buildings/garages to rear and staff house to side
Sherwood Lodge
Large, brick-built 18C house with pedimented front; used as location for Robin Hood
   Rifles' camps, 1886, 1887 and 1890; seat of Colonel Seely, CO, 1875–91; house demolished
   1974 for Police HQ; *lodges* of 1893 and 1903 remain
Southwell
*King Street, premises in use 1912; in 1912, base for H Coy, 8 Battalion, Notts &
   Derby Regiment
*Newark Road, *Drill Hall*, *c*.1914, single-storey front block, hall and small-arms range behind,
   by Brewill & Bailey, with later garage; in 1914, drill station A Squadron, South Notts Hussars,
   and base for H Coy, 8 Battalion, Notts and Derby Regiment; currently ACF Centre
*Normanton Road, Upton, outdoor rifle range; pre-existing cottage, butts and circular
   magazine with domed concrete roof; leased 1913–90; now rifle club
Sutton-in-Ashfield
*Alfreton Road, ex-*TAC*, 1938; two-storey block and bowstring-roof hall, with garages and
   other additions including staff flat, of 1953, behind; in 1914, base C Coy, 8 Battalion, Notts
   & Derby Regiment; then South Notts Hussars; in 1949, base for one company 8 (Motor)
   Battalion, Notts & Derby Regiment
Watnall
Hall, demolished 1962, home of Sir Lancelot Rollaston, Colonel of South Notts Hussars;
   probable venue; in 1914, base for B Squadron, South Notts Hussars
Welbeck Abbey
Possible use of riding school by Sherwood Rangers Yeomanry
Wiseton
In 1914 a drill station for Nottinghamshire RHA, possibly in Wiseton Hall where stables survive
Worksop
In 1910, Yeomanry stores, Infantry drill hall, Infantry stores and 30-yard range.
*Bridge Place, Cattle Market Hotel, demolished; in 1914, base for C Squadron, Sherwood Rangers
*Bridge Street, Officers' Mess of Rifle Volunteers, drills held in disused malt-kiln; in 1885,
   G Coy (late 7 Corps) 2 Nottinghamshire Rifle Volunteer Corps
*Potter Street, in use 1892; HQ 4 Notts Volunteer Battalion, Notts & Derby Regiment
*Newgate Street, HQ and stores, Sherwood Rangers, 1912
*Shaw Street, *Drill Hall*, built early 20C; in use 1912/14 as base for G Coy

8 Battalion, Notts & Derby Regiment; in 1949, base for one company 8 (Motor) Battalion, Notts & Derby Regiment

*Park Street, Scofton House, *TAC*; in 1949, base for one battery 528 (Notts) LAA (Mobile) Regiment RA TA; base for one company 307 (Northern Command) Battalion WRAC, TA; rebuilt and opened 29 June 1974 by Princess Anne; now *ACF*

Other locations in Nottinghamshire providing drill stations for Territorial units: *Basford, Burton Joyce, Calverton, Clumber, Daybrook, Eastwood, Farnsfield, Hucknall, Kirkby-in-Ashfield, Melton Ross, Misterton, Normanton, Pinxton, Plumtree, Ranskill, Shireoaks, Trent Port, Wollaton.*

Appendix 6

Locations Used by the Nottinghamshire Home Guard

Arnold, Bestwood Lodge: Home Guard training camp
Balderton, Turks Head PH: HQ Balderton platoon
Bestwood Colliery: HQ 5th Battalion
Caunton manor house: HQ Kelham/Caunton platoon
Clipstone Colliery: HQ 8th Battalion
Coddington House stable-block: platoon HQ
East Markham Hall: HQ (1) 10th Battalion, 1940
Kimberley Brewery; miniature indoor rifle range
Mansfield, Berry Hill Park: training camp, 1942
Mansfield, Fisher Lane Park: Blacker Bombard range, 1942
Mansfield, Chesterfield Road: HQ 6th Battalion
Newark-on-Trent: Borough Buildings, Balderton Gate: HQ 11th Battalion
Nottingham, 31 Derby Road: HQ (1) 14th Battalion (Trent River Patrol)
Nottingham, 47 Loughborough Road: HQ (2) 14th Battalion (Trent River Patrol)
Nottingham, 19, Bridgford Road: HQ 2nd Battalion
Retford, 19 Chapelgate: HQ (2) 10th Battalion

Appendix 7

Aviation-related Sites

Notes
*Drawing or Type Numbers used in several places show sequence/year of production:
the Watch Office for All Commands was built to the 343rd design to emerge from the
Air Ministry drawing office in 1943 – hence *343/43*.
*The term 'tb' refers to buildings with walls a single brick in width and officially 'temporary brick'.
*Where structures are recorded as surviving, that refers to the latest sighting pre-2013.
Figure 121 shows major airfield locations.

Babworth, Haygarth House was HQ No.5 Area Air Ministry Works Department, during
WWII, and continued into the 1950s as a training centre for RAF personnel involved in
operating and maintaining pumping equipment for POL installations.
Balderton opened in June 1941 as a bomber station with grass runways serving as a satellite of
25 FTS (Finningley); three hard runways were laid in 1943; following use as a HCU it was
transferred to the US IXth AAF Troop Carrier Command. The Meteor Flight Trials Unit
moved here from Hucknall 1943–44; after the war it was used by No.254 MU as No.1
Equipment Disposal Depot, then by No.93 MU for the storage of explosives until 1955.
Bircotes (Bawtry) was only ever a grass field with three hangars (1× T1, 1× B1 & 1× *Bessoneau*).
It served as the communications field for HQ No.1 Group RAF Bomber Command at
Bawtry Hall, and intermittently as a RLG for various OTUs. From 1945 it was used by
No.250 MU for MT storage. Very few traces remain.
Blidworth (SK573530) opened as No.35 SLG from 1941; it closed in 1945, and the guardroom
is now a bungalow at the entrance to the Scout Camp.
Coddington House was a RAF Depot and officers' mess and quarters for Winthorpe.
Cuckney, Budby Road, Warsop, was the base for 66 MU General Equipment Park.
East Retford: WWI aerodrome 1916–20+ (SK663813) on a site now occupied by HMP Ranby
and adjacent fields to north and west; used as a landing ground by 33 (Home Defence)
Squadron RFC, and later as a night-flying training station; four canvas *Bessoneau* hangars,
plus more permanent structures along the Worksop road; some brick huts survive from
the camp, opposite the prison which uses them as training-rooms, but the timber huts are
now gone; Ranby Hall accommodated pilots.
Gamston: opened in 1942 as a satellite of Ossington, No.14 (P)AFU; then a bomber field from
1943 with No.82 OTU; in 1944 No.91 Group Servicing Unit. It had four T2 hangars and
one B1. In 1945 it was No.9 Air Crew Holding Unit disposing of personnel surplus to
requirement, repatriating Commonwealth aircrew. It closed in 1945 but reopened in 1953
as a satellite of Worksop until 1957.
Grove Park (SK734796) opened as No.38 SLG closing in 1945, but safeguarded for future use;
the landing-strip was south of the village, and the guardhouse was the lodge to Grove Park.
Hucknall began as No.15 TDS for training pilots on DH9s in 1918. It was closed in 1919
but soon became Nottingham Flying Club, joined by the RAF in 1928. In 1934
Rolls-Royce moved onto site taking over two hangars, and developed the Merlin

engine there. Most of the war was spent as a Polish FTS. Development of the Meteor
jet-fighter also took place with test-flying moving to Balderton in 1943. Hucknall
was home to various RAuxAF units until its disbandment in 1957. It was HQ No.53
(Maintenance) Group RAF from 1947–56, closing in 1957. Club flying has lasted into
the new century and Rolls-Royce remain on site. The hangars consist of two double
GS (200ft × 172ft), one single Aircraft Repair Shed (100ft × 172ft), five Blisters,
two MAP Bellmans, and one MAP (200ft × 172ft).

Langar opened in September 1942 in No.5 Group as a satellite for Bottesford (Leicestershire)
flying bombing raids. In 1943 extra hangars were added for glider storage. The AVRO
works across the road repaired Lancasters from 1942. It then became Station 490 for
US IXth AAF Troop Carrier Command but for only a short while, returning to the RAF
as a HCU. After the war Langar became a supply base providing logistical support for the
1st Canadian Air Force serving with NATO on the Continent with warehousing and
an air-freight terminal being built. In 1961 Langar became redundant. Many buildings
including the Watch Office, T2 hangars and the MAP factory remain.

Misson (SK705975) operated as an inland bombing range used by OTUs based at Finningley
until at least 1948. In 1959/60 the site became a Bloodhound base for two fire units,
remaining operational until 1963. Now surplus military equipment dealers.

Newark-on-Trent, Lincoln Road was a RAF Maintenance Depot.

Newark-on-Trent, railway station and LMS yard was the location of No.4 Salvage Depot
which became No.58 MU Salvage and Repair Depot in 1940.

Newark-on-Trent, Langford was a RAF Petroleum Depot.

Newark-on-Trent, base for No.203 MU Supply Depot.

Newton opened in July 1940 having been planned as an Expansion Period bomber airfield, but
spent only the first year of its operational life flying sorties against enemy targets in France
and Germany. It joined Flying Training Command and hosted FTSs until 1946, and No.40
Initial Training Wing until 1944, using Orston as a satellite and Tollerton as a RLG. After
the war Newton was HQ 12 Group RAF Fighter Command, and HQ No.93 MU
(in 42 Group) from 1946–59. In 1959 the guided weapons courses arrived from Yatesbury
(Wiltshire) alongside No.9 School of Technical Training, 1958–74. From 1964–73, electrical
& instrument ground training also took place. In 1973 the RAF Police Dog School,
the RAF School of Education, and the RAF School of Management Training all moved in.
From 1995–2001 the station was run as an enclave of RAF College, Cranwell, 1995–2001.
Now in process of redevelopment.

Nottingham, Basford, was base for No.227 MU (formerly 'S'), a Barrack and Clothing Stores
Depot and RAF Ordnance Depot.

Orston was a satellite for Newton, closing in 1945.

Ossington was designed as a heavy bomber field with hard runways from the start but opened
in late 1941 as No.14 PFTS, then as No.14 (Pilot) Advanced Flying Unit, 1942–43,
and No.6 Lancaster Finishing School from 1945 until it closed in 1946.

Papplewick Moor was a RLG for Hucknall during both world wars. In 1945 it was put into
Care and Maintenance pending its disposal.

Plungar (SK762345) was a Landing Ground in the First World War.

Shelton 'RAF Shelton' appears on a 1941 defence map of the Newark-Ossington area.

Syerston was planned pre-war and opened in December 1940 as a satellite of Balderton.
Throughout 1941 it was an operational bomber for Polish and then Canadian squadrons.
After a closure for five months for runway laying, Conversion Flights arrived with
Lancasters, and then squadrons carrying out further bombing operations until the end of
1943, when training on bombers resumed, continuing to the end of the war, to be followed
by training on transport aircraft. From 1948–50 a RN Air Section course for FAA pilots ran
using Tollerton as RLG. In 1955 No.1 FTS formed, moving out after two years, followed by
No.2 FTS until 1970, using Jet Provosts. Since 1975 the Central Gliding School has been in
occupation, representing the chief use of Syerston to the present.

Thurgarton (SK680500) was a landing ground in the First World War.

Tollerton opened as Nottingham's civil aerodrome in 1930 and quickly became involved in pilot training for the RAF. In 1938 Field Aircraft Services moved in to carry out repairs to military aircraft and the airfield became a satellite of Newton. MAP left in 1949 but the RAF kept the airfield on as a satellite of Syerston until 1956. Club flying and, from 1963, the commercial operations of Truman Aviation, have kept the airfield active. Around 1980, two hangars from Desford (Leicestershire), put up for the RAFVR FTS in 1938, were dismantled and re-erected at Tollerton.

Wigsley (SK868703) was a landing ground in the First World War, and reopened in February 1942, on a different site, as a satellite for Swinderby (Lincolnshire) in No.5 Group, Bomber Command. Following occupation by an Australian bomber squadron, a number of HCUs used the base. At the end of the war No.28 Aircrew Holding Unit was here from 1945–46, and then Wigsley served as a RLG for Swinderby until 1958.

Winthorpe: opened September 1940 as satellite for Swinderby (Lincolnshire), being used by Polish bomber squadrons. It then served as a satellite for Ossington and Syerston until, in early 1942, it closed for the construction of three hard runways. Then HCUs were based there until the end of the war, after which Winthorpe became a storage facility until 1952 when the Central Servicing Development Establishment arrived, staying until the closure of the airfield in 1958; now Newark Air Museum.

Worksop opened for No.18 OTU in late 1943 for training Polish bomber crews as a satellite of Finningley (Yorkshire), replacing Bircotes with its grass strips, of particular use when Finningley was closed to receive its own hard runways. After the war it transferred to Flying Training Command and, although it closed in 1948, it underwent refurbishment and reopened in 1952 as No.211 Advanced Flying (Training) School, 1952–56 and No.4 Flying Training School, 1956–58, flying Meteors, Vampires and Provosts. From 1955–57 it was also home to a RAuxAF squadron flying Meteors, but closed in 1958, finally being de-requisitioned in 1960.

First World War landing-grounds: *Plungar*
Airfields in use in both world wars: **Hucknall**
Second World War airfields: Balderton

121 Map to show military airfields in Nottinghamshire.

Appendix 8

Air Defence

Bombing decoys

Barton in Fabis SK535314 *SF* for ROF Chilwell, A series Army decoys/ *QL* for Nottingham,
  (*MY*), C series Civil, Permanent *Starfish*
Clipston SK643337 *QL* for Nottingham (*MY*, Toton), C series Civil, Permanent *Starfish*
Cotgrave SK659358 *Q* for RAF Newton
Cropwell Butler SK653364 *QL* for Nottingham (*MY/LG*, Colwick), C series Civil, Permanent *Starfish*
Lowdham SK650455 *QL* for Nottingham (*MY/LG*, Gedling Colliery), C series Civil, Permanent *Starfish*
Kneeton SK717457 *Q* for RAF Syerston
Tithby SK709347 *Q* for RAF Newton and RAF Bottesford
Upton SK738564 *Q* for RAF Ossington

QL for Nottingham, C series Civil lasted October 1942 to May 1943
Permanent *Starfish*, lasted August 1941 to April 1943

Simulations:
Q and *QL* = night-time lights; *SF* = Special Fires/Starfish
MY = marshalling yards; *LG* = locomotive glows

Observer Corps (Royal from 1941)

Posts opened 1937–38
Blyth SK548969 (Yorks) then WWII re-site SK626863 then u/g SK635862
Burton Joyce/Lowdham SK675468 then SK643445 u/g
Cotgrave SK652345
Dunham-on-Trent SK804747 re-site SK822738 u/g
East Retford SK678070 (?) re-site SK704816 u/g
Edwinstowe/Ollerton SK648676 then SK656673 u/g
Farnsfield SK640577 re-site SK635586 u/g both destroyed
Hucknall SK518492 + u/g
Newark SK788523 re-site to Upton/Kelham SK753572 u/g

Posts opened 1941–43
Blyth resited to SK626863 (Notts)
East Markham SK729737 WW2 then u/g
Walkeringham/Wiseton SK770929 WWII (re-sited u/g SK756917)
Watnall, ROC Midland HQ at RAF 12 Group Filter Room, 1941–53

Posts opened 1948-49
Collingham SK837628, and u/g 1960s.
(Harby SK754306 now Leicestershire)
(u/g = underground, 1960s)

Appendix 9

Prisoner-of-War Camps

First World War
Babworth Hall, 'compound' camp for German POWs
Blyth (migratory gang)
Bulcote School, agricultural college
Bunny (migratory gang)
Carlton Depot
Carlton-on-Trent, Ossington Depot
Clayworth (migratory gang)
East Leake Depot
Gotham (migratory gang)
Halam Depot
Kegworth, German officers' camp
Kelham Brickfields
Langar Hall, Barnstone
Mansfield, Cuckney Depot
Misson (migratory gang)
Papplewick Depot
Plumtree Depot
Ranskill Depot
Retford Depot
Ruddington (migratory gang)
Shelford (migratory gang)
Sutton Bonington, Midland Agricultural & Dairy College
Tuxford Depot
Walkeringham (migratory gang)
Wiseton (migratory gang)
Woodborough Depot

Second World War
Arnold Lodge, Woodborough Road Camp (now Podders scrapyard)
No.143 Blyth, Serlby Hall Camp
No.633/656 Boughton Camp, New Ollerton (now industrial estate)
No.181/249: Carburton Camp, Youngrough Breck
No.143: Carlton Hall, Carlton-in-Lindrick
Caunton Camp
No.174 Cuckney, Norton Camp
No.262 Langar airfield
Mansfield, adjoining King's Mill Hospital
New Ollerton, Proteus Camp (now holiday accommodation)
No.52 Nether Headon Camp, East Retford (now industrial estate)

No.27 Nottingham, 3 Magdala Road
Ranby Camp (now prison)
Rufford Abbey
No.169/613 Tollerton Hall Camp
No.166 Wollaton Park

Appendix 10

Military Hospitals

First World War
Arnott Hall, VAD hospital
Babworth Hall, RAMC station then convalescent centre
Bayley Hospital, (affiliated to No.5 Northern General Hospital)
Beeston, 'The Cedars', Red Cross hospital 1914–18
Clipstone, hutted 356-bed military hospital at training camp
Eastwood, VAD (affiliated to No.5 Northern General Hospital)
Nottingham General Hospital, (affiliated to No.5 Northern General Hospital and known for
     the duration as Bagthorpe Military Hospital)
Radcliffe on Trent, Notts County War Hospital (Nottingham County Asylum)
Trent Bridge, VAD hospital (affiliated to No.5 Northern General Hospital)
Welbeck Abbey, military hospital in kitchen block 1914–19

Second World War
Edwalton Grange, Red Cross Convalescent Home/Auxiliary Hospital
Epperstone Manor, Red Cross Convalescent Home/Auxiliary Hospital
Lenton Firs, Red Cross Convalescent Home/Auxiliary Hospital
Lound Hall, Convalescent Home/Auxiliary Hospital serving Harlow Wood
Mansfield, Sutton Road, 30th US Eastern Base Section General Hospital, 600-bed emergency
     hospital, on original King's Mill site
Mansfield, Harlow Wood Hospital
Nottingham, City Hospital
Ruddington Hall, Red Cross Convalescent Home/Auxiliary Hospital
Southwell, Norwood Park, Red Cross Convalescent Home/Auxiliary Hospital
Thurgarton Priory, Red Cross Convalescent Home/Auxiliary Hospital

Appendix 11

Munitions Factories and Depots

First World War

Chilwell, No.6 NFF, filling 60-pounder and 6in howitzer shells with amatol
Old Radford, Canterbury Road Mills, JC Ley & Sons, cotton mill/cotton waste
Newark-on-Trent, Ransome's works
Nottingham, Kings Meadow Road, National Projectile Factory, Nottingham
Worksop, Anglo Shirley Aldred & Co. wood chemicals, acetate of lime for explosives

Second World War

Arnold, Coppice Road, J. Clarke & Co.'s Factory, Ministry of Supply
Arnold, Brookfield, Allen Solly & Co.'s Factory, RAOC sub MT Section
Balderton, Worthington Simpson Ltd, opened a new workshop in 1941 producing 5.5in
    Medium Guns and 17-pounder AT guns
Bunny, Gypsum mines
Clumber Park, ordnance storage and equipment trials
Hucknall, Rolls-Royce Experimental Unit, 1939–45
Langar, AVRoe Lancaster repair depot, 1942, MAP glider storage of Horsas, 1943
Mansfield, BSA, Lee-Enfield Mk IV (SMLE) 0.303 rifles
Mansfield, Barringer, Wallis and Manners (later Metal Box Company); Boys 0.55in AT rifles
    and Sten guns
Mansfield, Nottingham Road: Boneham and Turner, parts for Lancasters; parts for Bren guns
    and 20mm aircraft cannon
Newark-on-Trent, Northern Road, RHP (Ransome & Marles) made ball bearings for
    Rolls-Royce aero-engines and for gun-turrets
Newark-on-Trent, Blagg & Johnson, structural parts for Bailey Bridges, then from 1943, parts
    for landing-craft
Newark-on-Trent, Farrar Boiler Works, tank turrets, light reconnaissance tanks with AA guns,
    then from 1943 parts for landing-craft
Newark-on-Trent, Mumby & Sons, 315,000 uniforms for army and RAF; demob suits
Newark-on-Trent, Coopers clothing manufacturers made parachutes
Newstead Abbey, Ministry of Food Buffer Depot No.38
Nottingham, Kings Meadow Road, Royal Ordnance Factory making gun-barrels, tanks and artillery
Nottingham, shadow factory run by Rover building tanks
Nottingham, Barlock Typewriter Co. sears for Lee-Enfield 0.303 rifles
Nottingham, Dean Bros magazine cases and springs for Lee-Enfield 0.303 rifles Nottingham,
    Chelsea Street, New Basford, Herberts Ltd, sears, extractor springs, sear springs and sling
    swivels for Lee-Enfield 0.303 rifles
Nottingham, Raleigh Cycles manufactured jerrycans
Ranskill, ROF explosives, cordite manufacture
Ruddington, ROF FF No.14 explosives manufacture and shell-filling
Stapleford Wood, near Newark, Ministry of Supply home-grown timber depot

Sutton-in-Ashfield, Coxmoor Road, Ministry of Supply cold-store
Tollerton, Field Aircraft Services, maintenance & repair works for Lancasters and rebuilt
    Hampdens, converted Harrows to Sparrows etc., 1939–45 for MAP
Welbeck, Worksop, Royal Ordnance Depot

Cold War Buffer Depots
87 Gamston airfield
336 Main Road, Smalley Gate
336T Coxmoor Road, Sutton-in-Ashfield
ROF Ruddington, using existing rail links

Bibliography

Baldwin, D., *Robin Hood: The English Outlaw Unmasked* (Chalford, 2010)

Barley, M., *Nottingham Town Wall: Park Row Excavations 1964* (Transactions of the Thoroton Society of Nottinghamshire 69, 1965)

Beckett, J. (ed.), *A Centenary History of Nottingham* (Manchester, 1997)

Brewill, Lt-Col A.W., *The Robin Hoods* (Nottingham TF Association, 1921)

Brown, R.A., Colvin, H.M. and Taylor, A.J.: *The History of the King's Works Volume II The Middle Ages* (London, HMSO, London, 1963)

Butler, R.M., *The Civil War Defences of Nottingham* (Transactions of the Thoroton Society of Nottinghamshire 53, 1949)

Campbell, D., *War Plan UK* (London, 1982)

Challis, K. *et al.*, 'Computer Games and Virtual Landscapes' in *British Archaeology* 114, 2010

Chilwell 1939-45 (Leicester (Bell & Co., Leicester, n.d.)

Cocroft, W., *Dangerous Energy* (English Heritage, Swindon, 2000)

Cocroft, W. and Thomas R., *Cold War, Building for Nuclear Confrontation 1946–89* (English Heritage, Swindon, 2003)

Delve, K., *The Military Airfields of Britain: East Midlands* (Marlborough, 2008)

Dobinson, C., *Fields of Deception* (English Heritage and Methuen, London, 2000)

Dobinson, C., *AA Command* (English Heritage and Methuen, London, 2001)

Drage, C., *Nottingham Castle: A Place Full Royal* (Transactions of the Thoroton Society of Nottinghamshire 93, 1989)

Foulds, T., *The Siege of Nottingham Castle in 1194* (Transactions of the Thoroton Society of Nottinghamshire 95, 1991)

Gill, H., *Nottingham Castle* (Nottingham, 1904)

Halpenny, B.B., *Action Stations 2: Military airfields of Lincolnshire and the East Midlands* (Wellingborough, 1981)

Hardy, C. and Arthur, N., *Nottingham at War 1939–45* (*Nottingham Evening Post*, 1986)

Harwood, E., *Nottingham (Pevsner Architectural Guide)* (London & New Haven, 2008)

Iliffe, R. and Baguley, W., *The Robin Hood Rifles 1837–1901* (Nottingham, 1975)

Ingham, S., *Discovering the Civil War in Nottinghamshire* (Nottingham, 1992)

Kenyon, J., *Medieval Fortifications* (Leicester, 1990)

Kenyon, J., *Castles, Town Defences & Artillery Fortifications in the United Kingdom & Ireland: a Bibliography 1945–2006* (Donington, 2008)

King, D.J.C. & Alcock, L., *Ringworks of England and Wales*; in Chateau Gaillard III (1966), ed. Taylor, A.J. (Chichester, 1969)

King, D.J.C., *Castellarium Anglicanum (index & bibliography)* (New York, 1983)

Kinsley, G., *Recent Archaeological Work on the Mediaeval Castle at Nottingham* (Transactions of the Thoroton Society of Nottinghamshire 107, 2003)

Liddiard, R., *Castles in Context* (Macclesfield, 2005)

Marshall, P. and Samuels, J., *Recent Excavations at Newark Castle, Nottinghamshire* (Transactions of the Thoroton Society of Nottinghamshire 98, 1994)

Marshall, P. and Samuels, J., *Guardian of the Trent* (Newark, 1997)

McLynn, F.J., *Nottingham and the Jacobite rising of 1745* (Transactions of the Thoroton Society of Nottinghamshire 83, 1979)

Neville, Lt-Col W., *History of Nottingham High School Cadet Forces 1859–1980* (n.d.)

Nicholson, S., *The Great War in Nottinghamshire* (nottsheritagegateway.org.uk n.d.)

Nottinghamshire County Council: *Nottingham Citizens Handbook* (1995 facsimile of original edition issued by Nottingham Corporation, 1942)

Nunn, D., *World War I in Nottingham* (nottsheritagegateway.org.uk n.d.)

Old Mansfield Society, *Mansfield in World War II* (Mansfield, 2003)

Osborn, M., 'What made Langar linger longer' in *Airfield Review* 90 (Stockport, 2001)

Osborne, M., *20th Century Defences in Britain: the East Midlands* (Market Deeping, 2003)

Osborne, M., *Defending Britain* (Stroud, 2004)

Osborne, M., *Sieges & Fortifications of the Civil Wars in Britain* (Leigh-on-Sea, 2004)

Osborne, M., *Always Ready, the drill halls of Britain's volunteer forces* (Leigh-on-Sea, 2006)

Osborne, M., *Pillboxes of Britain and Ireland* (Stroud, 2008)

Patterson, M., *Roman Nottinghamshire* (Nottingham, 2011)

Pevsner, N., *Buildings of England: Nottinghamshire* (Harmondsworth, 1951)

Pevsner, N. and Williamson, E., *Buildings of England: Nottinghamshire* (London & New Haven, 2003)

Ponsford, M.W., *Nottingham town wall: Park Row excavations 1967* (Transactions of the Thoroton Society of Nottinghamshire 75, 1971)

Ponsford, M.W. and Carter A., *Nottingham town wall: Park Row excavations 1967 and 1968* (Transactions of the Thoroton Society of Nottinghamshire 75, 1971)

Royal Commission on Historical Monuments, *Newark-on-Trent: The Civil War Siegeworks* (London, 1964)

Ruddy, A., *To the Last Round: the Leicestershire & Rutland Home Guard 1940-1945* (Derby, 2007)

Salter, M., *The Castles of the East Midlands* (Malvern, Folly Publications, Malvern, 2002)

Seward, D., *The Wars of the Roses* (London, 1995)

Speight, S., *Early medieval castle sites in Nottinghamshire* (Transactions of the Thoroton Society of Nottinghamshire 98, 1994)

Speight, S., *Four more early medieval 'castle' sites in Nottinghamshire* (Transactions of the Thoroton Society of Nottinghamshire 99, 1995)

Speight, S. and Franklin G., *Egmanton near Laxton: Nottinghamshire's second finest motte and bailey castle* (Transactions of the Thoroton Society of Nottinghamshire 107, 2003)

Stocker, D., *England's Landscape: the East Midlands* (London, 2006)

Summers, N., *Manor Farm, Halloughton* (Transactions of the Thoroton Society of Nottinghamshire 69, 1965)

Thomas, R.J.C., *RAF Misson* (Airfield Review 99, Stockport, 1997)

Trent & Peak Archaeological Unit, University of Nottingham: *Margidunum Roman villa and small town* (Nottingham, 2004)

Turner, J., *'Nellie' The History of Churchill's Lincoln-built Trenching Machine* (Occasional Papers in Lincolnshire History & Archaeology 7, Lincoln, 1988)

Webster, G., *The Roman Invasion of Britain* (London, 1980 & 1993)

Wilson, D. and Moorhouse, S., Note on 'Anglo-Saxon fortifications of Nottingham' (1970) in *Medieval Archaeology XV*, 1971

Wood, A., *Nottinghamshire in the Civil War* (Oxford, 1937 (reprinted 1971))

Wood, A., *The Duke of Kingston's Regiment of Light Horse* (Transactions of the Thoroton Society of Nottinghamshire, 49, 1945)

Wood, D., *Attack Warning Red* (Portsmouth, 1976/1992)

Wright, J., *Castles of Nottinghamshire* (Nottingham, 2008)

Websites

www.dukeswoodoilmuseum.co.uk

www.nottsheritagegateway.org.uk

www.sthubertsrangers.org/bestwoodpark

www.subbrit.org.uk/rsg/sites/n/nottingham_war_room/index.html

Index

Page numbers in **bold** denote illustrations